THE BRAVE
AND THE BOLD

BATMAN AND
WONDER WOMAN

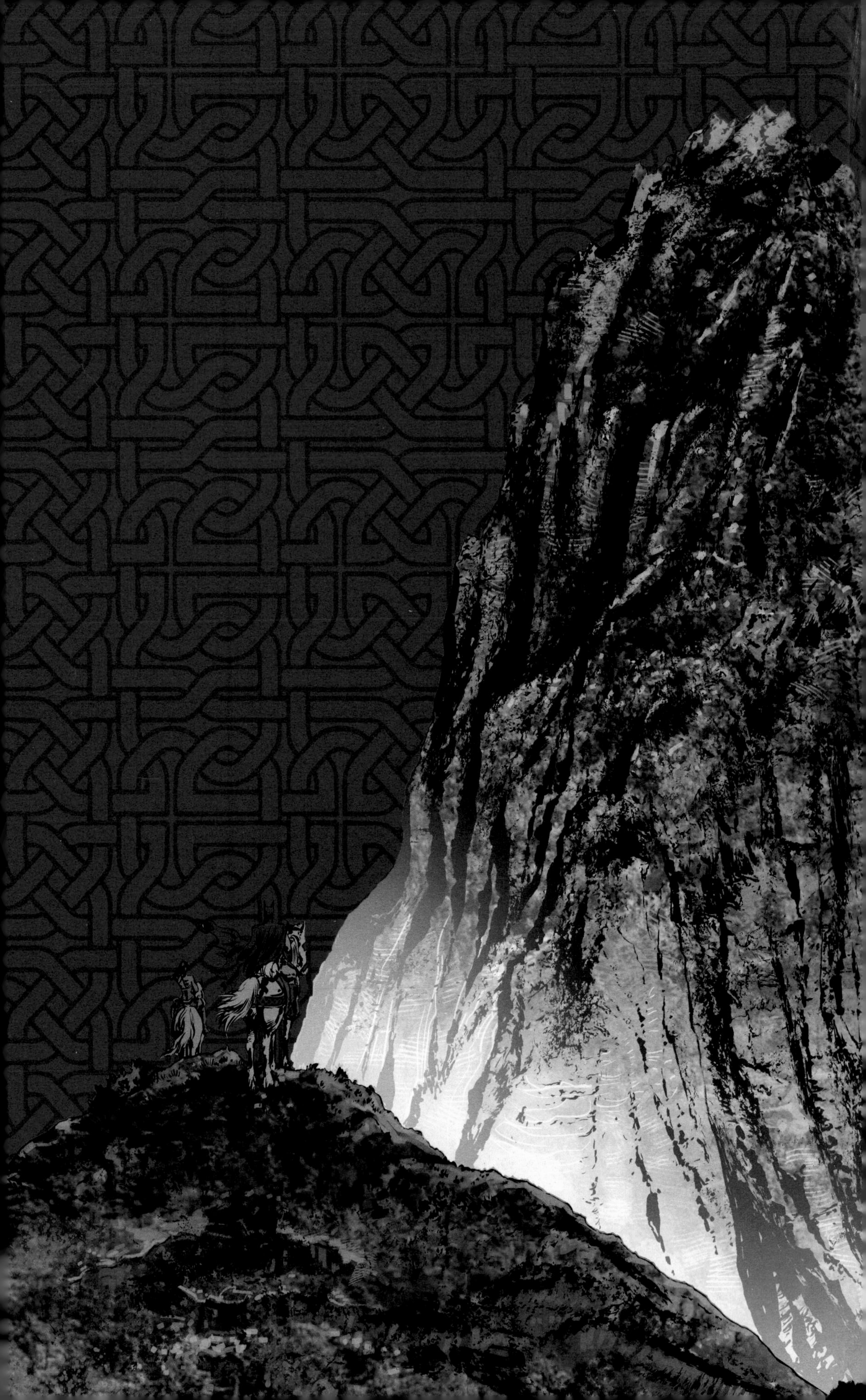

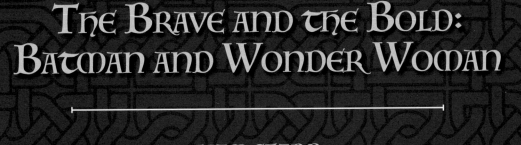

THE BRAVE AND THE BOLD: BATMAN AND WONDER WOMAN

LIAM SHARP
writer and artist

ROMULO FAJARDO JR.
colorist

ALW'S TROY PETERI
letterer

SHARP and FAJARDO JR.
collection cover artists

BATMAN created by BOB KANE with BILL FINGER
WONDER WOMAN created by WILLIAM MOULTON MARSTON

In loving memory of Danny McCormack

Jessica Chen, Mike Cotton Editors – Original Series
Rob Levin Associate Editor – Original Series
Jeb Woodard Group Editor – Collected Editions
Tyler-Marie Evans Editor – Collected Edition
Steve Cook Design Director – Books
Megen Bellersen Publication Design

Bob Harras Senior VP – Editor-in-Chief, DC Comics
Pat McCallum Executive Editor, DC Comics

Dan DiDio Publisher
Jim Lee Publisher & Chief Creative Officer
Amit Desai Executive VP – Business & Marketing Strategy,
Direct to Consumer & Global Franchise Management
Bobbie Chase VP & Executive Editor, Young Reader & Talent Development
Mark Chiarello Senior VP – Art, Design & Collected Editions
John Cunningham Senior VP – Sales & Trade Marketing
Briar Darden VP – Business Affairs
Anne DePies Senior VP – Business Strategy, Finance & Administration
Don Falletti VP – Manufacturing Operations
Lawrence Ganem VP – Editorial Administration & Talent Relations
Alison Gill Senior VP – Manufacturing & Operations
Jason Greenberg VP – Business Strategy & Finance
Hank Kanalz Senior VP – Editorial Strategy & Administration
Jay Kogan Senior VP – Legal Affairs
Nick J. Napolitano VP – Manufacturing Administration
Lisette Osterloh VP – Digital Marketing & Events
Eddie Scannell VP – Consumer Marketing
Courtney Simmons Senior VP – Publicity & Communications
Jim (Ski) Sokolowski VP – Comic Book Specialty Sales & Trade Marketing
Nancy Spears VP – Mass, Book, Digital Sales & Trade Marketing
Michele R. Wells VP – Content Strategy

THE BRAVE AND THE BOLD: BATMAN AND WONDER WOMAN

DC Comics, 2900 West Alameda Ave., Burbank, CA 91505
Printed by LSC Communications, Kendallville, IN, USA. 10/12/18. First Printing.
ISBN: 978-1-4012-8343-8

Library of Congress Cataloging-in-Publication Data is available.

PEFC Certified
Printed on paper from sustainably managed forests and controlled sources
PEFC/29-31-337   www.pefc.org

Introduction
By Jim FitzPatrick

When I was a kid growing up in Dublin, Ireland, there was only one constant source of artistic inspiration for kids like me, and that was the comics, both British and American.

I slaved endlessly learning to draw from them. The artists I learned from most are now lost to history, except for a few we remember, like the greatest of them all, Jack Kirby, and, of course, Hal Foster and his wonderful creation Prince Valiant.

These were my teachers, along with an unknown artist I copied from endlessly who I later discovered was the "Michelangelo of the Comic Strip," Burne Hogarth. The comic strip was, of course, his extraordinary rendition of *Tarzan*.

His work made it my way via a relative from America who sent comics pages from the *Chicago Herald Tribune* for us little Irish kids to pore over and enjoy.

When everyone else was finished with them, I held on to the battered pages and drew the Tarzan figure over and over until eventually I could present a passable imitation to the girls I was desperate to impress.

I failed miserably, and it was only much later, in my early teens, that I struck on the magic formula: I drew the likes of teen idols James Dean and Elvis Presley with panache and (as I thought) with great flourish and style, presented them to my intended and whooooooo, I was away.

Fast-forward to now, the year is 2018, and Liam Sharp, an artist whose work I am very familiar with and really enjoy, releases on Twitter pages of his sketches, inks and colors for his latest venture, a graphic novel of THE BRAVE AND THE BOLD.

Lo and behold, this wonderful artist credits me, Jim FitzPatrick, and my book *The Silver Arm*, published way back in 1981, as a seminal influence, one that brought Irish and Celtic mythology alive for him.

From this well of inspiration sprang this beautiful volume: rich, decorative, structurally powerful, textured with layers of visual meaning and finely scripted, too. A delight for the eye and the imagination. Even the title, THE BRAVE AND THE BOLD, seems apt for a story born of myth and legend.

As an artist, I am indeed happy to be honored with the task of introducing this magnificent volume. I must say Liam has done his homework on the mythology and stayed faithful to his sources, while adding his own particular flavor. It's a very modern take on a very ancient tale of warriors, male and female, wizards and warlocks, heroes and villains, all clothed in the garments of today's great comic book heroes.

It's a long way from the earliest voices of early Irish civilization to modern Americana, but this only continues a fine tradition of universal borrowing, learning, improving and improvising, all to create new art and new meanings.

Last but not at all least, a volume like this not only brings the work of Liam Sharp to a much larger world audience, but reminds us artists and creators, young and old, that in some other little room somewhere on this spinning planet, there will emerge into the light a kid like me or Liam, inspired to delve into the drawings and the mythology that inspired this book, and who will one day take it all to yet another level and inspire *another* new generation of kids with the lifeblood of art burning in their veins.

I was that kid once, and I'm pretty sure Liam was, too.

Over to the next generation. *Venceremos!*

Jim FitzPatrick
August 2018

Jim FitzPatrick is the internationally acclaimed author and artist of two books of Irish myths, The Book of Conquests *and* The Silver Arm, *and the creator of the famed 1968 Che Guevara revolutionary poster.*

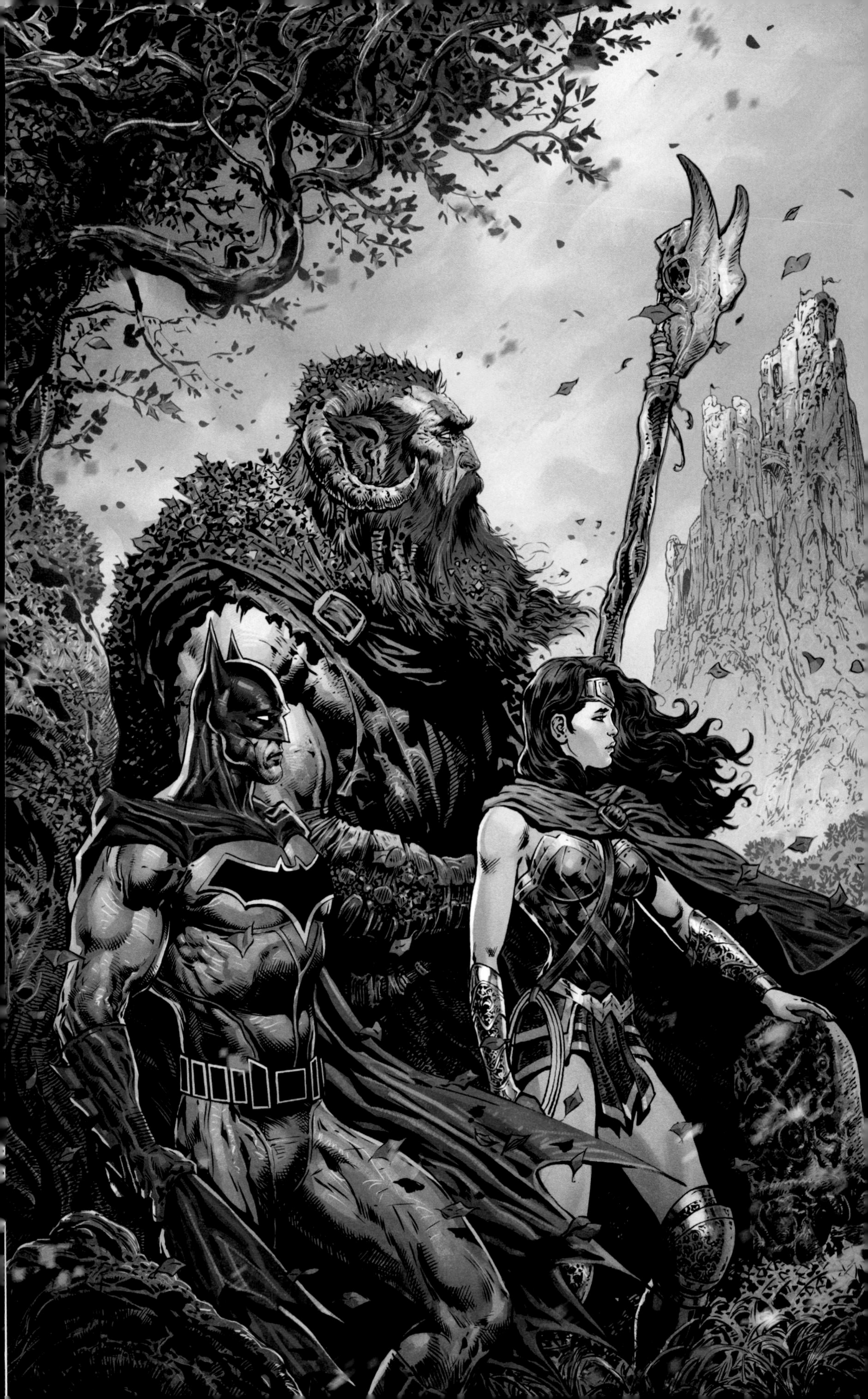

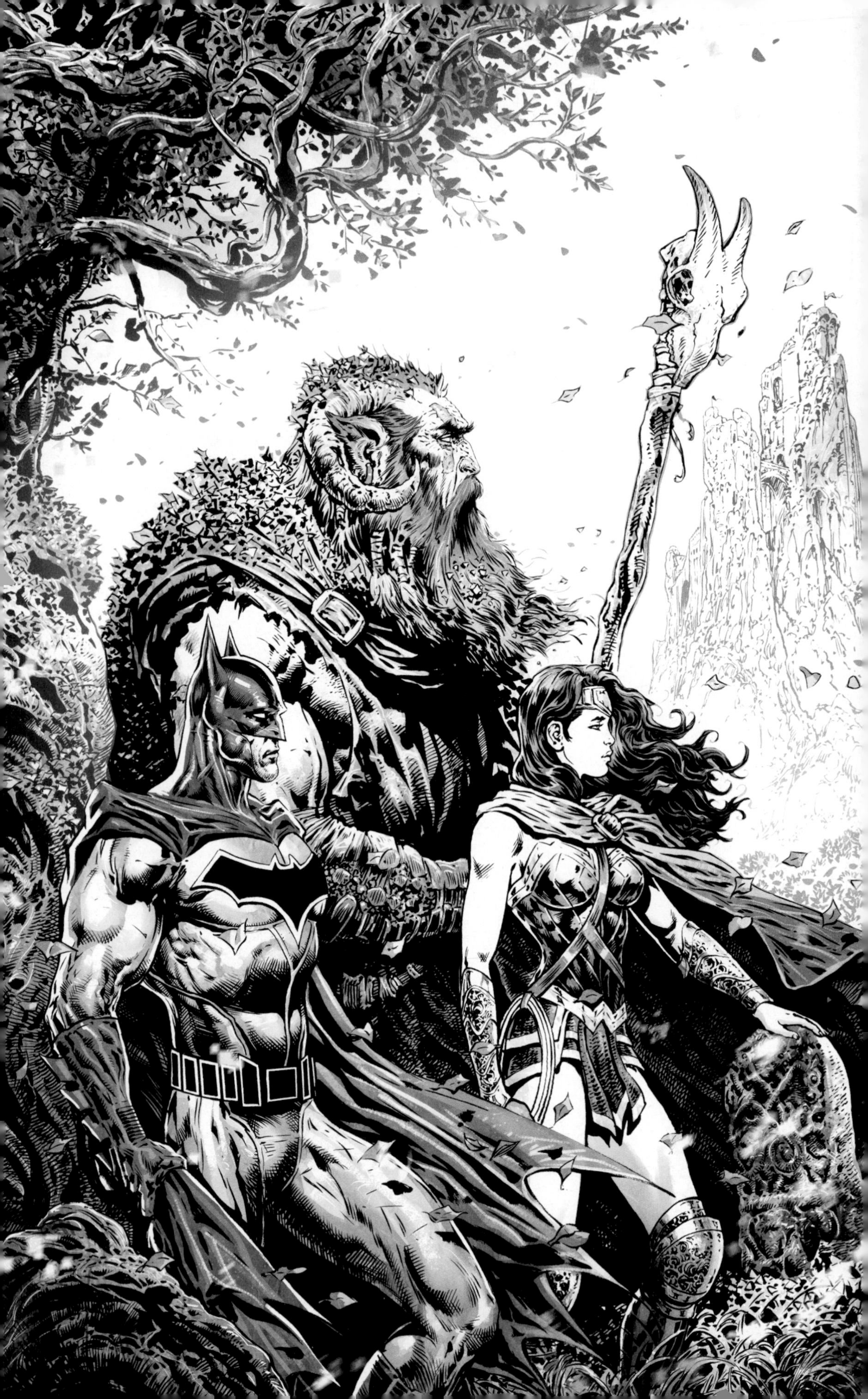

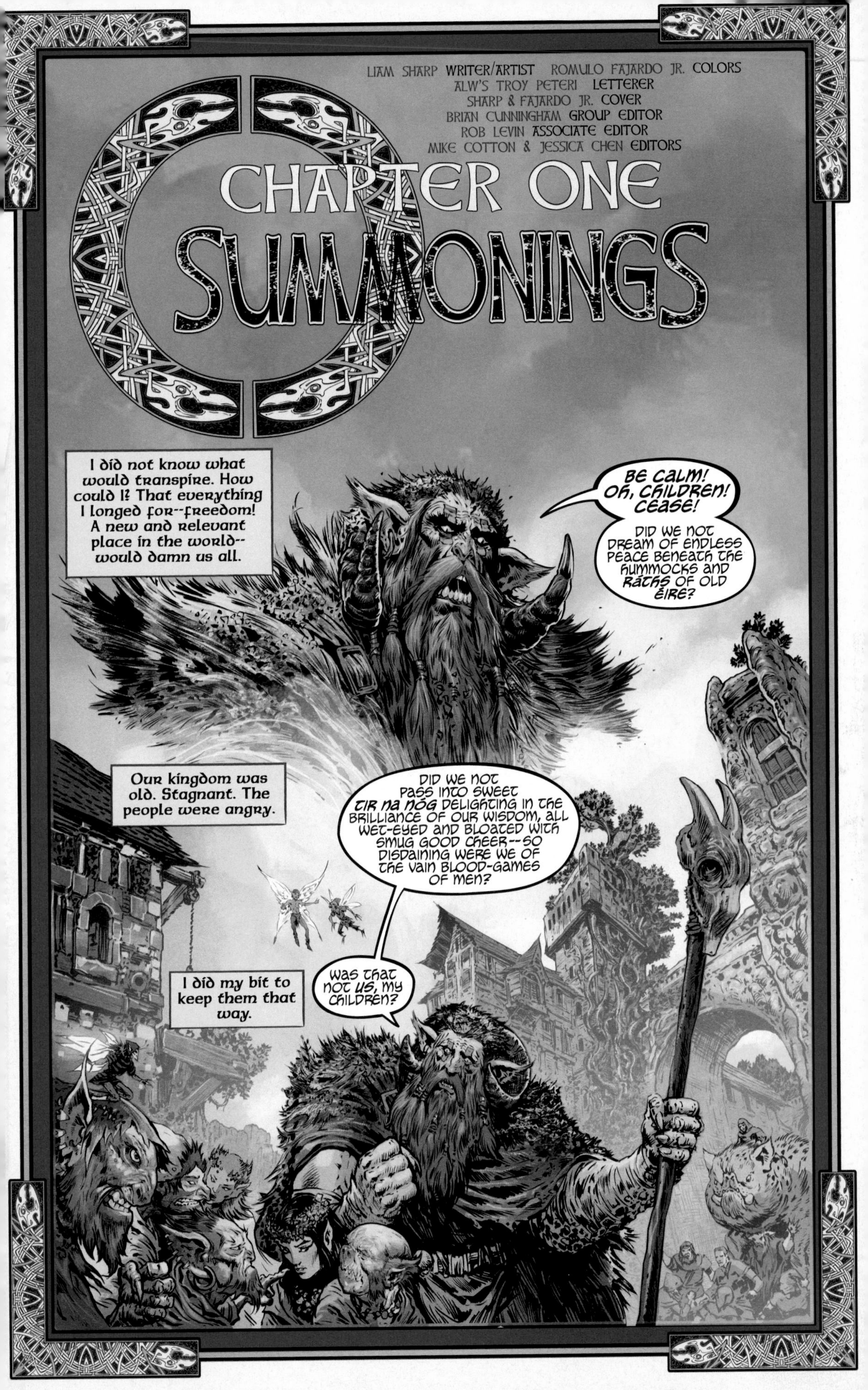

LIAM SHARP WRITER/ARTIST ROMULO FAJARDO JR. COLORS
ALW'S TROY PETERI LETTERER
SHARP & FAJARDO JR. COVER
BRIAN CUNNINGHAM GROUP EDITOR
ROB LEVIN ASSOCIATE EDITOR
MIKE COTTON & JESSICA CHEN EDITORS
CHAPTER ONE
SUMMONINGS
I did not know what would transpire. How could I? That everything I longed for--freedom! A new and relevant place in the world--would damn us all.
BE CALM! OH, CHILDREN! CEASE!
DID WE NOT DREAM OF ENDLESS PEACE BENEATH THE HUMMOCKS AND RATHS OF OLD EIRE?
Our kingdom was old. Stagnant. The people were angry.
DID WE NOT PASS INTO SWEET TIR NA NÓG DELIGHTING IN THE BRILLIANCE OF OUR WISDOM, ALL WET-EYED AND BLOATED WITH SMUG GOOD CHEER--SO DISDAINING WERE WE OF THE VAIN BLOOD-GAMES OF MEN?
I did my bit to keep them that way.
WAS THAT NOT US, MY CHILDREN?

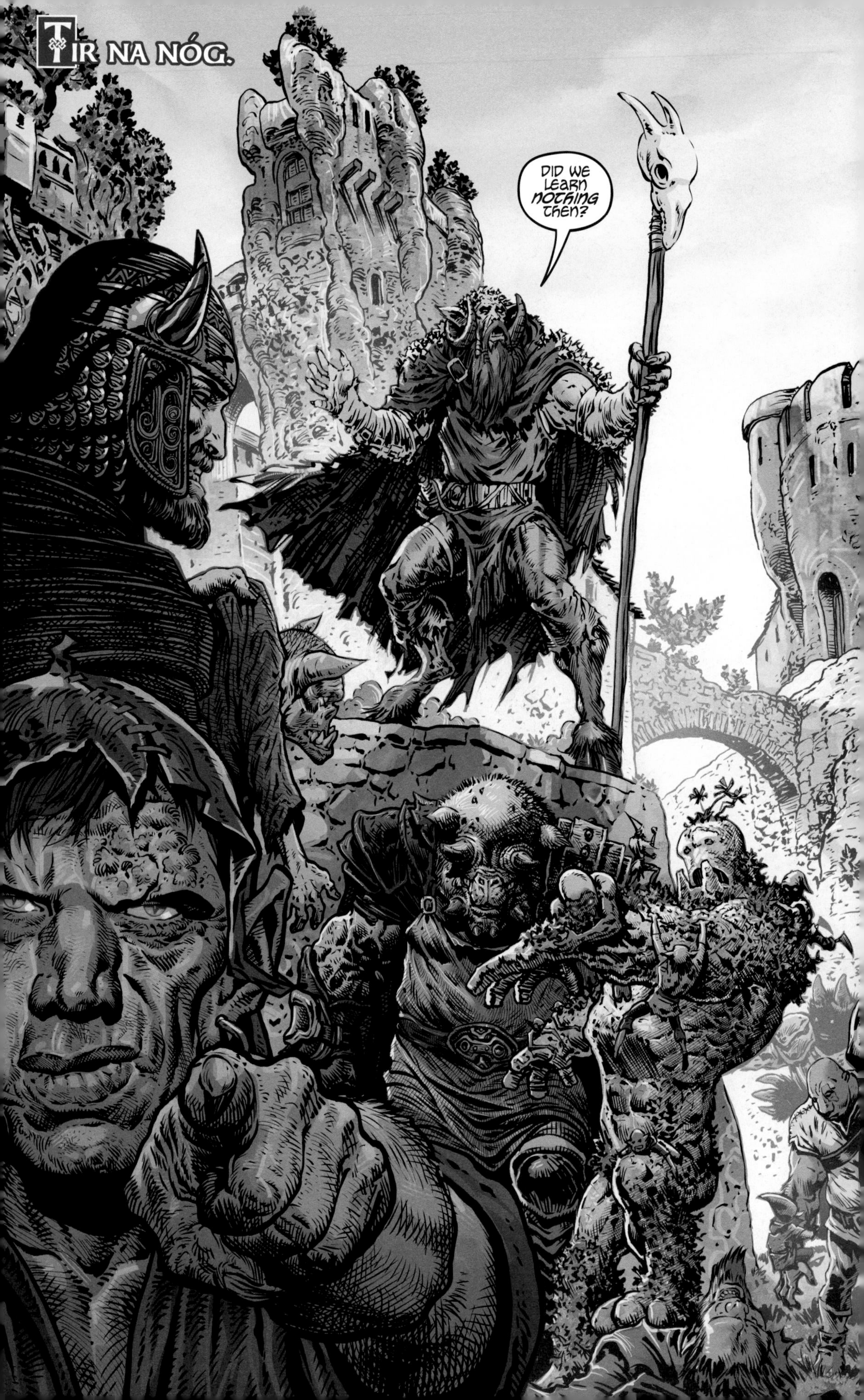
TIR NA NÓG.
DID WE LEARN NOTHING THEN?

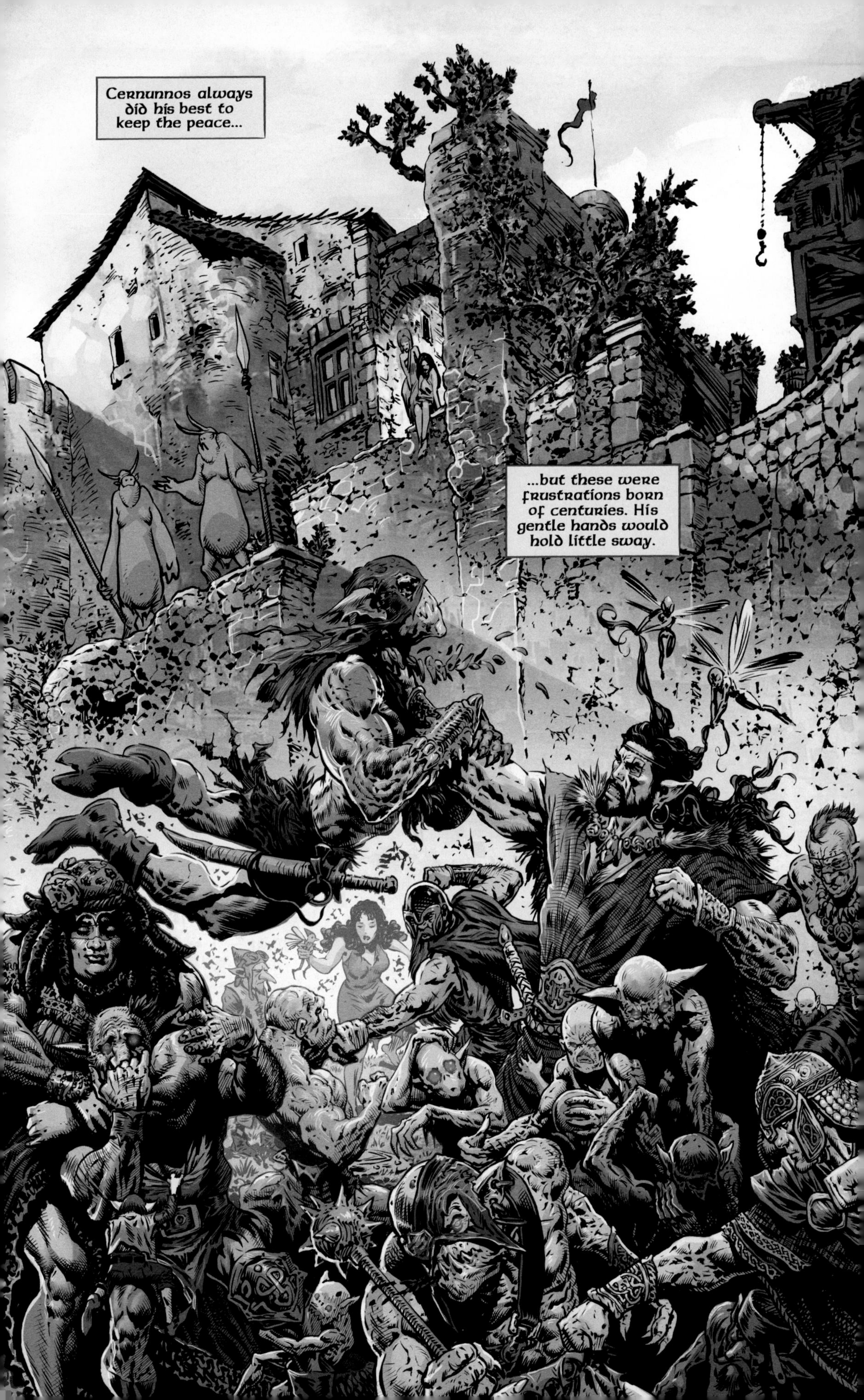
Cernunnos always did his best to keep the peace...
...but these were frustrations born of centuries. His gentle hands would hold little sway.

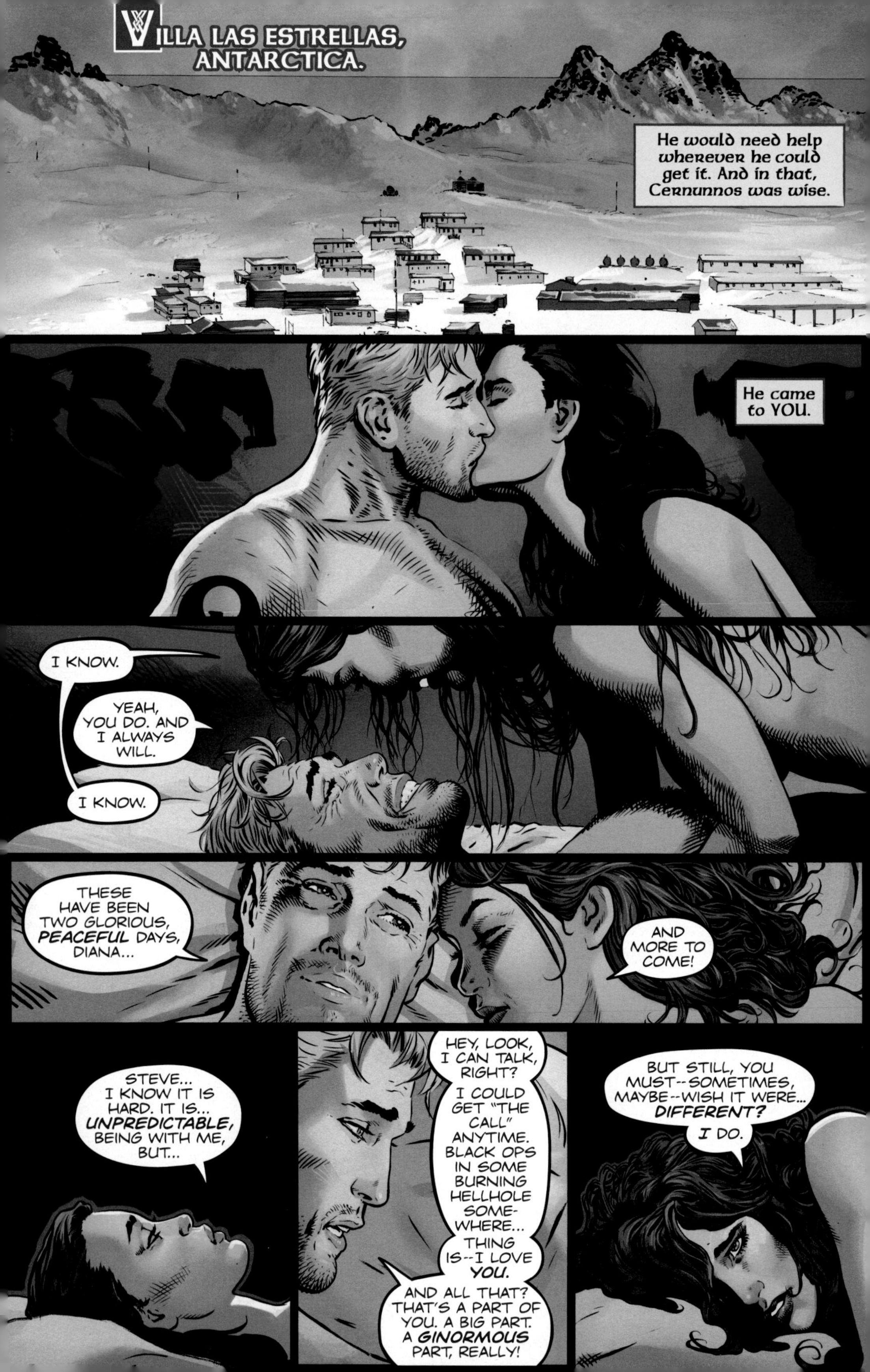
VILLA LAS ESTRELLAS, ANTARCTICA.
He would need help wherever he could get it. And in that, Cernunnos was wise.
He came to YOU.
I KNOW.
YEAH, YOU DO. AND I ALWAYS WILL.
I KNOW.
THESE HAVE BEEN TWO GLORIOUS, *PEACEFUL* DAYS, DIANA...
AND MORE TO COME!
STEVE... I KNOW IT IS HARD. IT IS... *UNPREDICTABLE,* BEING WITH ME, BUT...
HEY, LOOK, I CAN TALK, RIGHT?
I COULD GET "THE CALL" ANYTIME. BLACK OPS IN SOME BURNING HELLHOLE SOME-WHERE...
THING IS--I LOVE *YOU.*
AND ALL THAT? THAT'S A PART OF YOU. A BIG PART. A *GINORMOUS* PART, REALLY!
BUT STILL, YOU MUST--SOMETIMES, MAYBE--WISH IT WERE... *DIFFERENT?*
I DO.

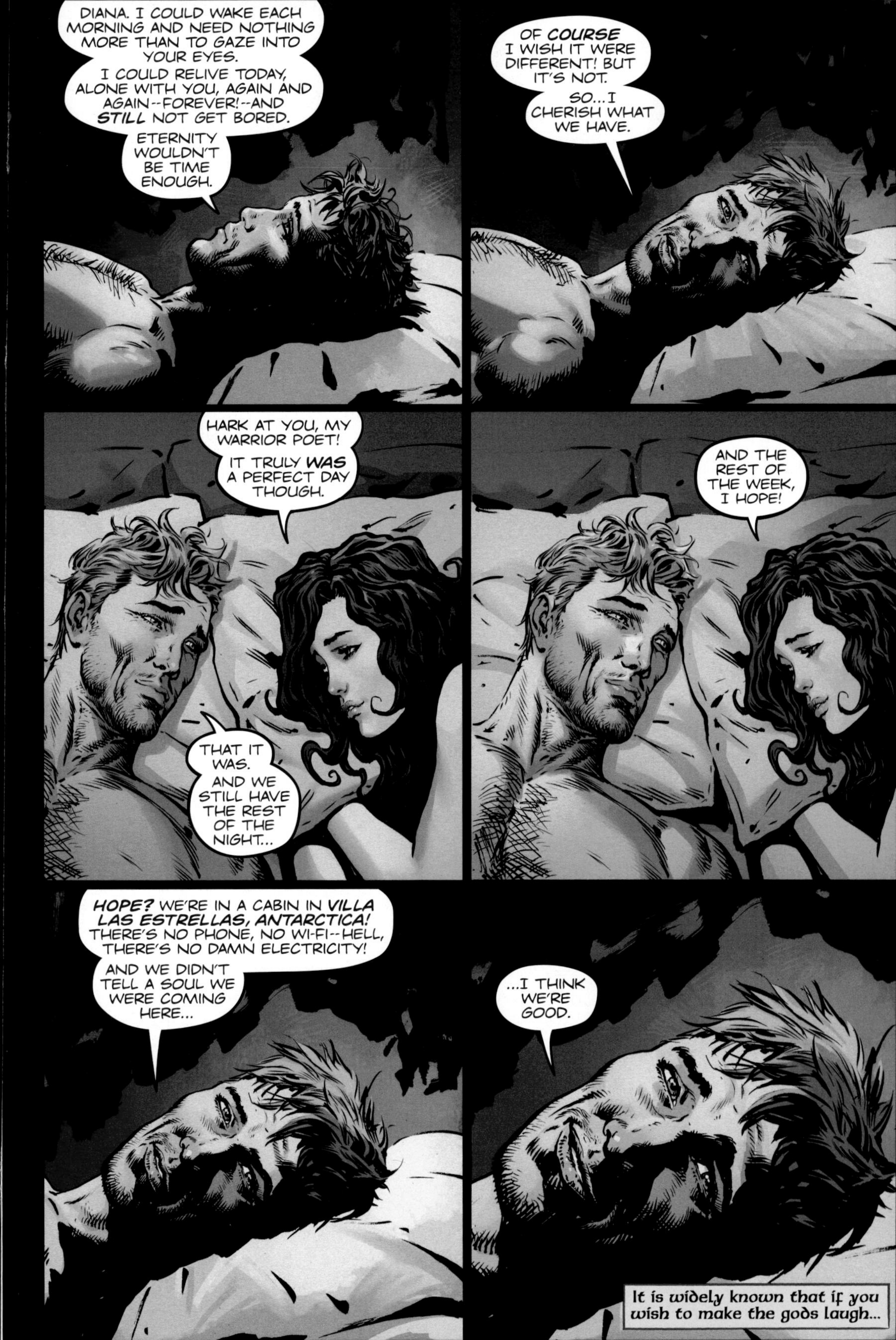
DIANA. I COULD WAKE EACH MORNING AND NEED NOTHING MORE THAN TO GAZE INTO YOUR EYES.
I COULD RELIVE TODAY, ALONE WITH YOU, AGAIN AND AGAIN--FOREVER!--AND STILL NOT GET BORED.
ETERNITY WOULDN'T BE TIME ENOUGH.
OF COURSE I WISH IT WERE DIFFERENT! BUT IT'S NOT.
SO...I CHERISH WHAT WE HAVE.
HARK AT YOU, MY WARRIOR POET!
IT TRULY WAS A PERFECT DAY THOUGH.
THAT IT WAS.
AND WE STILL HAVE THE REST OF THE NIGHT...
AND THE REST OF THE WEEK, I HOPE!
HOPE? WE'RE IN A CABIN IN VILLA LAS ESTRELLAS, ANTARCTICA! THERE'S NO PHONE, NO WI-FI--HELL, THERE'S NO DAMN ELECTRICITY!
AND WE DIDN'T TELL A SOUL WE WERE COMING HERE...
...I THINK WE'RE GOOD.
It is widely known that if you wish to make the gods laugh...

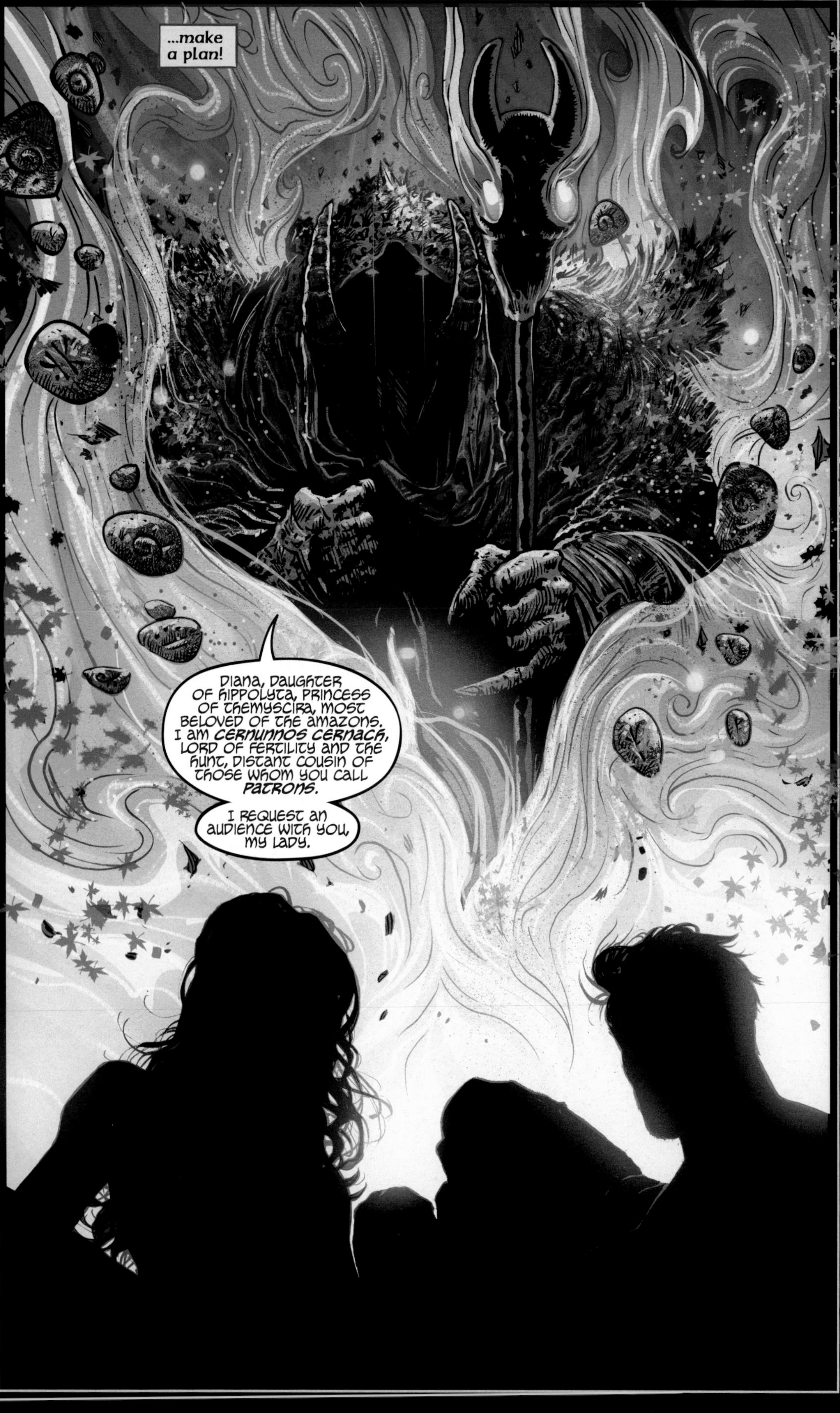
...make a plan!
Diana, daughter of Hippolyta, princess of Themyscira, most beloved of the amazons. I am Cernunnos Cernach, lord of fertility and the hunt, distant cousin of those whom you call Patrons.
I request an audience with you, my lady.

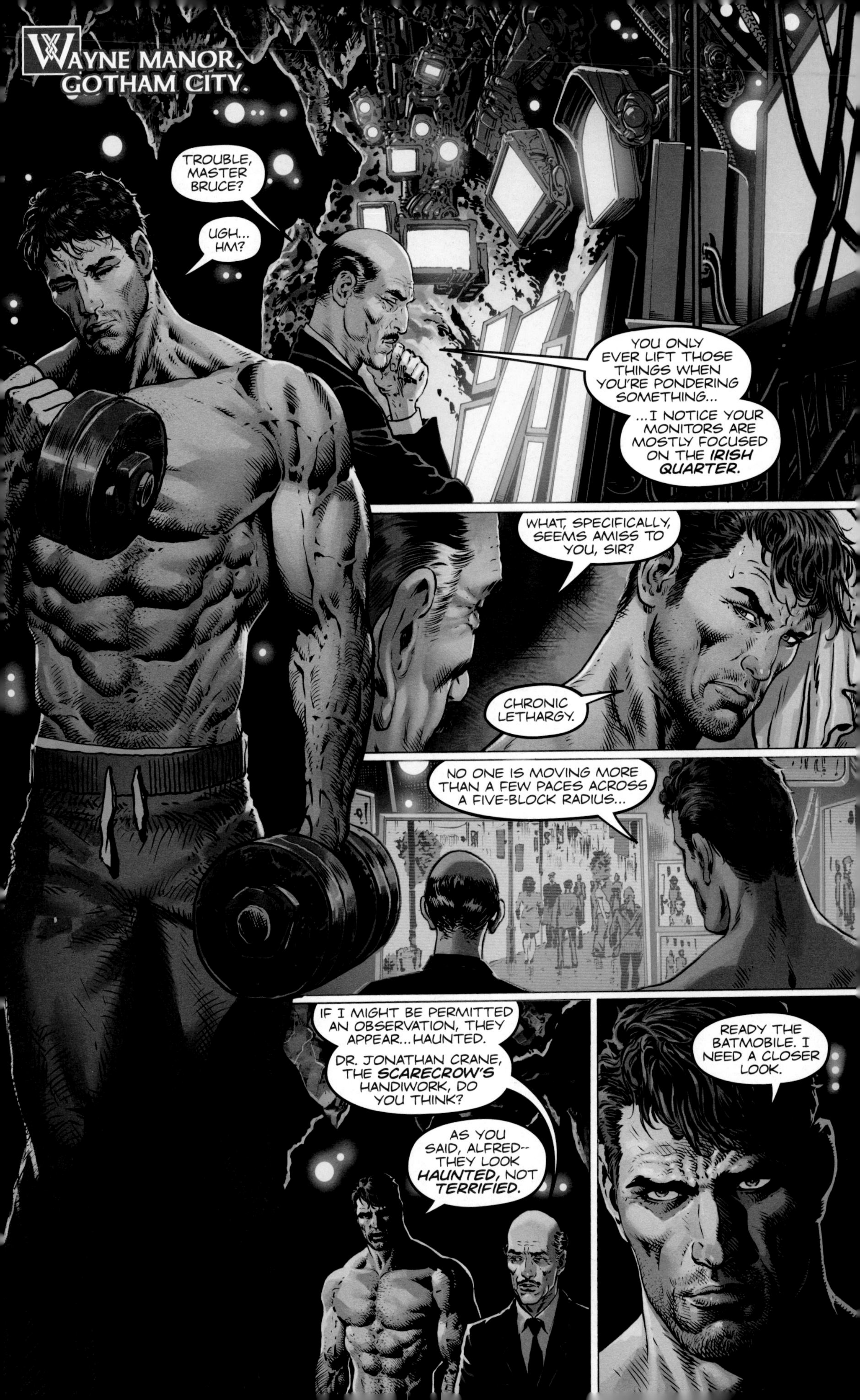
WAYNE MANOR, GOTHAM CITY.
TROUBLE, MASTER BRUCE?
UGH... HM?
YOU ONLY EVER LIFT THOSE THINGS WHEN YOU'RE PONDERING SOMETHING...
...I NOTICE YOUR MONITORS ARE MOSTLY FOCUSED ON THE IRISH QUARTER.
WHAT, SPECIFICALLY, SEEMS AMISS TO YOU, SIR?
CHRONIC LETHARGY.
NO ONE IS MOVING MORE THAN A FEW PACES ACROSS A FIVE-BLOCK RADIUS...
IF I MIGHT BE PERMITTED AN OBSERVATION, THEY APPEAR...HAUNTED.
DR. JONATHAN CRANE, THE SCARECROW'S HANDIWORK, DO YOU THINK?
AS YOU SAID, ALFRED-- THEY LOOK HAUNTED, NOT TERRIFIED.
READY THE BATMOBILE. I NEED A CLOSER LOOK.

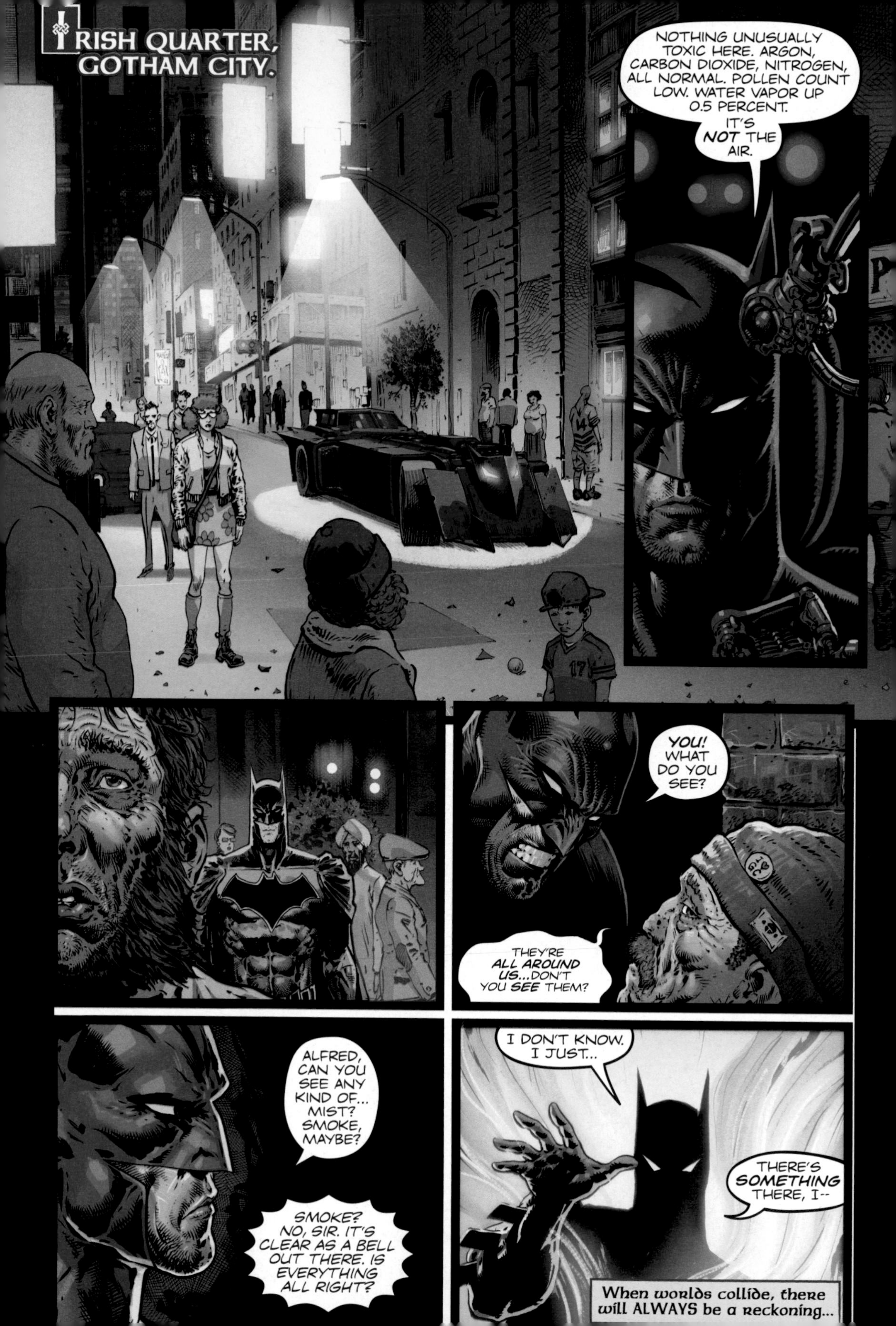
IRISH QUARTER, GOTHAM CITY.
NOTHING UNUSUALLY TOXIC HERE. ARGON, CARBON DIOXIDE, NITROGEN, ALL NORMAL. POLLEN COUNT LOW. WATER VAPOR UP 0.5 PERCENT.
IT'S NOT THE AIR.
YOU! WHAT DO YOU SEE?
THEY'RE ALL AROUND US...DON'T YOU SEE THEM?
ALFRED, CAN YOU SEE ANY KIND OF... MIST? SMOKE, MAYBE?
SMOKE? NO, SIR. IT'S CLEAR AS A BELL OUT THERE. IS EVERYTHING ALL RIGHT?
I DON'T KNOW. I JUST...
THERE'S SOMETHING THERE, I--
When worlds collide, there will ALWAYS be a reckoning...

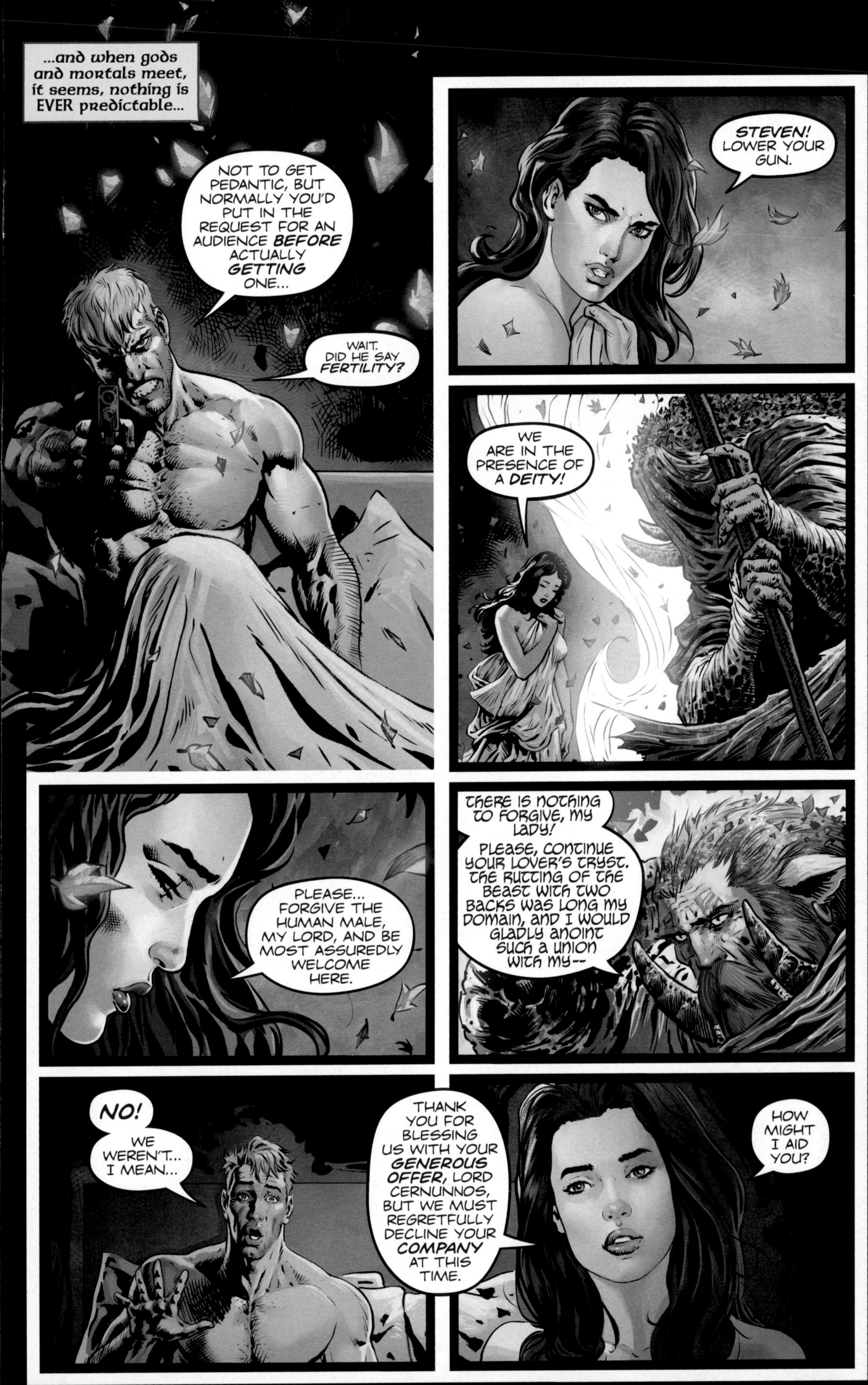
...and when gods and mortals meet, it seems, nothing is EVER predictable...
NOT TO GET PEDANTIC, BUT NORMALLY YOU'D PUT IN THE REQUEST FOR AN AUDIENCE BEFORE ACTUALLY GETTING ONE...
WAIT. DID HE SAY FERTILITY?
STEVEN! LOWER YOUR GUN.
WE ARE IN THE PRESENCE OF A DEITY!
PLEASE... FORGIVE THE HUMAN MALE, MY LORD, AND BE MOST ASSUREDLY WELCOME HERE.
THERE IS NOTHING TO FORGIVE, MY LADY!
PLEASE, CONTINUE YOUR LOVER'S TRYST. THE RUTTING OF THE BEAST WITH TWO BACKS WAS LONG MY DOMAIN, AND I WOULD GLADLY ANOINT SUCH A UNION WITH MY--
NO!
WE WEREN'T... I MEAN...
THANK YOU FOR BLESSING US WITH YOUR GENEROUS OFFER, LORD CERNUNNOS, BUT WE MUST REGRETFULLY DECLINE YOUR COMPANY AT THIS TIME.
HOW MIGHT I AID YOU?

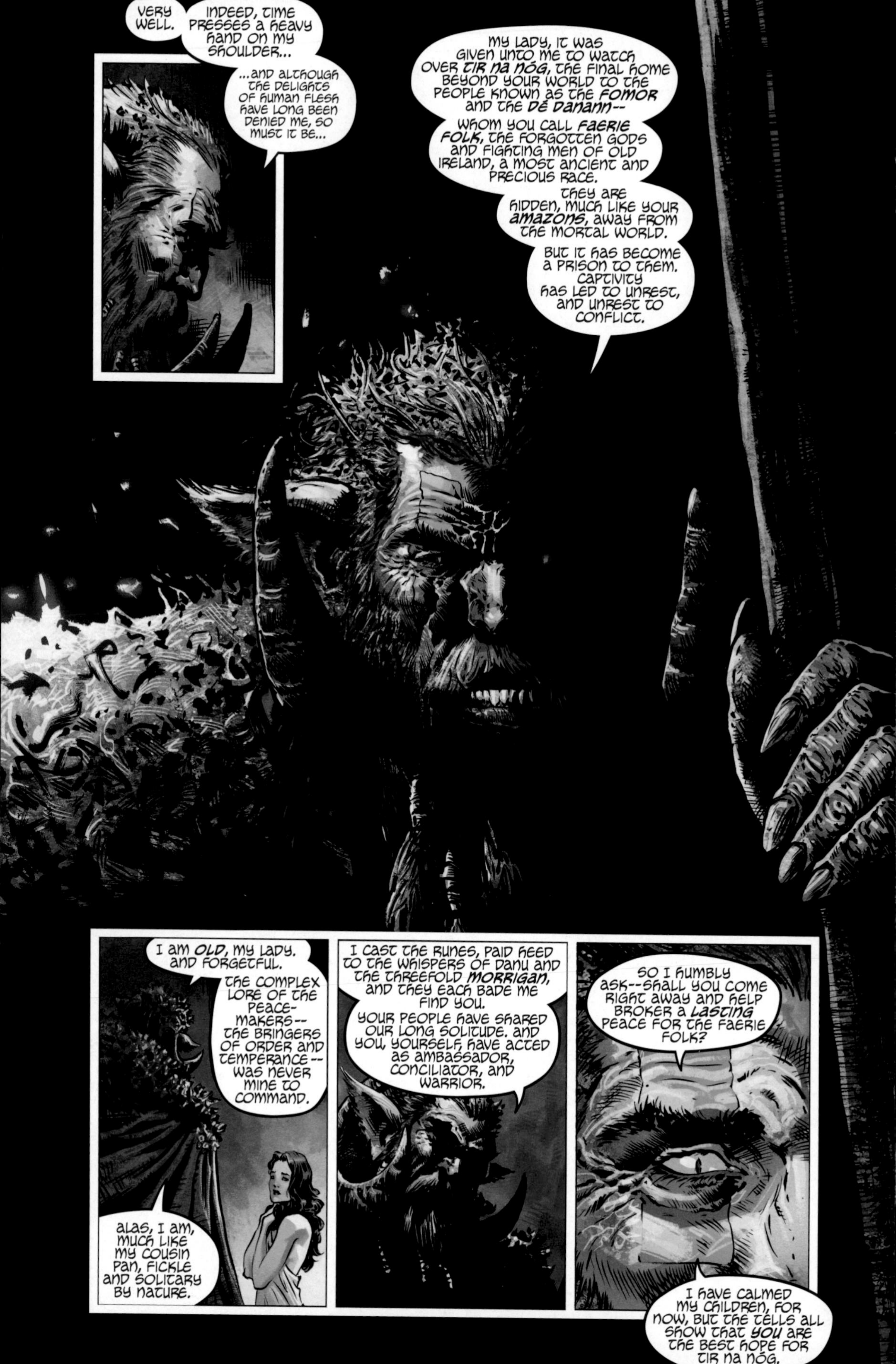
VERY WELL.
INDEED, TIME PRESSES A HEAVY HAND ON MY SHOULDER...
...AND ALTHOUGH THE DELIGHTS OF HUMAN FLESH HAVE LONG BEEN DENIED ME, SO MUST IT BE...
MY LADY, IT WAS GIVEN UNTO ME TO WATCH OVER TIR NA NÓG, THE FINAL HOME BEYOND YOUR WORLD TO THE PEOPLE KNOWN AS THE FOMOR AND THE DÉ DANANN--
WHOM YOU CALL FAERIE FOLK, THE FORGOTTEN GODS AND FIGHTING MEN OF OLD IRELAND, A MOST ANCIENT AND PRECIOUS RACE.
THEY ARE HIDDEN, MUCH LIKE YOUR AMAZONS, AWAY FROM THE MORTAL WORLD.
BUT IT HAS BECOME A PRISON TO THEM. CAPTIVITY HAS LED TO UNREST, AND UNREST TO CONFLICT.
I AM OLD, MY LADY. AND FORGETFUL.
THE COMPLEX LORE OF THE PEACE-MAKERS--THE BRINGERS OF ORDER AND TEMPERANCE--WAS NEVER MINE TO COMMAND.
ALAS, I AM, MUCH LIKE MY COUSIN PAN, FICKLE AND SOLITARY BY NATURE.
I CAST THE RUNES, PAID HEED TO THE WHISPERS OF DANU AND THE THREEFOLD MORRIGAN, AND THEY EACH BADE ME FIND YOU.
YOUR PEOPLE HAVE SHARED OUR LONG SOLITUDE. AND YOU, YOURSELF, HAVE ACTED AS AMBASSADOR, CONCILIATOR, AND WARRIOR.
SO I HUMBLY ASK--SHALL YOU COME RIGHT AWAY AND HELP BROKER A LASTING PEACE FOR THE FAERIE FOLK?
I HAVE CALMED MY CHILDREN, FOR NOW, BUT THE TELLS ALL SHOW THAT YOU ARE THE BEST HOPE FOR TIR NA NÓG.

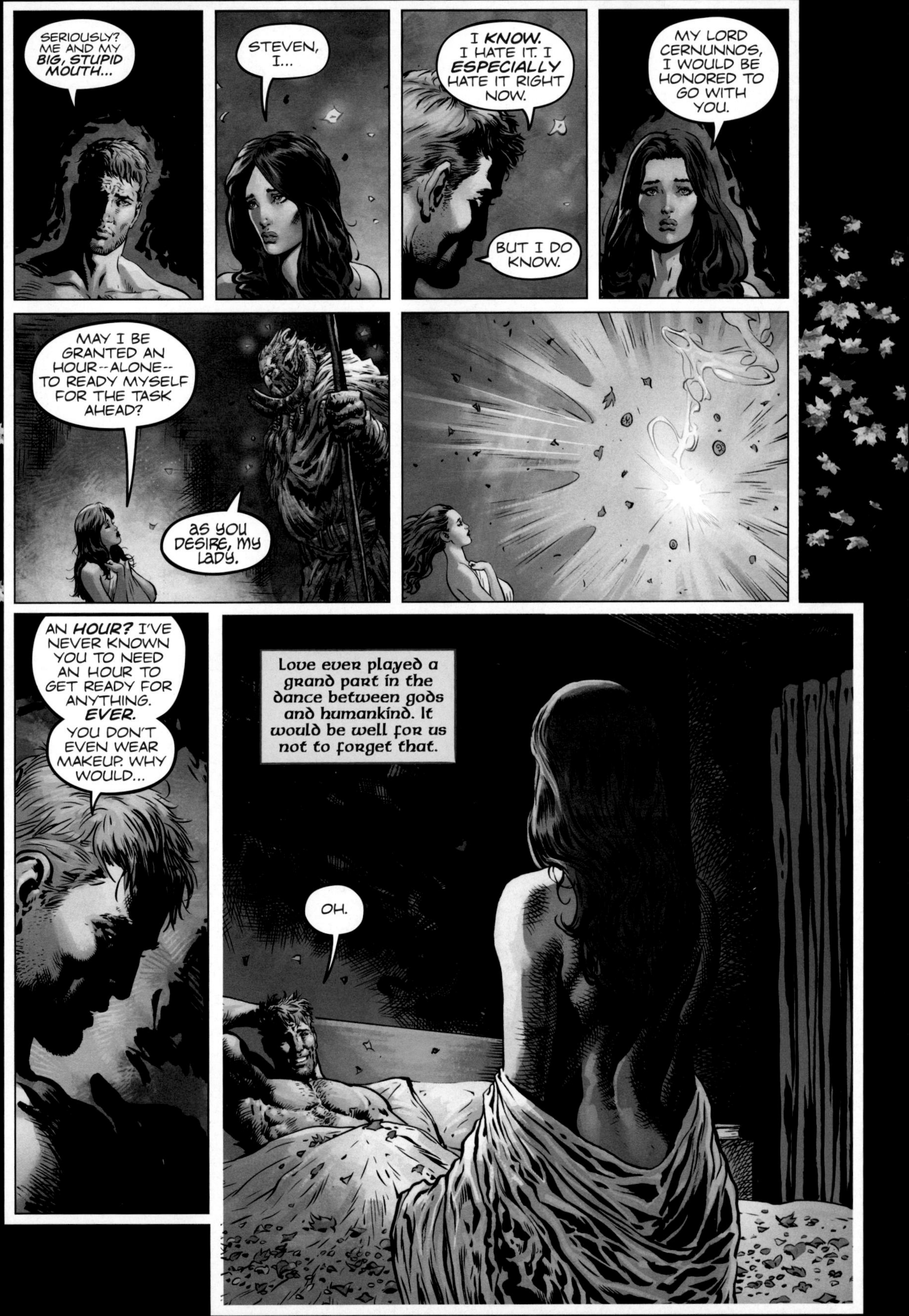
SERIOUSLY? ME AND MY BIG, STUPID MOUTH...
STEVEN, I...
I KNOW. I HATE IT. I ESPECIALLY HATE IT RIGHT NOW.
BUT I DO KNOW.
MY LORD CERNUNNOS, I WOULD BE HONORED TO GO WITH YOU.
MAY I BE GRANTED AN HOUR--ALONE--TO READY MYSELF FOR THE TASK AHEAD?
AS YOU DESIRE, MY LADY.
AN HOUR? I'VE NEVER KNOWN YOU TO NEED AN HOUR TO GET READY FOR ANYTHING. EVER.
YOU DON'T EVEN WEAR MAKEUP. WHY WOULD...
Love ever played a grand part in the dance between gods and humankind. It would be well for us not to forget that.
OH.

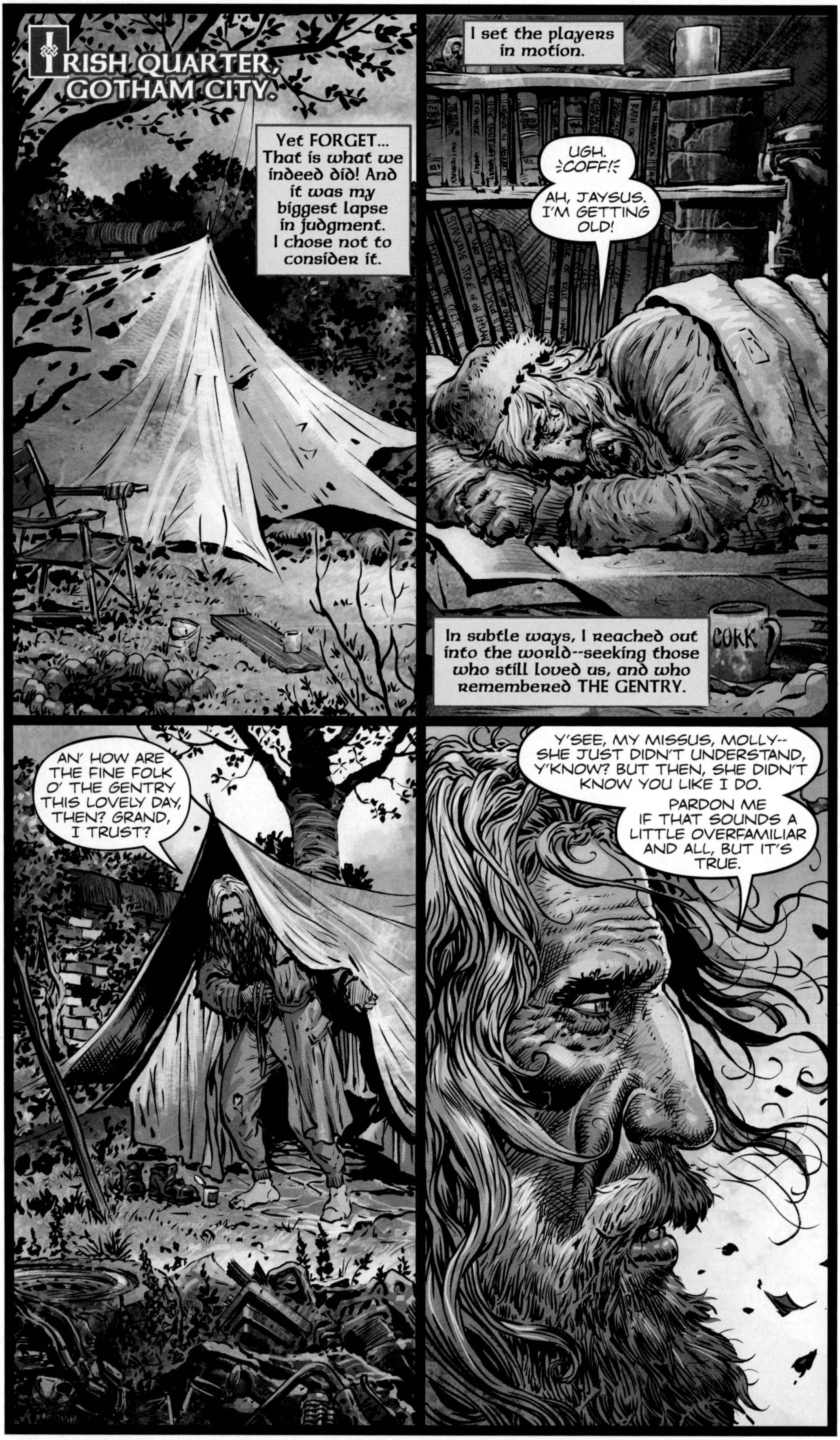
IRISH QUARTER, GOTHAM CITY.
Yet FORGET... That is what we indeed did! And it was my biggest lapse in judgment. I chose not to consider it.
I set the players in motion.
UGH. COFF!
AH, JAYSUS. I'M GETTING OLD!
In subtle ways, I reached out into the world--seeking those who still loved us, and who remembered THE GENTRY.
CORK
AN' HOW ARE THE FINE FOLK O' THE GENTRY THIS LOVELY DAY, THEN? GRAND, I TRUST?
Y'SEE, MY MISSUS, MOLLY--SHE JUST DIDN'T UNDERSTAND, Y'KNOW? BUT THEN, SHE DIDN'T KNOW YOU LIKE I DO.
PARDON ME IF THAT SOUNDS A LITTLE OVERFAMILIAR AND ALL, BUT IT'S TRUE.

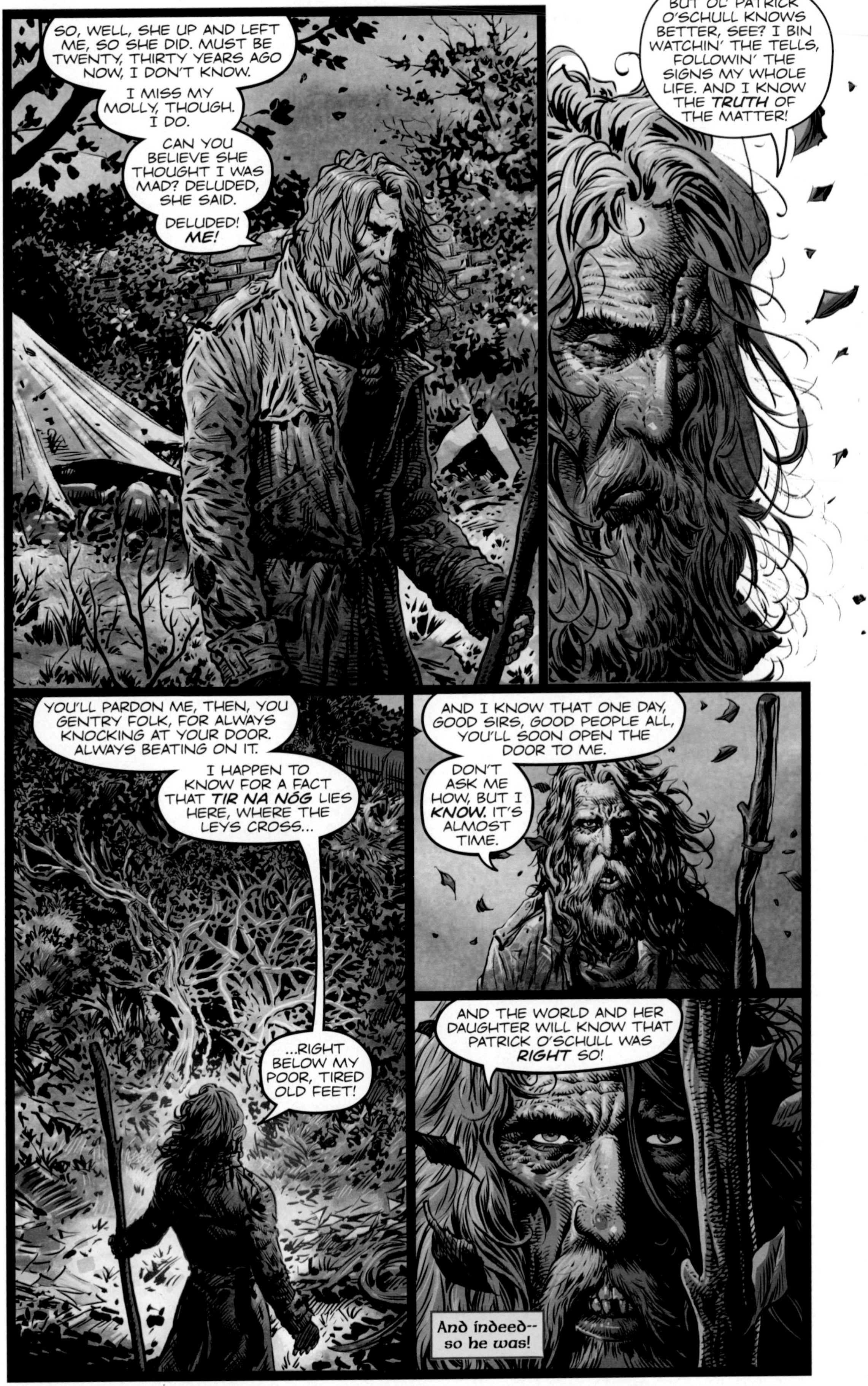
SO, WELL, SHE UP AND LEFT ME, SO SHE DID. MUST BE TWENTY, THIRTY YEARS AGO NOW, I DON'T KNOW.
I MISS MY MOLLY, THOUGH. I DO.
CAN YOU BELIEVE SHE THOUGHT I WAS MAD? DELUDED, SHE SAID.
DELUDED! ME!
BUT OL' PATRICK O'SCHULL KNOWS BETTER, SEE? I BIN WATCHIN' THE TELLS, FOLLOWIN' THE SIGNS MY WHOLE LIFE. AND I KNOW THE TRUTH OF THE MATTER!
YOU'LL PARDON ME, THEN, YOU GENTRY FOLK, FOR ALWAYS KNOCKING AT YOUR DOOR. ALWAYS BEATING ON IT.
I HAPPEN TO KNOW FOR A FACT THAT TIR NA NÓG LIES HERE, WHERE THE LEYS CROSS...
...RIGHT BELOW MY POOR, TIRED OLD FEET!
AND I KNOW THAT ONE DAY, GOOD SIRS, GOOD PEOPLE ALL, YOU'LL SOON OPEN THE DOOR TO ME.
DON'T ASK ME HOW, BUT I KNOW. IT'S ALMOST TIME.
AND THE WORLD AND HER DAUGHTER WILL KNOW THAT PATRICK O'SCHULL WAS RIGHT SO!
And indeed-- so he was!

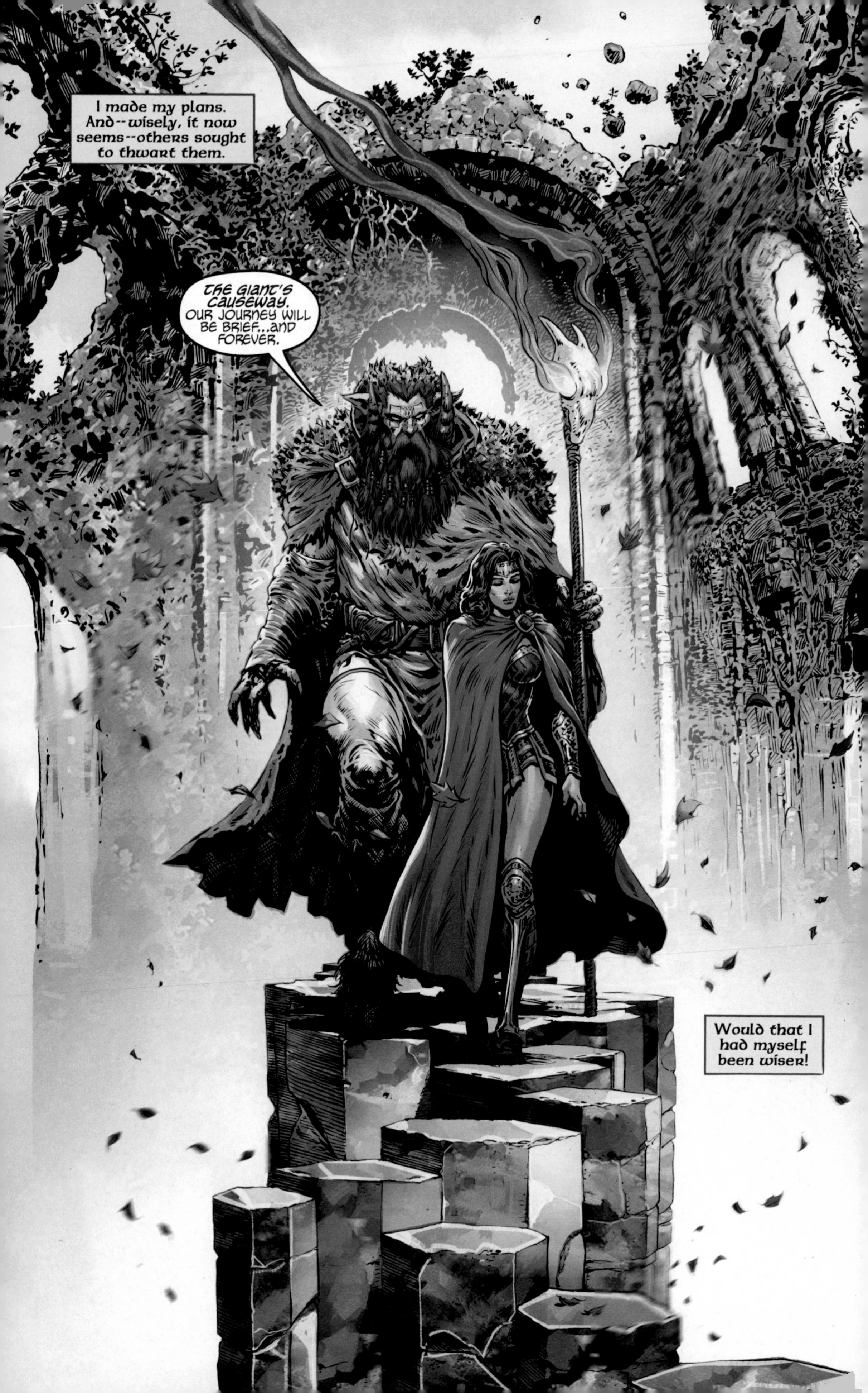
I made my plans. And--wisely, it now seems--others sought to thwart them.
THE GIANT'S CAUSEWAY. OUR JOURNEY WILL BE BRIEF...AND FOREVER.
Would that I had myself been wiser!

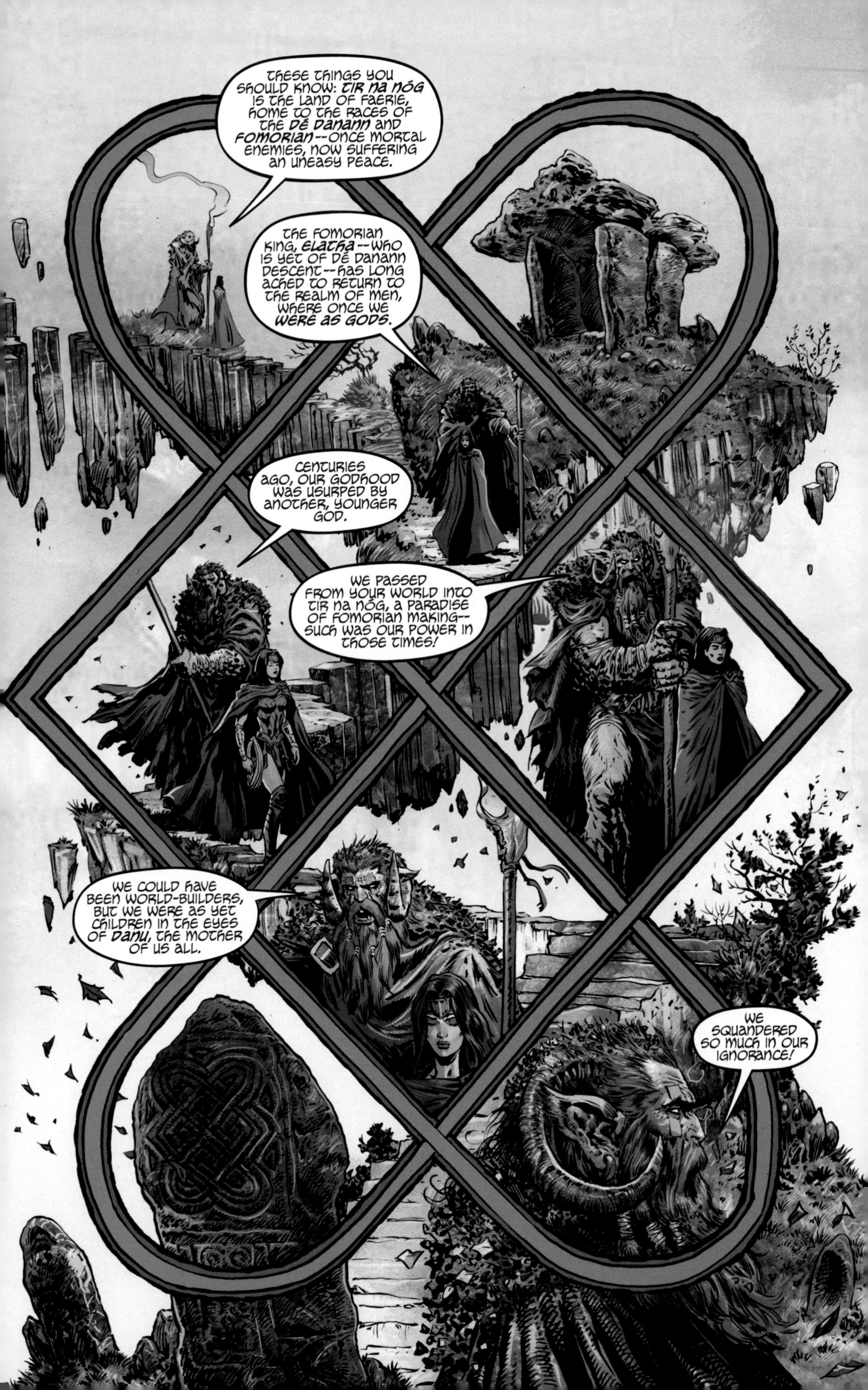
THESE THINGS YOU SHOULD KNOW: TIR NA NÓG IS THE LAND OF FAERIE, HOME TO THE RACES OF THE DÉ DANANN AND FOMORIAN--ONCE MORTAL ENEMIES, NOW SUFFERING AN UNEASY PEACE.
THE FOMORIAN KING, ELATHA--WHO IS YET OF DÉ DANANN DESCENT--HAS LONG ACHED TO RETURN TO THE REALM OF MEN, WHERE ONCE WE WERE AS GODS.
CENTURIES AGO, OUR GODHOOD WAS USURPED BY ANOTHER, YOUNGER GOD.
WE PASSED FROM YOUR WORLD INTO TIR NA NÓG, A PARADISE OF FOMORIAN MAKING--SUCH WAS OUR POWER IN THOSE TIMES!
WE COULD HAVE BEEN WORLD-BUILDERS, BUT WE WERE AS YET CHILDREN IN THE EYES OF DANU, THE MOTHER OF US ALL.
WE SQUANDERED SO MUCH IN OUR IGNORANCE!

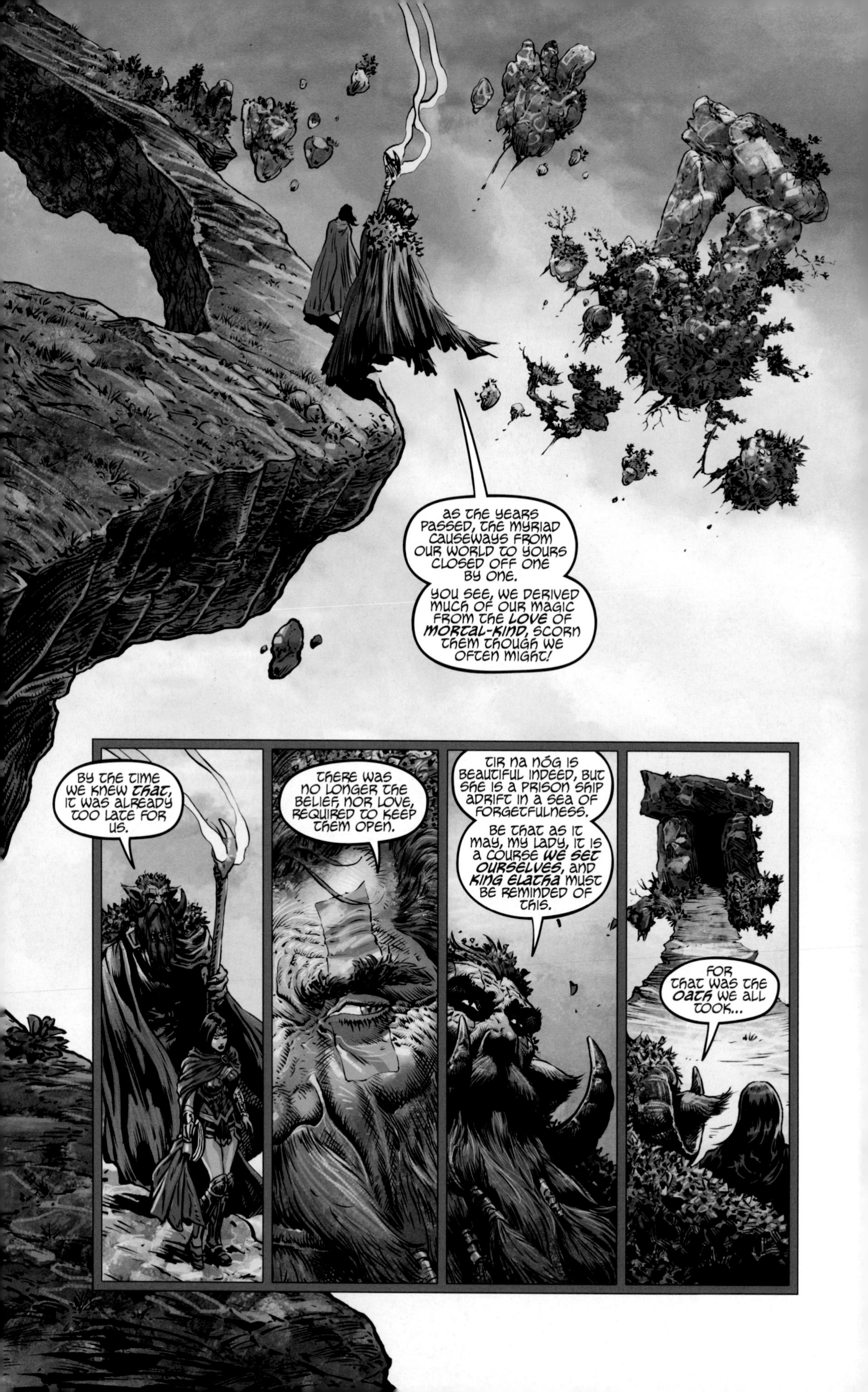
AS THE YEARS PASSED, THE MYRIAD CAUSEWAYS FROM OUR WORLD TO YOURS CLOSED OFF ONE BY ONE.
YOU SEE, WE DERIVED MUCH OF OUR MAGIC FROM THE LOVE OF MORTAL-KIND, SCORN THEM THOUGH WE OFTEN MIGHT!
BY THE TIME WE KNEW THAT, IT WAS ALREADY TOO LATE FOR US.
THERE WAS NO LONGER THE BELIEF, NOR LOVE, REQUIRED TO KEEP THEM OPEN.
TIR NA NÓG IS BEAUTIFUL INDEED, BUT SHE IS A PRISON SHIP ADRIFT IN A SEA OF FORGETFULNESS.
BE THAT AS IT MAY, MY LADY, IT IS A COURSE WE SET OURSELVES, AND KING ELATHA MUST BE REMINDED OF THIS.
FOR THAT WAS THE OATH WE ALL TOOK...

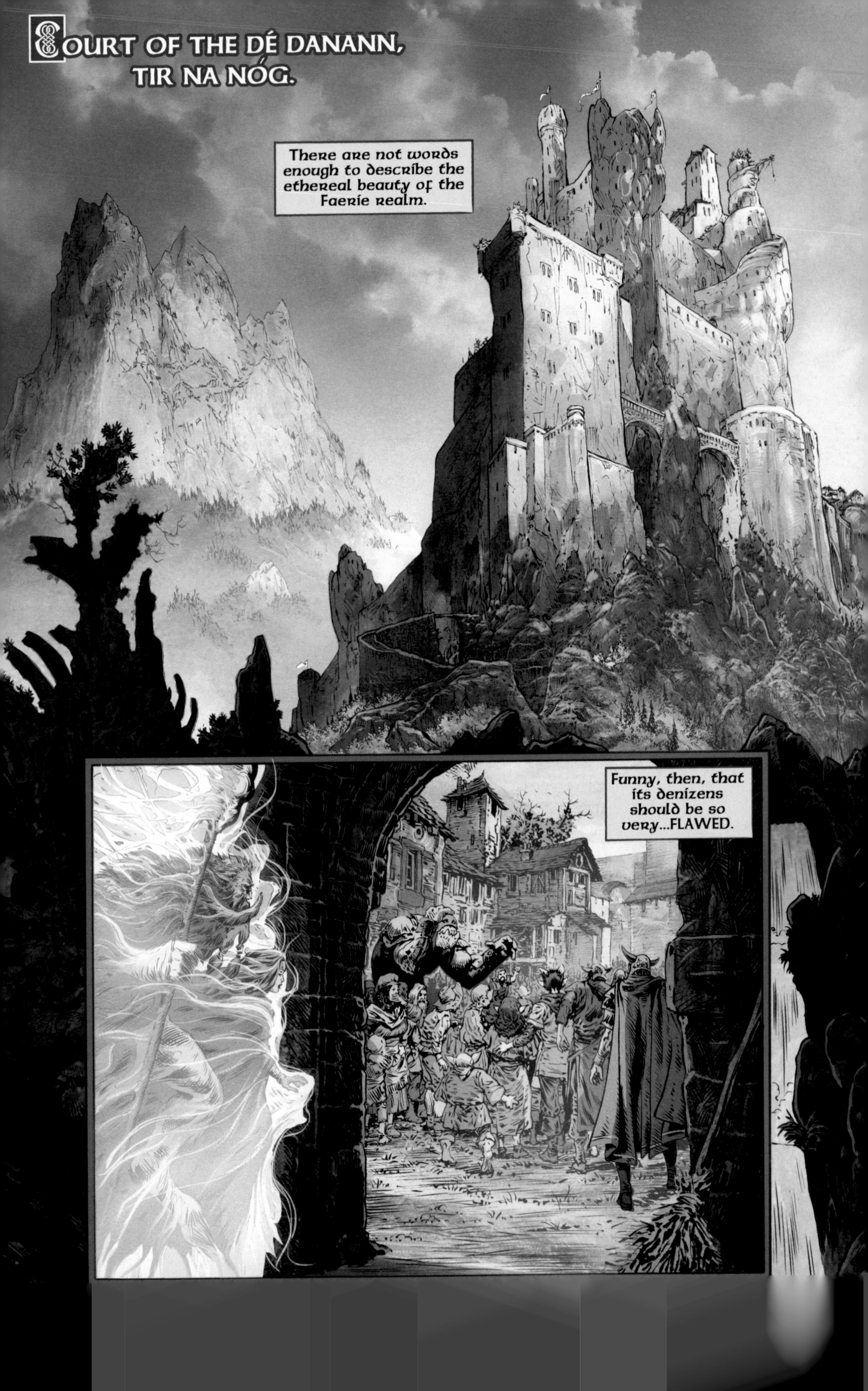
COURT OF THE DÉ DANANN, TIR NA NÓG.
There are not words enough to describe the ethereal beauty of the Faerie realm.
Funny, then, that its denizens should be so very...FLAWED.

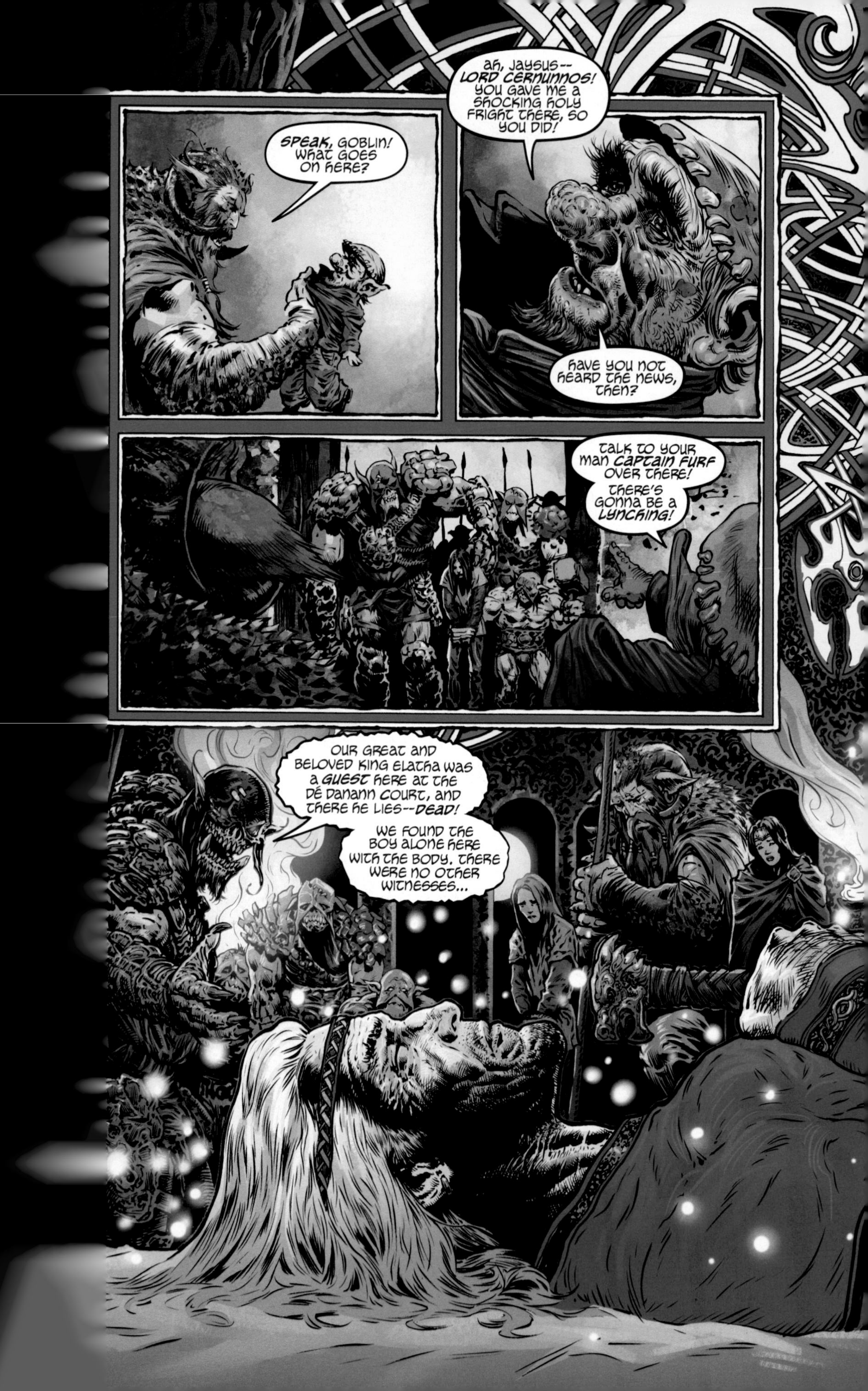
SPEAK, GOBLIN! WHAT GOES ON HERE?
AH, JAYSUS--LORD CERNUNNOS! YOU GAVE ME A SHOCKING HOLY FRIGHT THERE, SO YOU DID!
HAVE YOU NOT HEARD THE NEWS, THEN?
TALK TO YOUR MAN CAPTAIN FURF OVER THERE! THERE'S GONNA BE A LYNCHING!
OUR GREAT AND BELOVED KING ELATHA WAS A GUEST HERE AT THE DÉ DANANN COURT, AND THERE HE LIES--DEAD!
WE FOUND THE BOY ALONE HERE WITH THE BODY. THERE WERE NO OTHER WITNESSES...

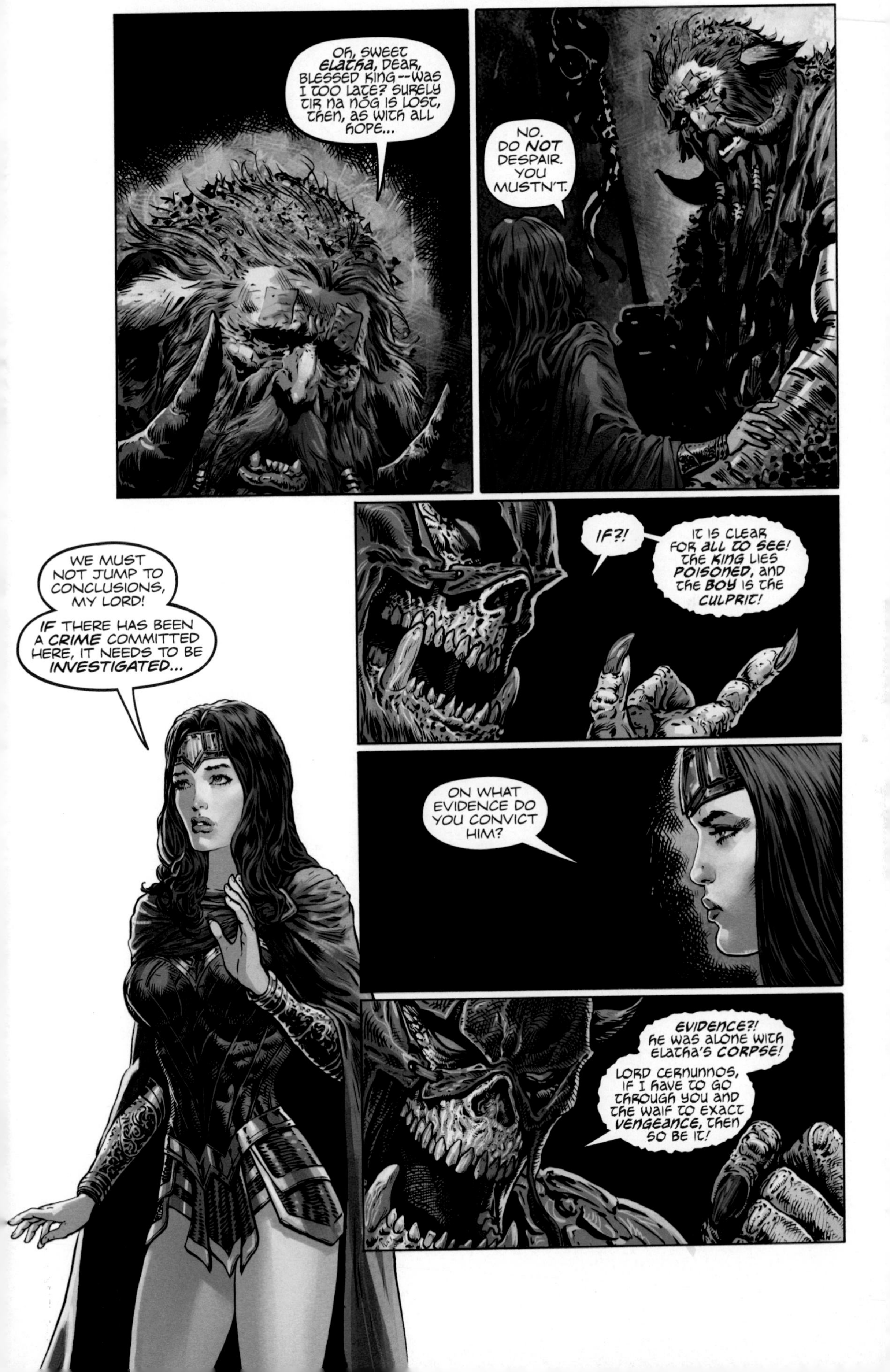
OH, SWEET ELATHA, DEAR, BLESSED KING--WAS I TOO LATE? SURELY TIR NA NÓG IS LOST, THEN, AS WITH ALL HOPE...
NO. DO NOT DESPAIR. YOU MUSTN'T.
IF?!
IT IS CLEAR FOR ALL TO SEE! THE KING LIES POISONED, AND THE BOY IS THE CULPRIT!
WE MUST NOT JUMP TO CONCLUSIONS, MY LORD!
IF THERE HAS BEEN A CRIME COMMITTED HERE, IT NEEDS TO BE INVESTIGATED...
ON WHAT EVIDENCE DO YOU CONVICT HIM?
EVIDENCE?! HE WAS ALONE WITH ELATHA'S CORPSE!
LORD CERNUNNOS, IF I HAVE TO GO THROUGH YOU AND THE WAIF TO EXACT VENGEANCE, THEN SO BE IT!

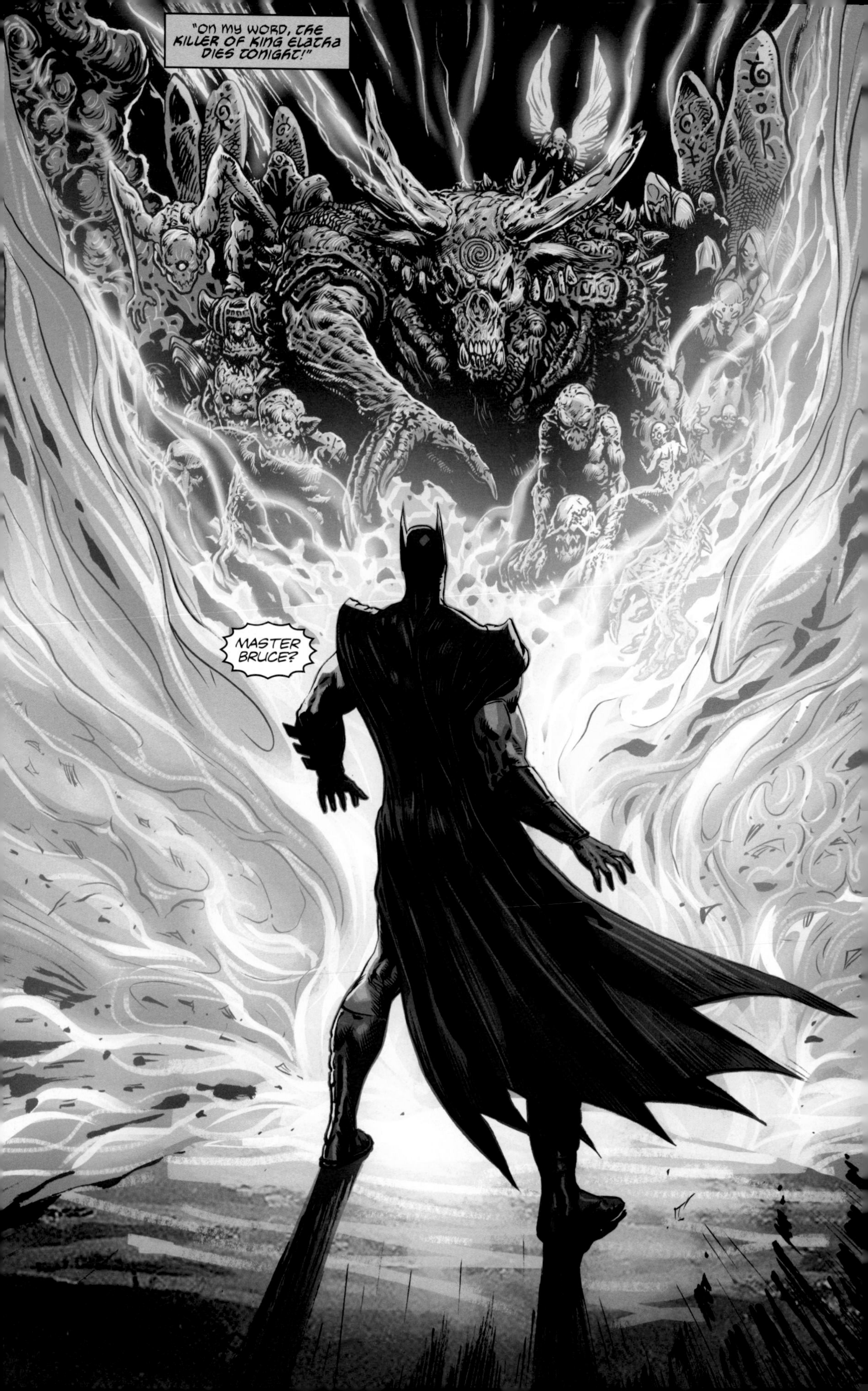
"ON MY WORD, THE KILLER OF KING ELATHA DIES TONIGHT!"
MASTER BRUCE?

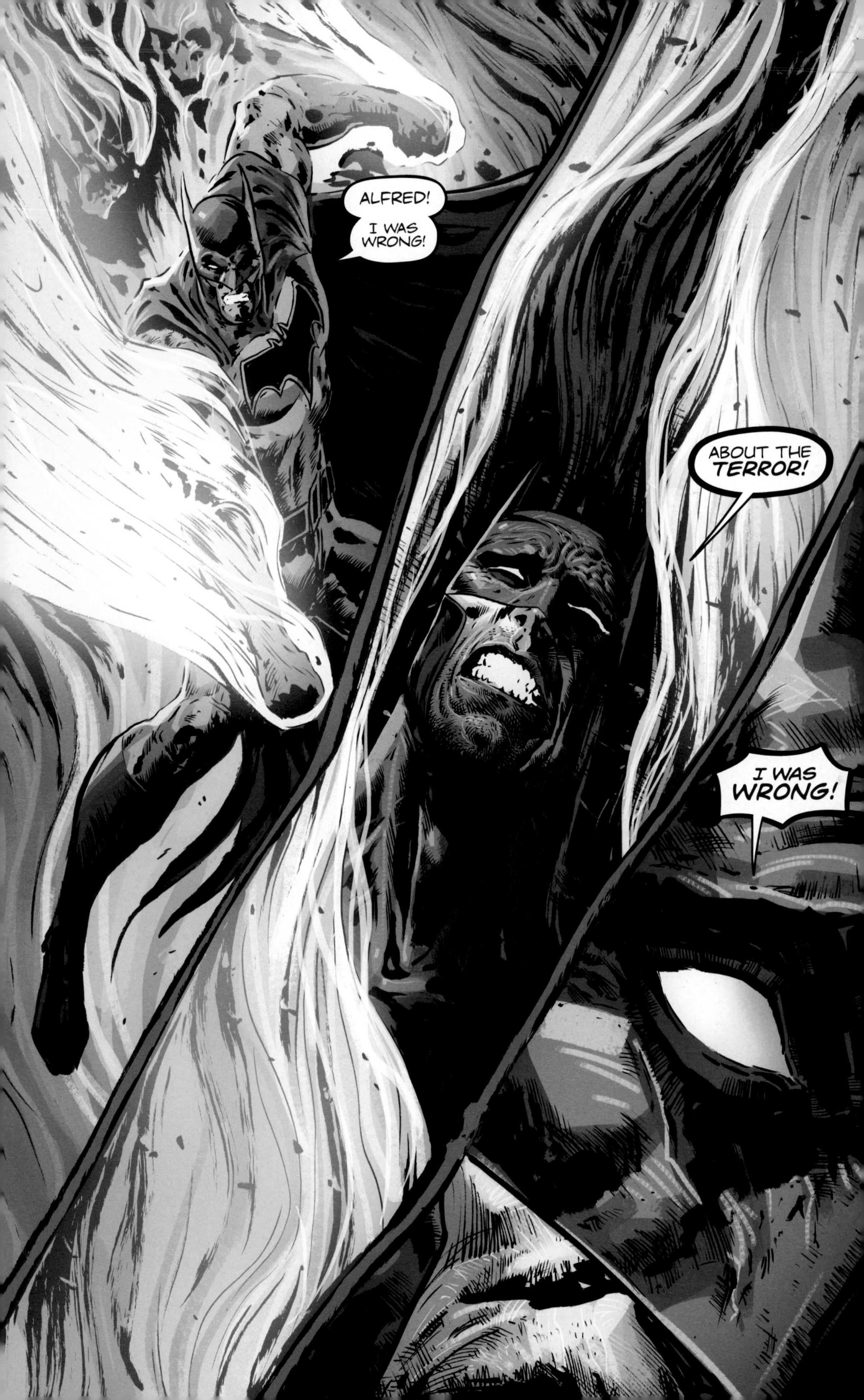
ALFRED! I WAS WRONG!
ABOUT THE TERROR!
I WAS WRONG!

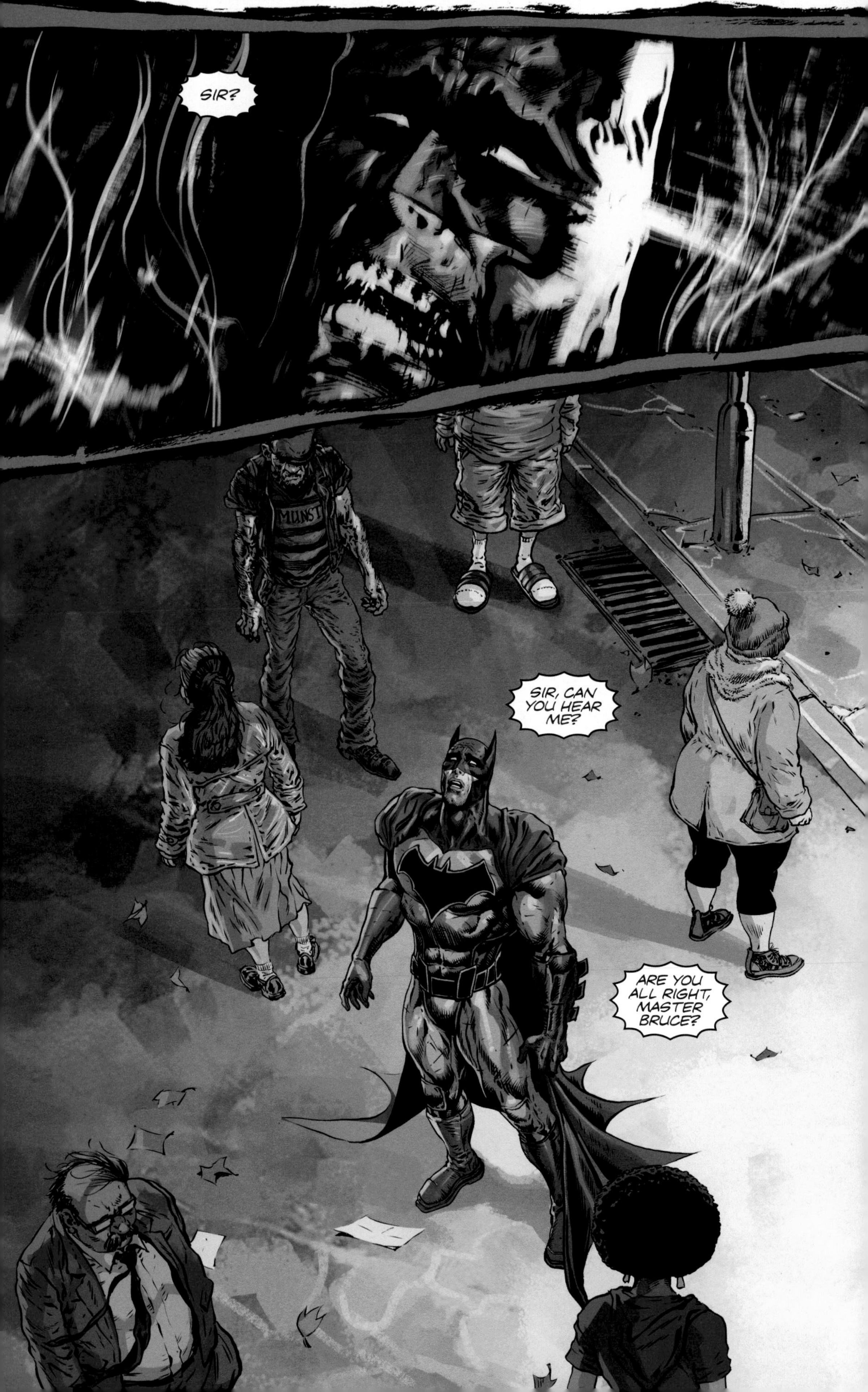
SIR?
SIR, CAN YOU HEAR ME?
ARE YOU ALL RIGHT, MASTER BRUCE?
MUNST

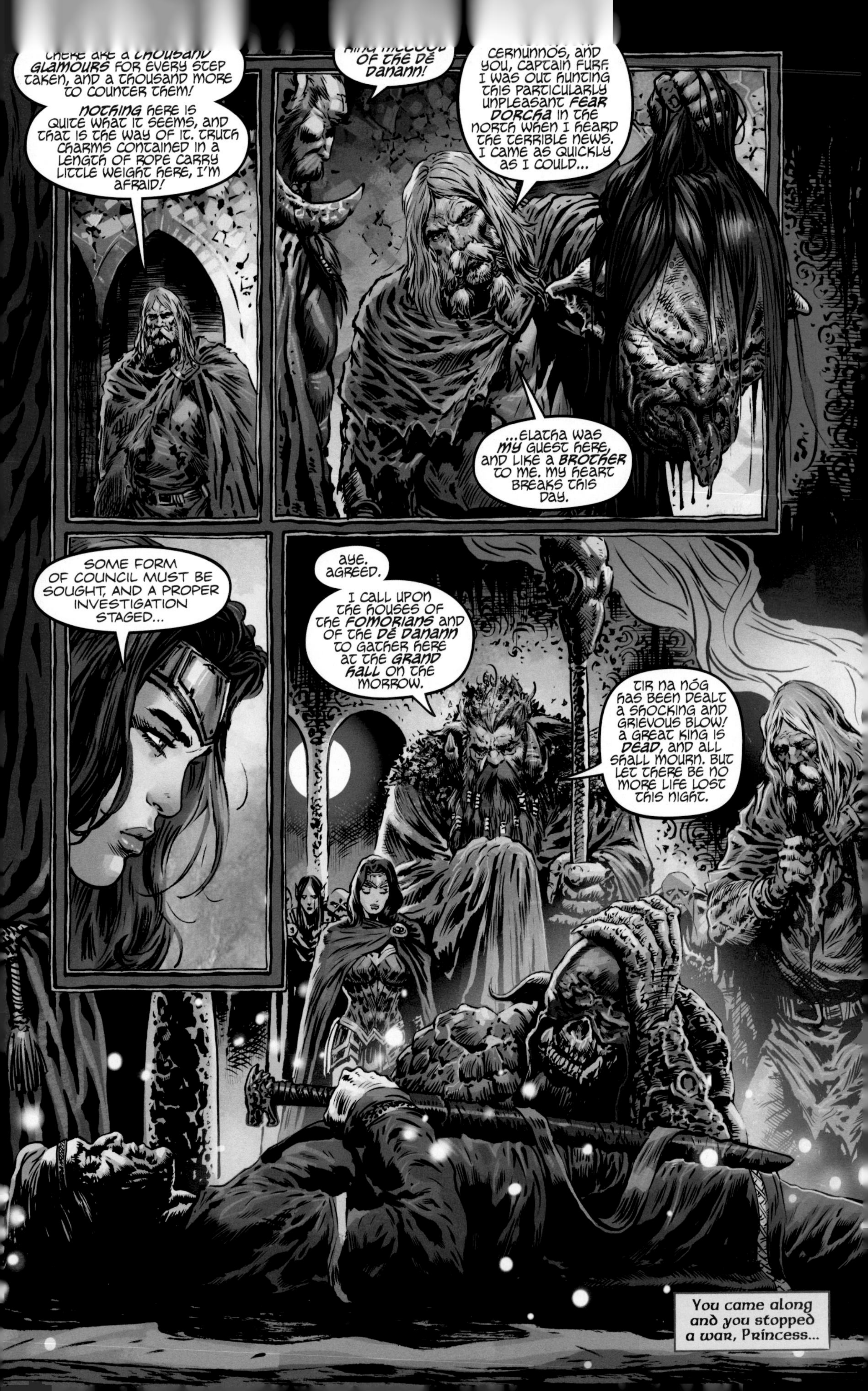
There are a thousand glamours for every step taken, and a thousand more to counter them!
Nothing here is quite what it seems, and that is the way of it. Truth charms contained in a length of rope carry little weight here, I'm afraid!
...of the Dé Danann!
Cernunnos, and you, Captain Furf. I was out hunting this particularly unpleasant Fear Dorcha in the north when I heard the terrible news. I came as quickly as I could...
...Elatha was my guest here, and like a brother to me. My heart breaks this day.
Some form of council must be sought, and a proper investigation staged...
Aye. Agreed.
I call upon the houses of the Fomorians and of the Dé Danann to gather here at the Grand Hall on the morrow.
Tir na Nóg has been dealt a shocking and grievous blow! A great king is dead, and all shall mourn. But let there be no more life lost this night.
You came along and you stopped a war, Princess...

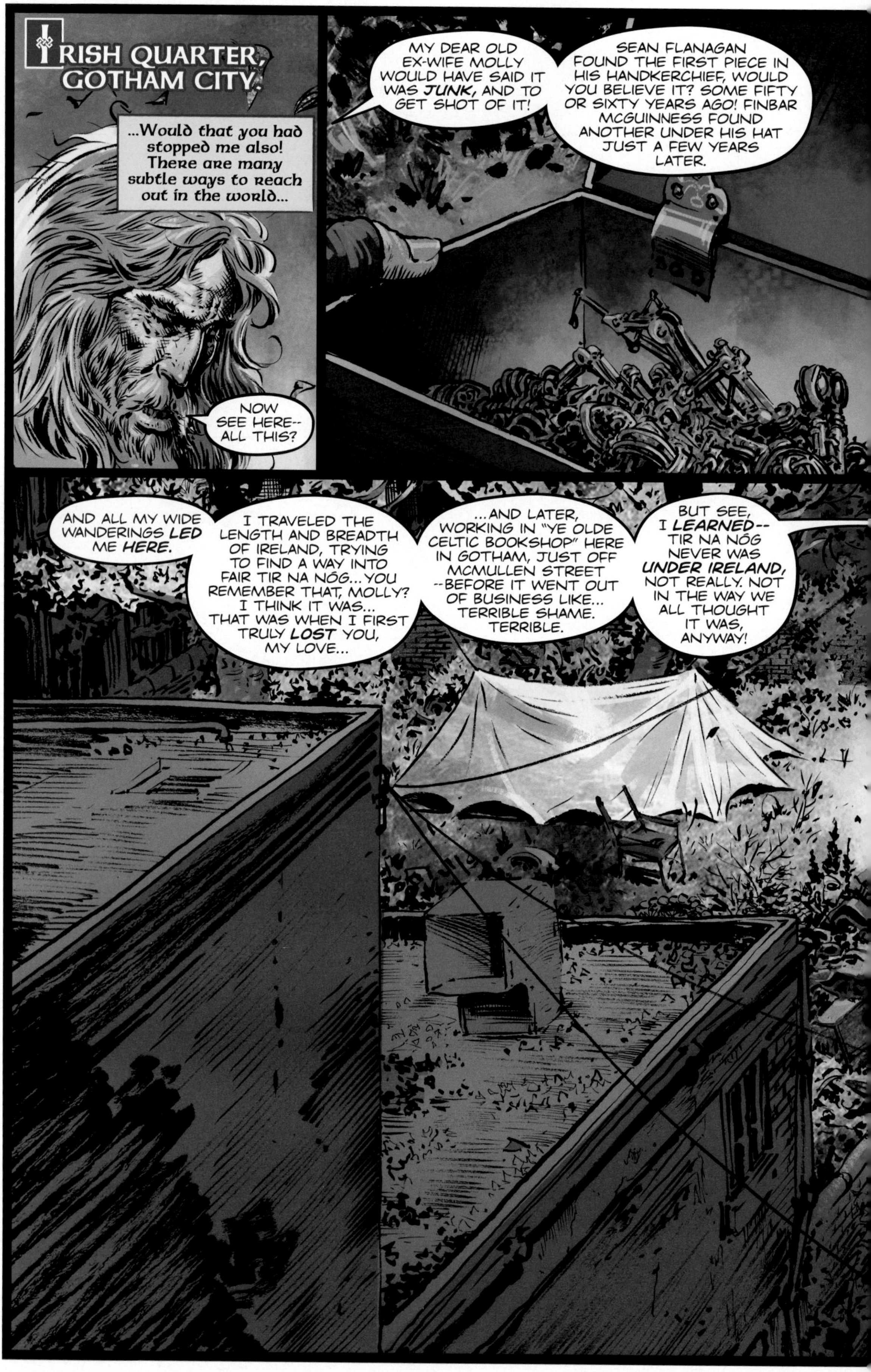
IRISH QUARTER, GOTHAM CITY.
...Would that you had stopped me also! There are many subtle ways to reach out in the world...
NOW SEE HERE-- ALL THIS?
MY DEAR OLD EX-WIFE MOLLY WOULD HAVE SAID IT WAS JUNK, AND TO GET SHOT OF IT!
SEAN FLANAGAN FOUND THE FIRST PIECE IN HIS HANDKERCHIEF, WOULD YOU BELIEVE IT? SOME FIFTY OR SIXTY YEARS AGO! FINBAR MCGUINNESS FOUND ANOTHER UNDER HIS HAT JUST A FEW YEARS LATER.
AND ALL MY WIDE WANDERINGS LED ME HERE.
I TRAVELED THE LENGTH AND BREADTH OF IRELAND, TRYING TO FIND A WAY INTO FAIR TIR NA NÓG...YOU REMEMBER THAT, MOLLY? I THINK IT WAS... THAT WAS WHEN I FIRST TRULY LOST YOU, MY LOVE...
...AND LATER, WORKING IN "YE OLDE CELTIC BOOKSHOP" HERE IN GOTHAM, JUST OFF MCMULLEN STREET --BEFORE IT WENT OUT OF BUSINESS LIKE... TERRIBLE SHAME. TERRIBLE.
BUT SEE, I LEARNED-- TIR NA NÓG NEVER WAS UNDER IRELAND, NOT REALLY. NOT IN THE WAY WE ALL THOUGHT IT WAS, ANYWAY!

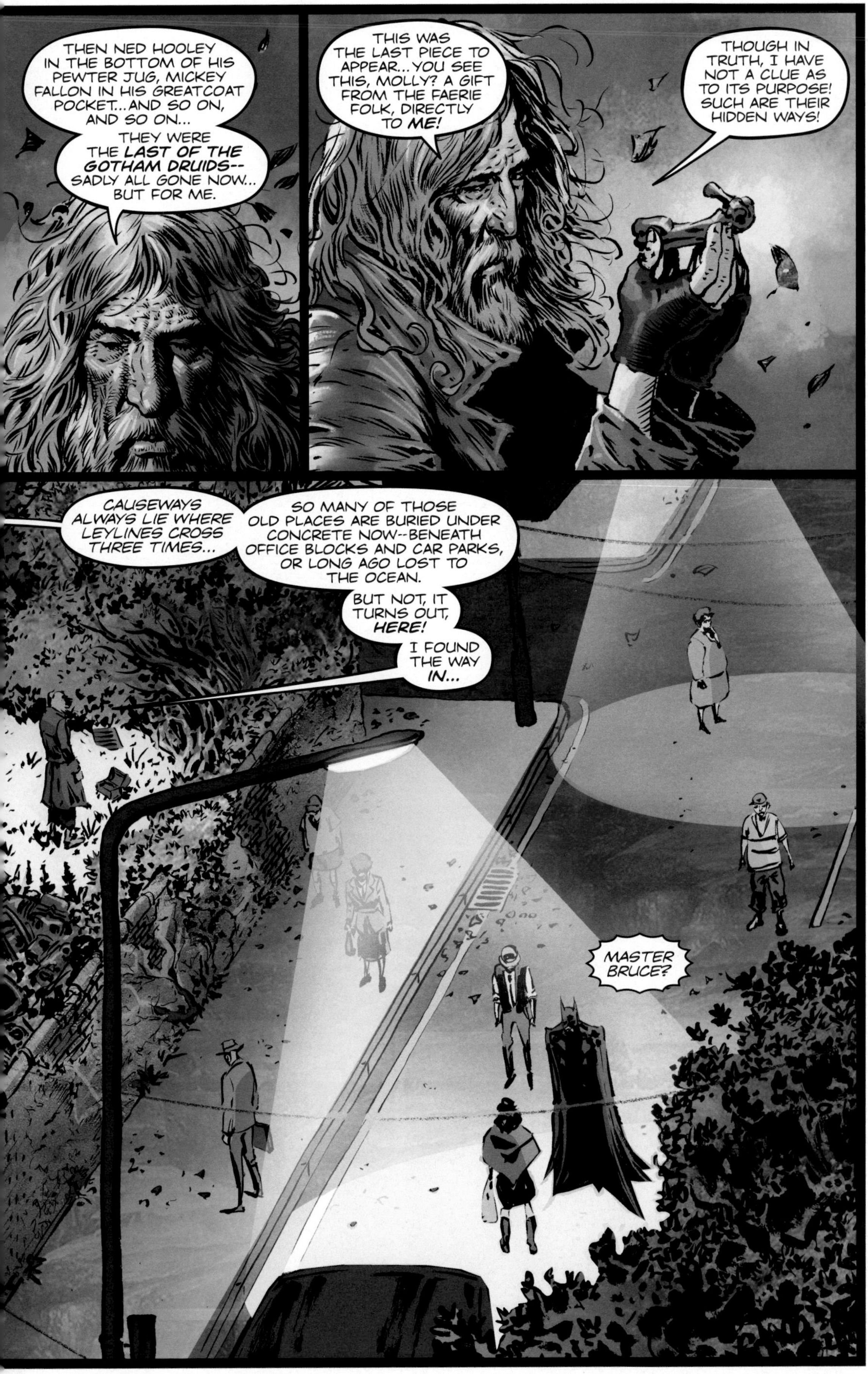
THEN NED HOOLEY IN THE BOTTOM OF HIS PEWTER JUG, MICKEY FALLON IN HIS GREATCOAT POCKET...AND SO ON, AND SO ON...
THEY WERE THE **LAST OF THE GOTHAM DRUIDS--** SADLY ALL GONE NOW... BUT FOR ME.
THIS WAS THE LAST PIECE TO APPEAR...YOU SEE THIS, MOLLY? A GIFT FROM THE FAERIE FOLK, DIRECTLY TO **ME!**
THOUGH IN TRUTH, I HAVE NOT A CLUE AS TO ITS PURPOSE! SUCH ARE THEIR HIDDEN WAYS!
CAUSEWAYS ALWAYS LIE WHERE LEYLINES CROSS THREE TIMES...
SO MANY OF THOSE OLD PLACES ARE BURIED UNDER CONCRETE NOW--BENEATH OFFICE BLOCKS AND CAR PARKS, OR LONG AGO LOST TO THE OCEAN.
BUT NOT, IT TURNS OUT, **HERE!**
I FOUND THE WAY **IN...**
MASTER BRUCE?

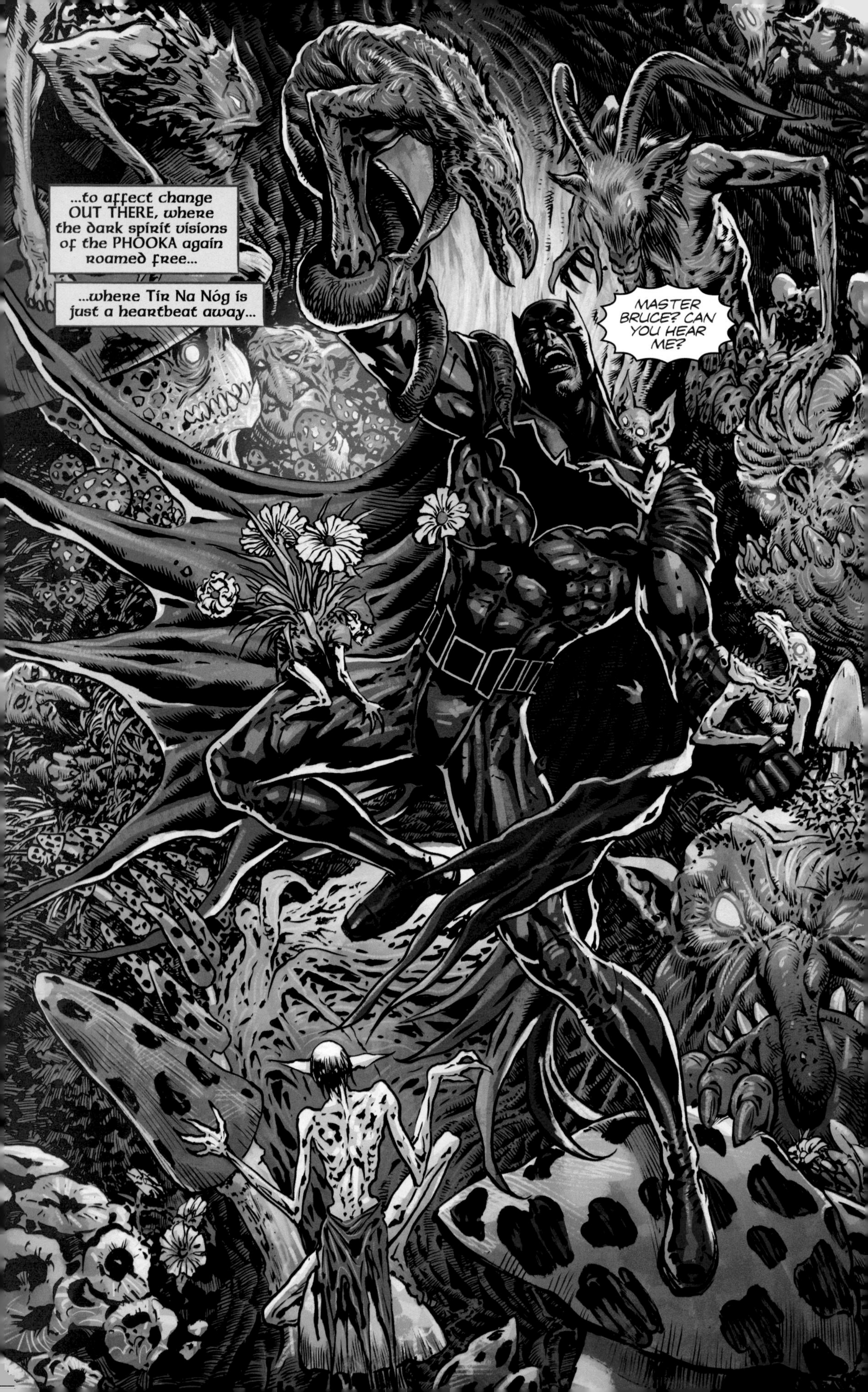
...to affect change OUT THERE, where the dark spirit visions of the PHOOKA again roamed free...
...where Tír Na Nóg is just a heartbeat away...
MASTER BRUCE? CAN YOU HEAR ME?

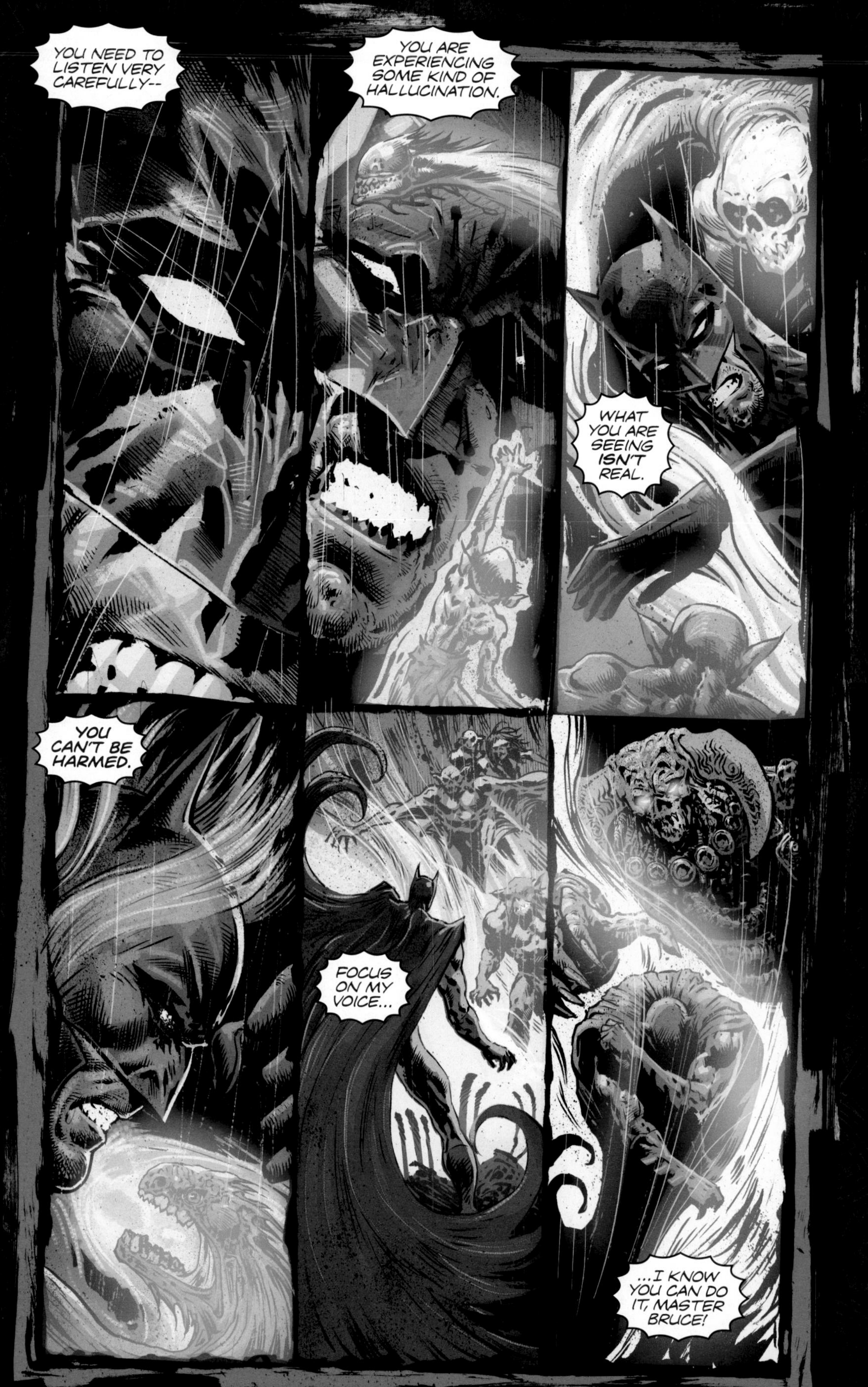
YOU NEED TO LISTEN VERY CAREFULLY--
YOU ARE EXPERIENCING SOME KIND OF HALLUCINATION.
WHAT YOU ARE SEEING ISN'T REAL.
YOU CAN'T BE HARMED.
FOCUS ON MY VOICE...
...I KNOW YOU CAN DO IT, MASTER BRUCE!

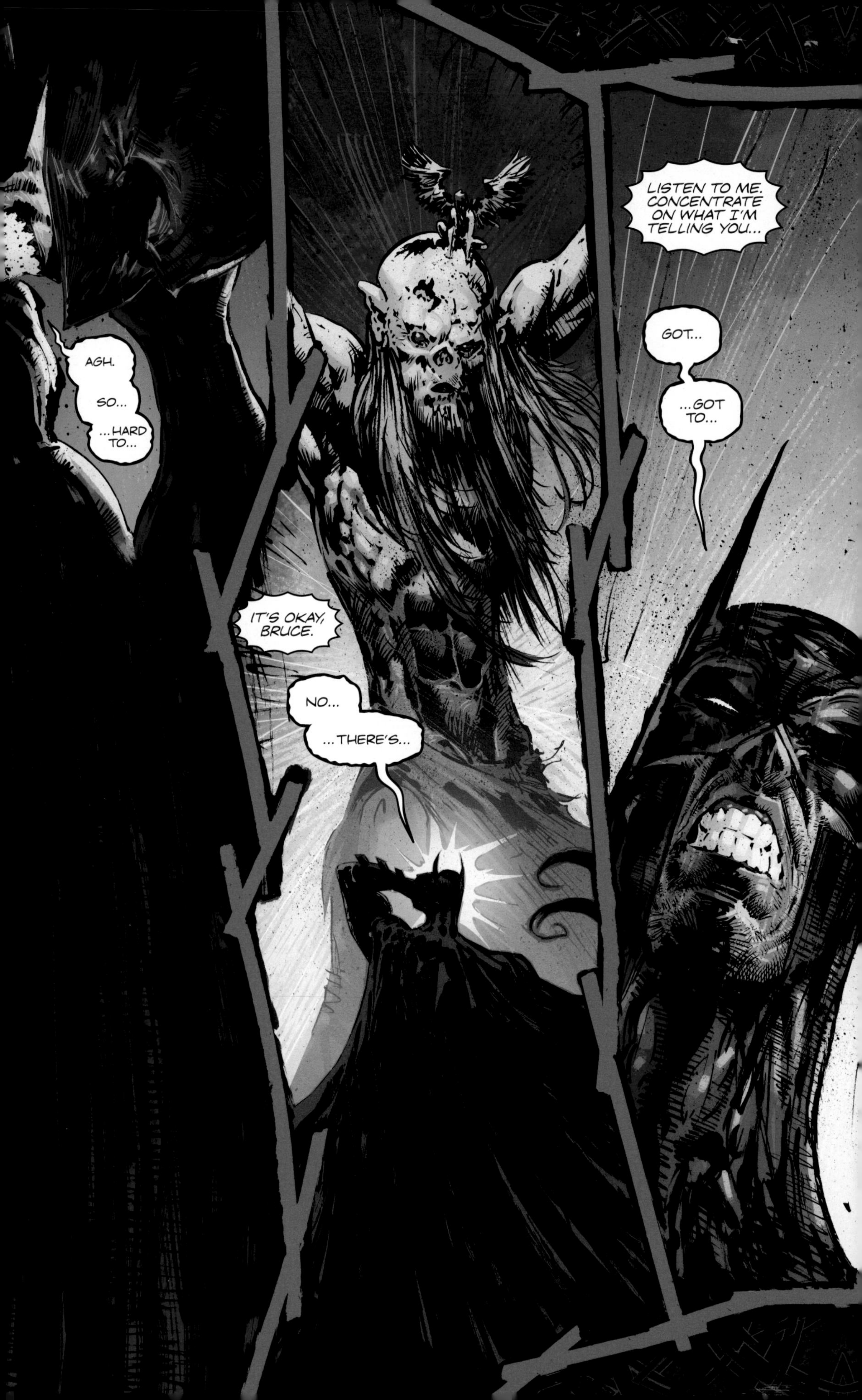
AGH.
SO...
...HARD TO...
IT'S OKAY, BRUCE.
NO...
...THERE'S...
LISTEN TO ME. CONCENTRATE ON WHAT I'M TELLING YOU...
GOT...
...GOT TO...

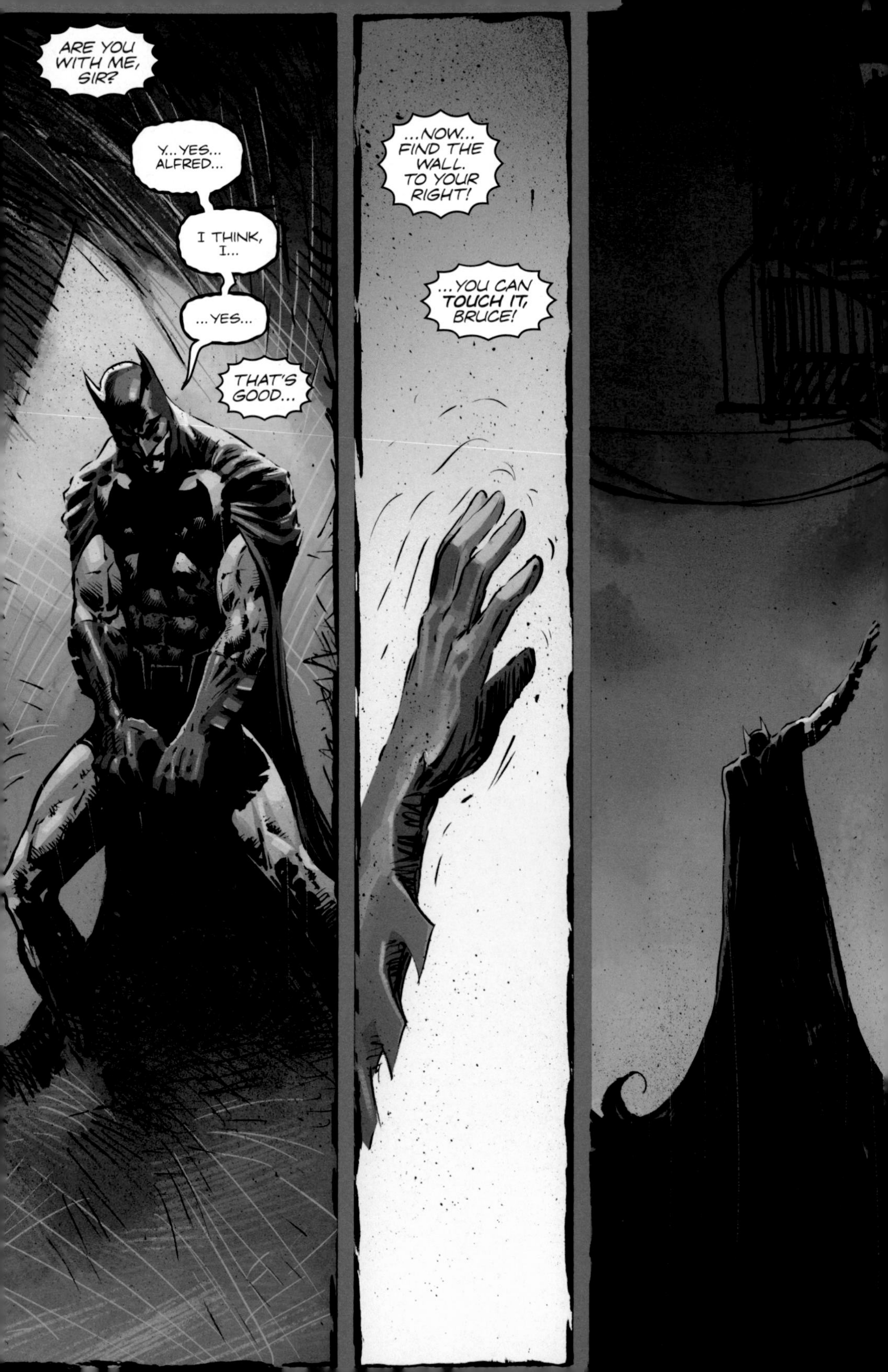
ARE YOU WITH ME, SIR?
Y...YES... ALFRED...
I THINK, I...
...YES...
THAT'S GOOD...
...NOW... FIND THE WALL. TO YOUR RIGHT!
...YOU CAN TOUCH IT, BRUCE!

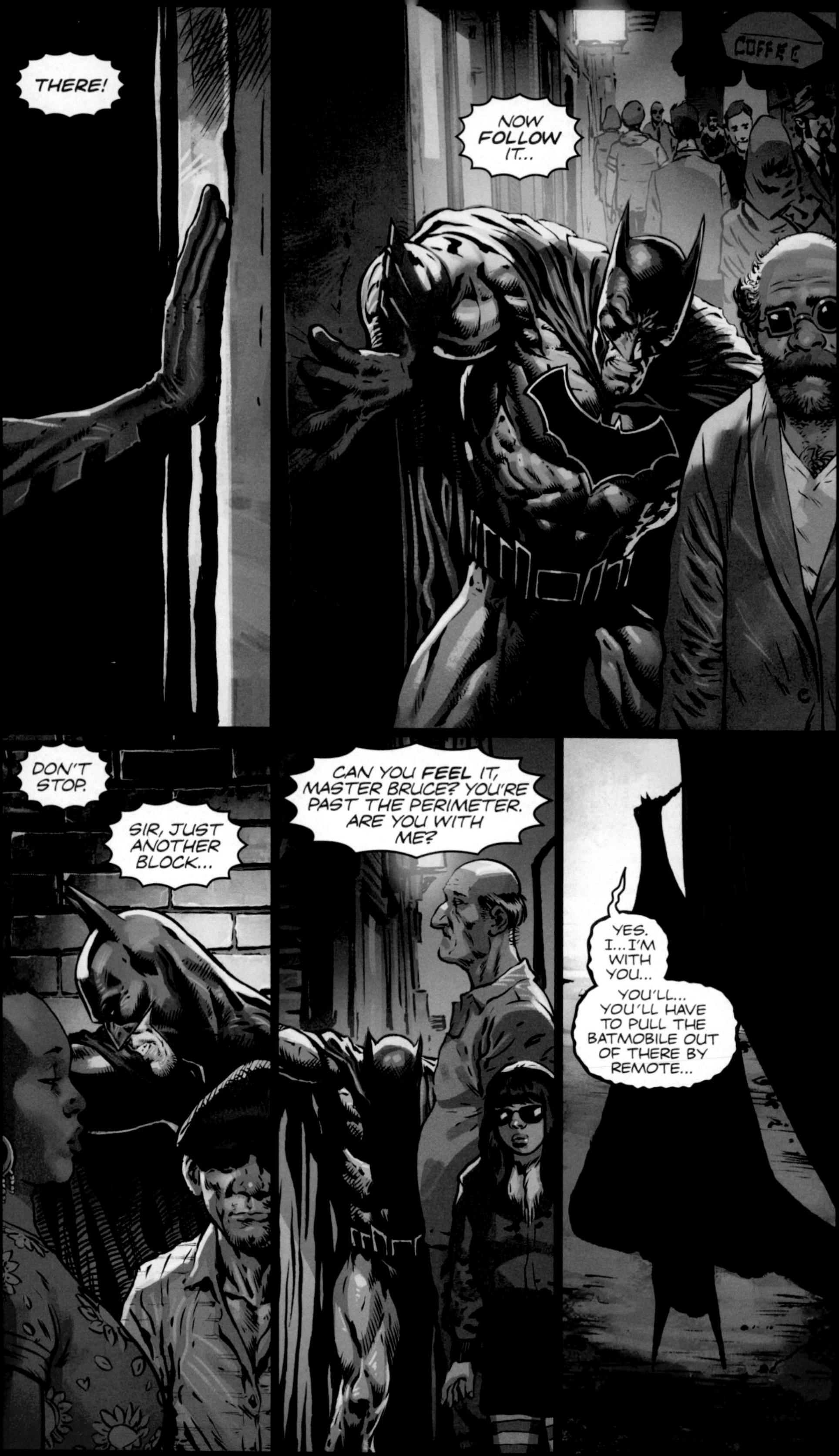
THERE!
COFFEE
NOW FOLLOW IT...
DON'T STOP.
SIR, JUST ANOTHER BLOCK...
CAN YOU FEEL IT, MASTER BRUCE? YOU'RE PAST THE PERIMETER. ARE YOU WITH ME?
YES. I...I'M WITH YOU...
YOU'LL... YOU'LL HAVE TO PULL THE BATMOBILE OUT OF THERE BY REMOTE...

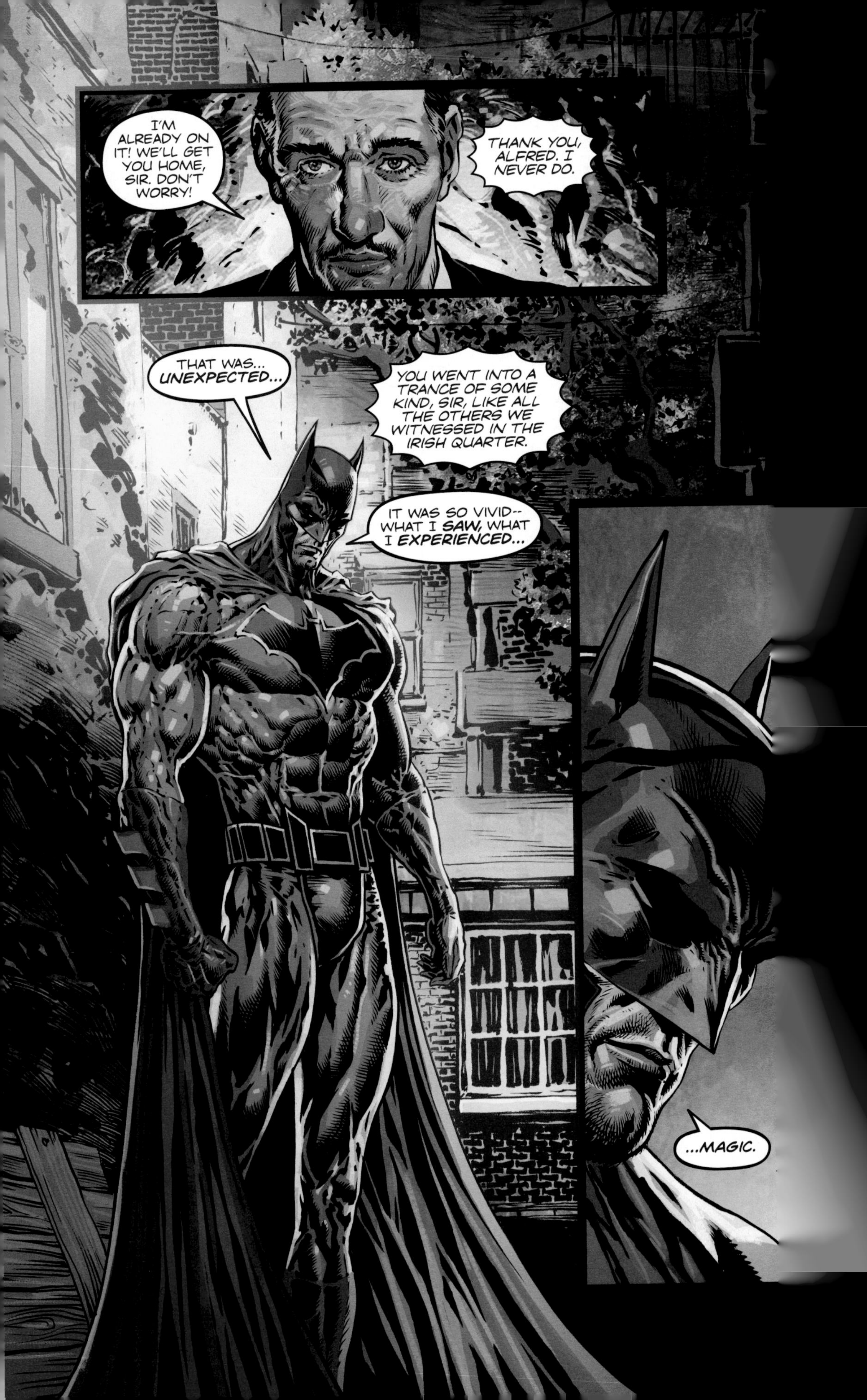
I'M ALREADY ON IT! WE'LL GET YOU HOME, SIR. DON'T WORRY!
THANK YOU, ALFRED. I NEVER DO.
THAT WAS... UNEXPECTED...
YOU WENT INTO A TRANCE OF SOME KIND, SIR, LIKE ALL THE OTHERS WE WITNESSED IN THE IRISH QUARTER.
IT WAS SO VIVID-- WHAT I SAW, WHAT I EXPERIENCED...
...MAGIC.

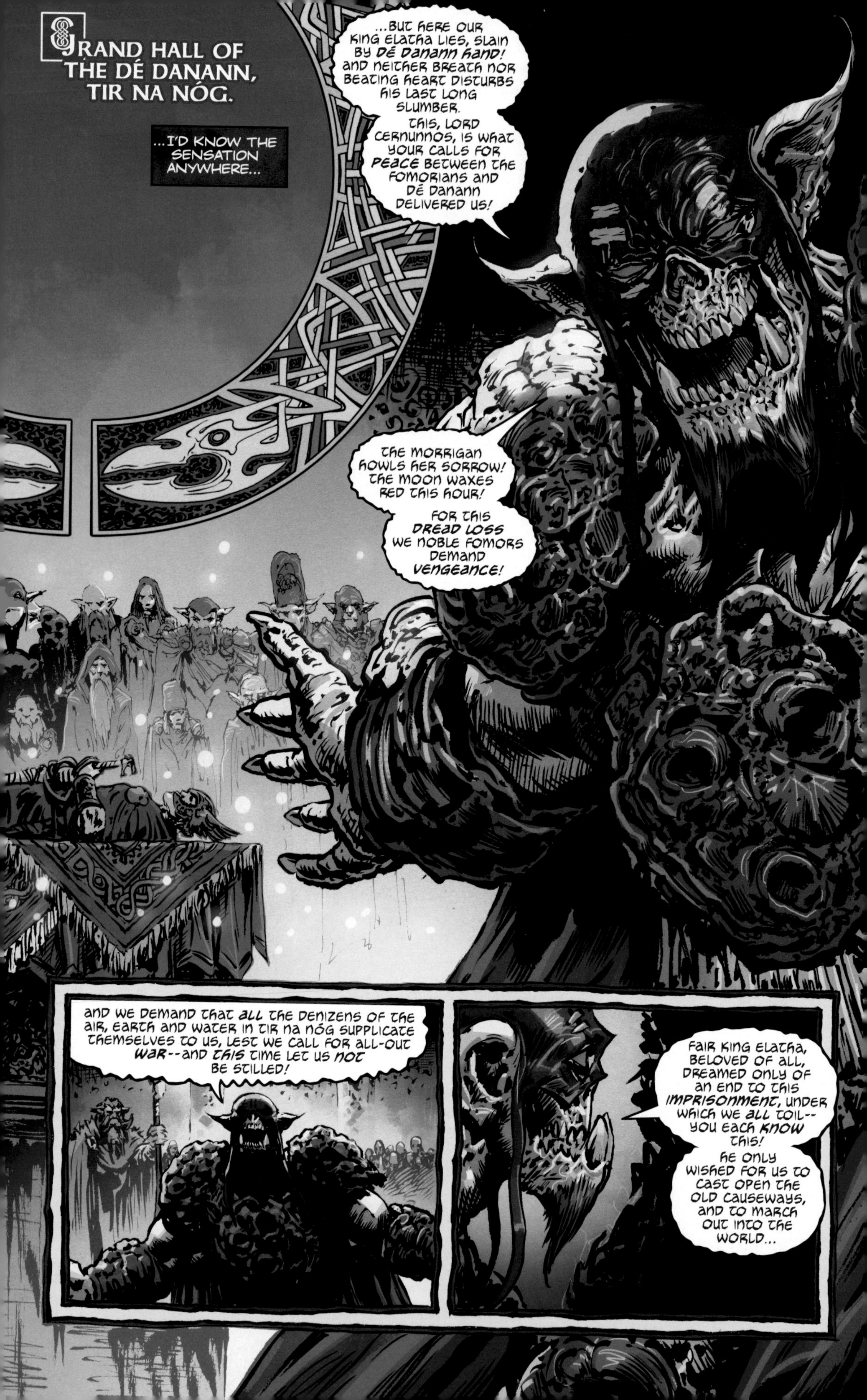
GRAND HALL OF THE DÉ DANANN, TIR NA NÓG.
...I'D KNOW THE SENSATION ANYWHERE...
...BUT HERE OUR KING ELATHA LIES, SLAIN BY DÉ DANANN HAND! AND NEITHER BREATH NOR BEATING HEART DISTURBS HIS LAST LONG SLUMBER.
THIS, LORD CERNUNNOS, IS WHAT YOUR CALLS FOR PEACE BETWEEN THE FOMORIANS AND DÉ DANANN DELIVERED US!
THE MORRIGAN HOWLS HER SORROW! THE MOON WAXES RED THIS HOUR!
FOR THIS DREAD LOSS WE NOBLE FOMORS DEMAND VENGEANCE!
AND WE DEMAND THAT ALL THE DENIZENS OF THE AIR, EARTH AND WATER IN TIR NA NÓG SUPPLICATE THEMSELVES TO US, LEST WE CALL FOR ALL-OUT WAR--AND THIS TIME LET US NOT BE STILLED!
FAIR KING ELATHA, BELOVED OF ALL, DREAMED ONLY OF AN END TO THIS IMPRISONMENT, UNDER WHICH WE ALL TOIL--YOU EACH KNOW THIS!
HE ONLY WISHED FOR US TO CAST OPEN THE OLD CAUSEWAYS, AND TO MARCH OUT INTO THE WORLD...

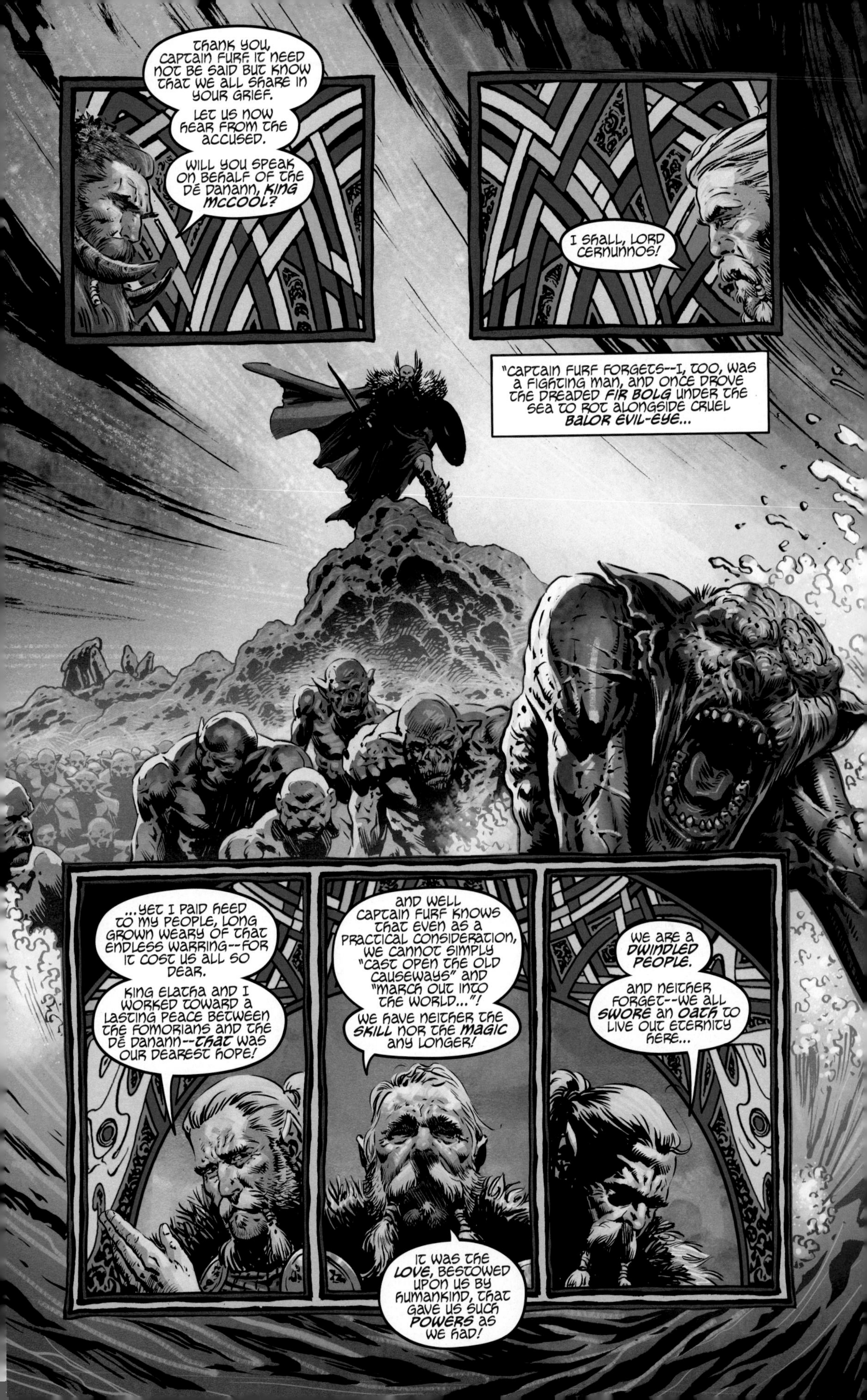
THANK YOU, CAPTAIN FURF. IT NEED NOT BE SAID BUT KNOW THAT WE ALL SHARE IN YOUR GRIEF.
LET US NOW HEAR FROM THE ACCUSED.
WILL YOU SPEAK ON BEHALF OF THE DÉ DANANN, KING MCCOOL?
I SHALL, LORD CERNUNNOS!
"CAPTAIN FURF FORGETS--I, TOO, WAS A FIGHTING MAN, AND ONCE DROVE THE DREADED FIR BOLG UNDER THE SEA TO ROT ALONGSIDE CRUEL BALOR EVIL-EYE...
...YET I PAID HEED TO MY PEOPLE, LONG GROWN WEARY OF THAT ENDLESS WARRING--FOR IT COST US ALL SO DEAR.
KING ELATHA AND I WORKED TOWARD A LASTING PEACE BETWEEN THE FOMORIANS AND THE DÉ DANANN--THAT WAS OUR DEAREST HOPE!
AND WELL CAPTAIN FURF KNOWS THAT EVEN AS A PRACTICAL CONSIDERATION, WE CANNOT SIMPLY "CAST OPEN THE OLD CAUSEWAYS" AND "MARCH OUT INTO THE WORLD..."!
WE HAVE NEITHER THE SKILL NOR THE MAGIC ANY LONGER!
IT WAS THE LOVE, BESTOWED UPON US BY HUMANKIND, THAT GAVE US SUCH POWERS AS WE HAD!
WE ARE A DWINDLED PEOPLE.
AND NEITHER FORGET--WE ALL SWORE AN OATH TO LIVE OUT ETERNITY HERE...

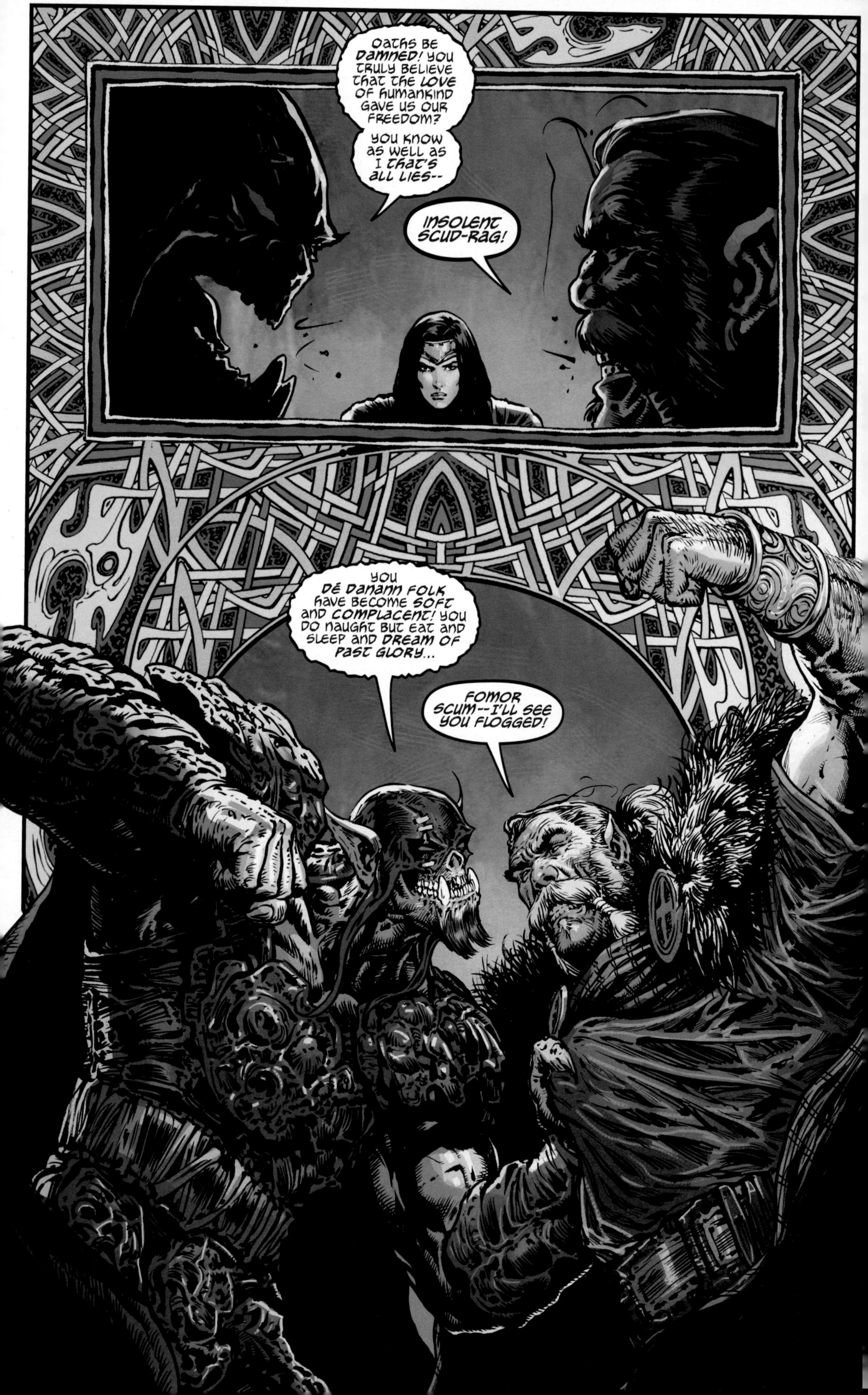

OATHS BE DAMNED! YOU TRULY BELIEVE THAT THE LOVE OF HUMANKIND GAVE US OUR FREEDOM?
YOU KNOW AS WELL AS I THAT'S ALL LIES--
INSOLENT SCUD-RAG!
YOU DÉ DANANN FOLK HAVE BECOME SOFT AND COMPLACENT! YOU DO NAUGHT BUT EAT AND SLEEP AND DREAM OF PAST GLORY...
FOMOR SCUM--I'LL SEE YOU FLOGGED!

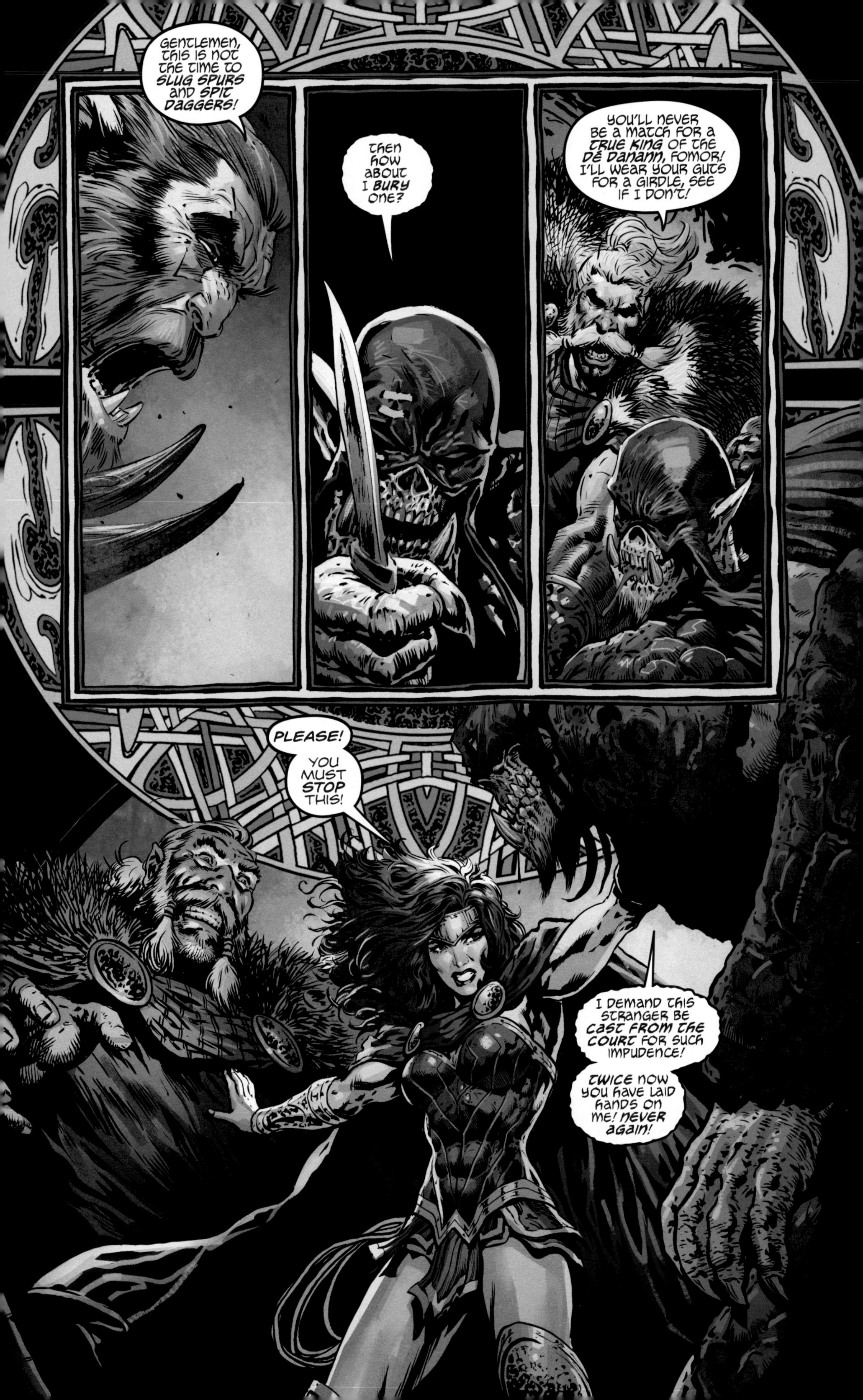
GENTLEMEN, THIS IS NOT THE TIME TO SLUG SPURS AND SPIT DAGGERS!
THEN HOW ABOUT I BURY ONE?
YOU'LL NEVER BE A MATCH FOR A TRUE KING OF THE DÉ DANANN, FOMOR! I'LL WEAR YOUR GUTS FOR A GIRDLE, SEE IF I DON'T!
PLEASE!
YOU MUST STOP THIS!
I DEMAND THIS STRANGER BE CAST FROM THE COURT FOR SUCH IMPUDENCE!
TWICE NOW YOU HAVE LAID HANDS ON ME! NEVER AGAIN!

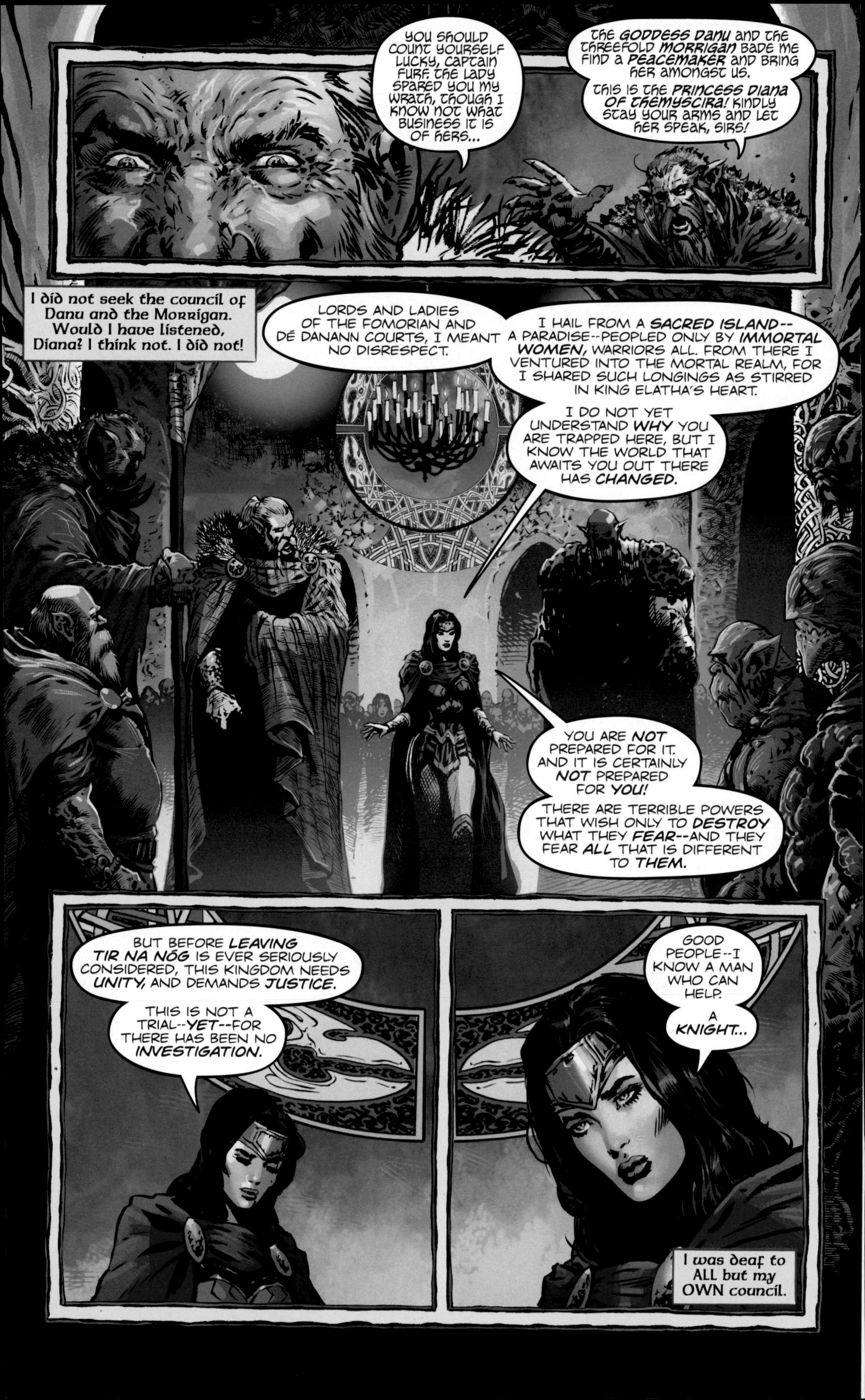

YOU SHOULD COUNT YOURSELF LUCKY, CAPTAIN FURF. THE LADY SPARED YOU MY WRATH, THOUGH I KNOW NOT WHAT BUSINESS IT IS OF HERS...
THE GODDESS DANU AND THE THREEFOLD MORRIGAN BADE ME FIND A PEACEMAKER AND BRING HER AMONGST US.
THIS IS THE PRINCESS DIANA OF THEMYSCIRA! KINDLY STAY YOUR ARMS AND LET HER SPEAK, SIRS!
I did not seek the council of Danu and the Morrigan. Would I have listened, Diana? I think not. I did not!
LORDS AND LADIES OF THE FOMORIAN AND DÉ DANANN COURTS, I MEANT NO DISRESPECT.
I HAIL FROM A SACRED ISLAND--A PARADISE--PEOPLED ONLY BY IMMORTAL WOMEN, WARRIORS ALL. FROM THERE I VENTURED INTO THE MORTAL REALM, FOR I SHARED SUCH LONGINGS AS STIRRED IN KING ELATHA'S HEART.
I DO NOT YET UNDERSTAND WHY YOU ARE TRAPPED HERE, BUT I KNOW THE WORLD THAT AWAITS YOU OUT THERE HAS CHANGED.
YOU ARE NOT PREPARED FOR IT. AND IT IS CERTAINLY NOT PREPARED FOR YOU!
THERE ARE TERRIBLE POWERS THAT WISH ONLY TO DESTROY WHAT THEY FEAR--AND THEY FEAR ALL THAT IS DIFFERENT TO THEM.
BUT BEFORE LEAVING TIR NA NÓG IS EVER SERIOUSLY CONSIDERED, THIS KINGDOM NEEDS UNITY, AND DEMANDS JUSTICE.
THIS IS NOT A TRIAL--YET--FOR THERE HAS BEEN NO INVESTIGATION.
GOOD PEOPLE--I KNOW A MAN WHO CAN HELP.
A KNIGHT...
I was deaf to ALL but my OWN council.

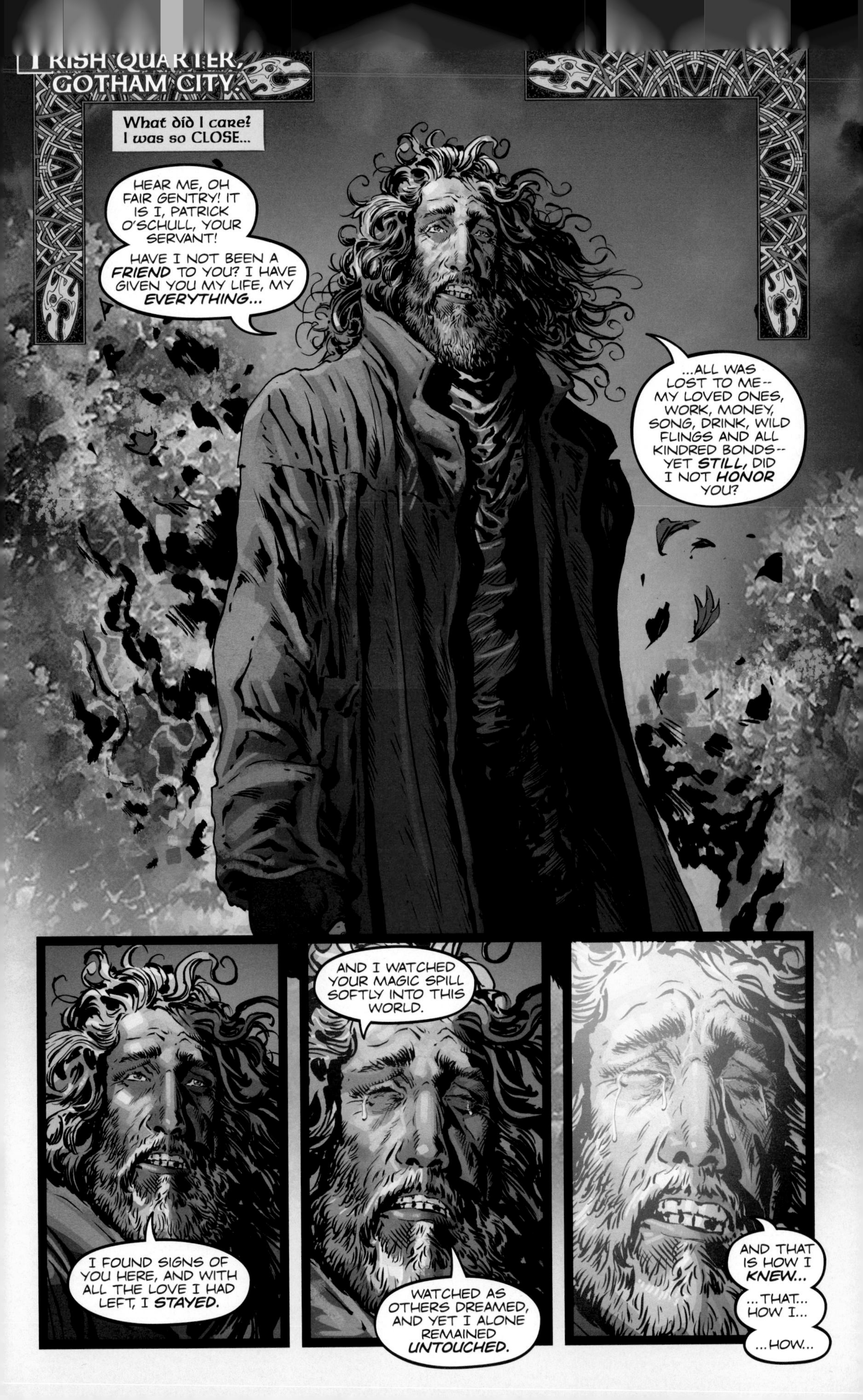

IRISH QUARTER, GOTHAM CITY.
What did I care? I was so CLOSE...
HEAR ME, OH FAIR GENTRY! IT IS I, PATRICK O'SCHULL, YOUR SERVANT!
HAVE I NOT BEEN A FRIEND TO YOU? I HAVE GIVEN YOU MY LIFE, MY EVERYTHING...
...ALL WAS LOST TO ME-- MY LOVED ONES, WORK, MONEY, SONG, DRINK, WILD FLINGS AND ALL KINDRED BONDS-- YET STILL, DID I NOT HONOR YOU?
I FOUND SIGNS OF YOU HERE, AND WITH ALL THE LOVE I HAD LEFT, I STAYED.
AND I WATCHED YOUR MAGIC SPILL SOFTLY INTO THIS WORLD.
WATCHED AS OTHERS DREAMED, AND YET I ALONE REMAINED UNTOUCHED.
AND THAT IS HOW I KNEW...
...THAT... HOW I...
...HOW...

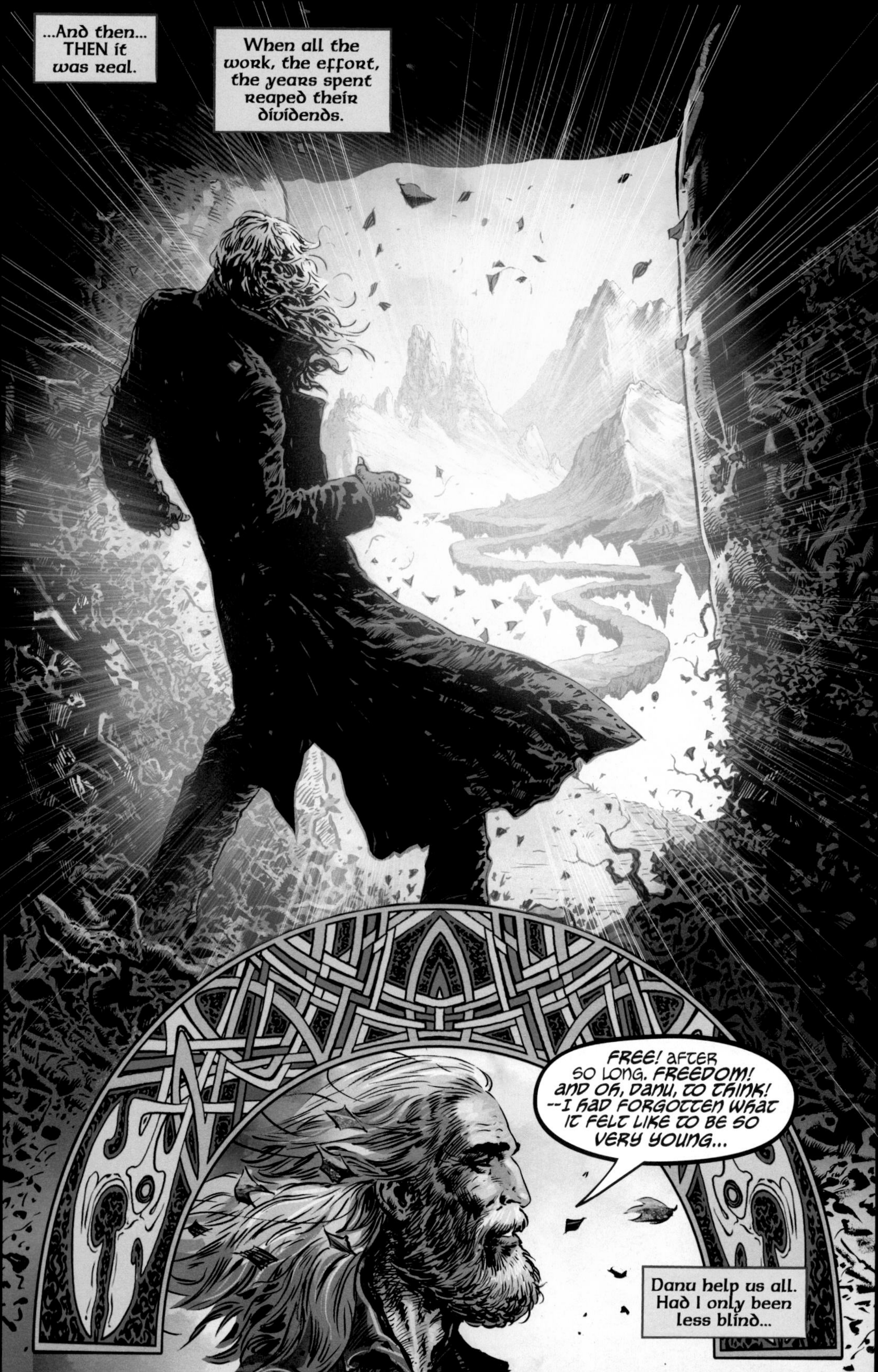
...And then... THEN it was real.
When all the work, the effort, the years spent reaped their dividends.
FREE! AFTER SO LONG. FREEDOM! AND OH, DANU, TO THINK! --I HAD FORGOTTEN WHAT IT FELT LIKE TO BE SO VERY YOUNG...
Danu help us all. Had I only been less blind...

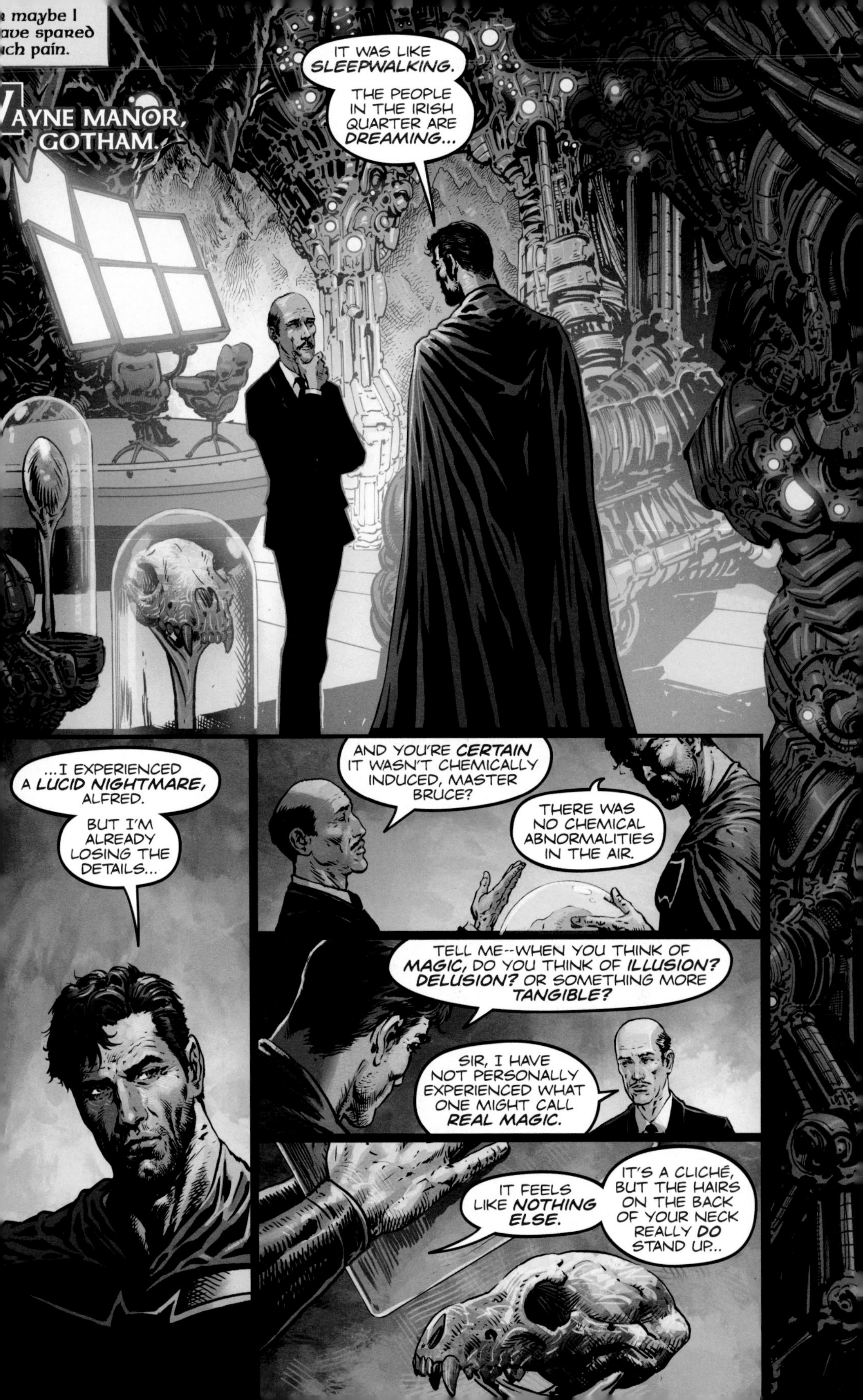

...n maybe I ...ave spared ...uch pain.
WAYNE MANOR, GOTHAM.
IT WAS LIKE SLEEPWALKING.
THE PEOPLE IN THE IRISH QUARTER ARE DREAMING...
...I EXPERIENCED A LUCID NIGHTMARE, ALFRED.
BUT I'M ALREADY LOSING THE DETAILS...
AND YOU'RE CERTAIN IT WASN'T CHEMICALLY INDUCED, MASTER BRUCE?
THERE WAS NO CHEMICAL ABNORMALITIES IN THE AIR.
TELL ME--WHEN YOU THINK OF MAGIC, DO YOU THINK OF ILLUSION? DELUSION? OR SOMETHING MORE TANGIBLE?
SIR, I HAVE NOT PERSONALLY EXPERIENCED WHAT ONE MIGHT CALL REAL MAGIC.
IT FEELS LIKE NOTHING ELSE.
IT'S A CLICHÉ, BUT THE HAIRS ON THE BACK OF YOUR NECK REALLY DO STAND UP...

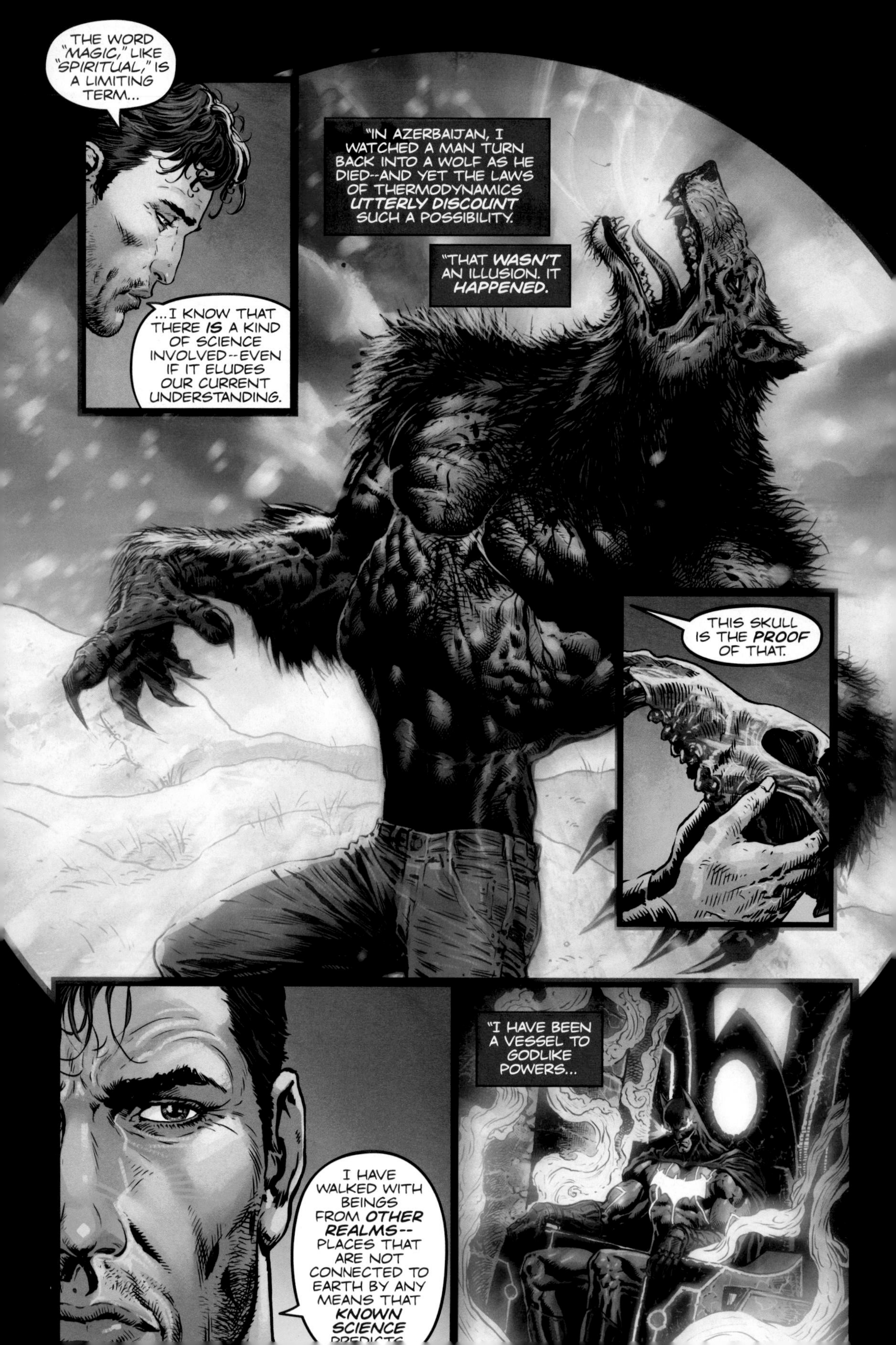
THE WORD "MAGIC," LIKE "SPIRITUAL," IS A LIMITING TERM...
...I KNOW THAT THERE IS A KIND OF SCIENCE INVOLVED--EVEN IF IT ELUDES OUR CURRENT UNDERSTANDING.
"IN AZERBAIJAN, I WATCHED A MAN TURN BACK INTO A WOLF AS HE DIED--AND YET THE LAWS OF THERMODYNAMICS UTTERLY DISCOUNT SUCH A POSSIBILITY.
"THAT WASN'T AN ILLUSION. IT HAPPENED.
THIS SKULL IS THE PROOF OF THAT.
"I HAVE BEEN A VESSEL TO GODLIKE POWERS...
I HAVE WALKED WITH BEINGS FROM OTHER REALMS--PLACES THAT ARE NOT CONNECTED TO EARTH BY ANY MEANS THAT KNOWN SCIENCE

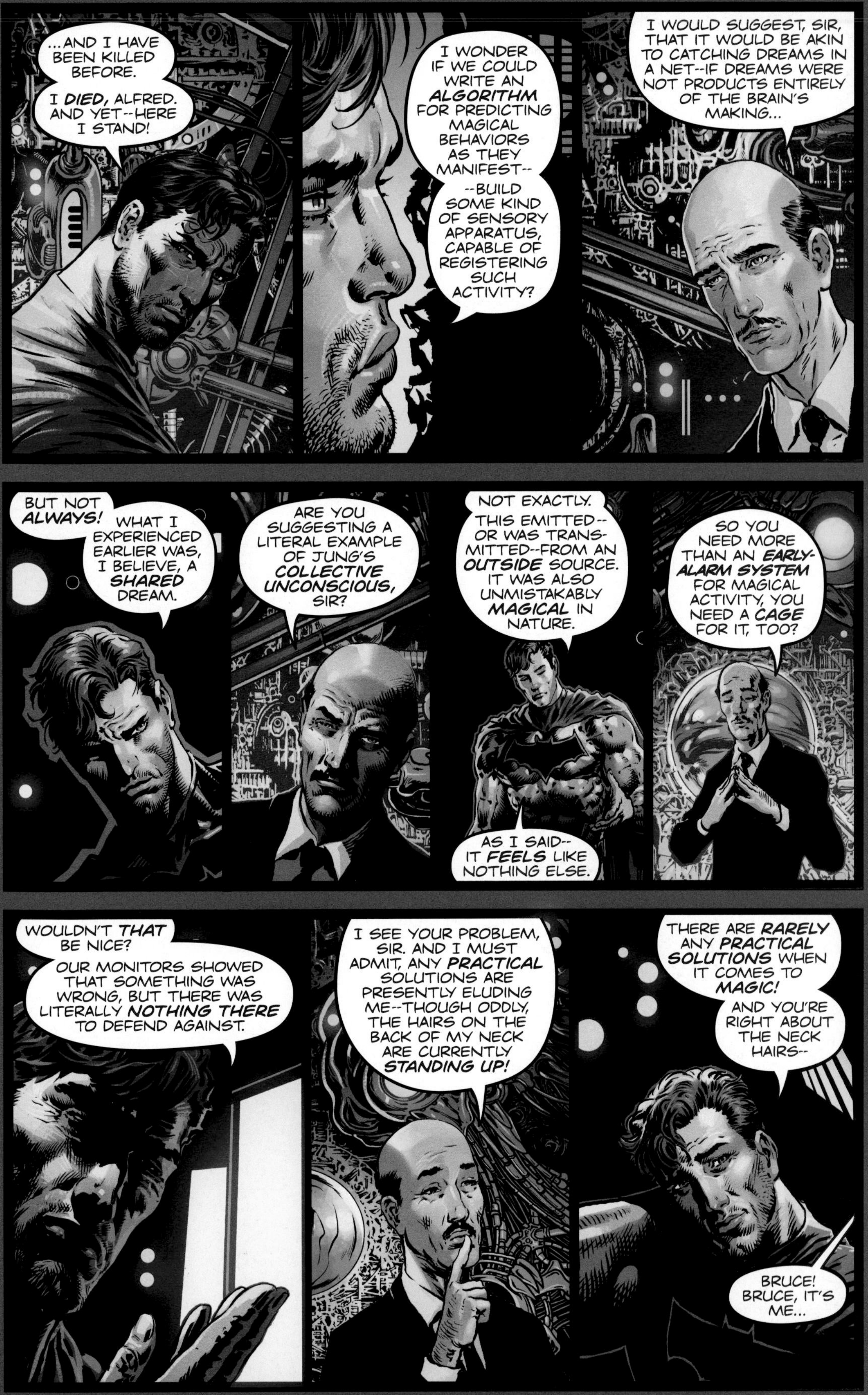
...AND I HAVE BEEN KILLED BEFORE.
I DIED, ALFRED. AND YET--HERE I STAND!
I WONDER IF WE COULD WRITE AN ALGORITHM FOR PREDICTING MAGICAL BEHAVIORS AS THEY MANIFEST--
--BUILD SOME KIND OF SENSORY APPARATUS, CAPABLE OF REGISTERING SUCH ACTIVITY?
I WOULD SUGGEST, SIR, THAT IT WOULD BE AKIN TO CATCHING DREAMS IN A NET--IF DREAMS WERE NOT PRODUCTS ENTIRELY OF THE BRAIN'S MAKING...
BUT NOT ALWAYS!
WHAT I EXPERIENCED EARLIER WAS, I BELIEVE, A SHARED DREAM.
ARE YOU SUGGESTING A LITERAL EXAMPLE OF JUNG'S COLLECTIVE UNCONSCIOUS, SIR?
NOT EXACTLY.
THIS EMITTED--OR WAS TRANS-MITTED--FROM AN OUTSIDE SOURCE. IT WAS ALSO UNMISTAKABLY MAGICAL IN NATURE.
AS I SAID--IT FEELS LIKE NOTHING ELSE.
SO YOU NEED MORE THAN AN EARLY-ALARM SYSTEM FOR MAGICAL ACTIVITY, YOU NEED A CAGE FOR IT, TOO?
WOULDN'T THAT BE NICE?
OUR MONITORS SHOWED THAT SOMETHING WAS WRONG, BUT THERE WAS LITERALLY NOTHING THERE TO DEFEND AGAINST.
I SEE YOUR PROBLEM, SIR. AND I MUST ADMIT, ANY PRACTICAL SOLUTIONS ARE PRESENTLY ELUDING ME--THOUGH ODDLY, THE HAIRS ON THE BACK OF MY NECK ARE CURRENTLY STANDING UP!
THERE ARE RARELY ANY PRACTICAL SOLUTIONS WHEN IT COMES TO MAGIC!
AND YOU'RE RIGHT ABOUT THE NECK HAIRS--
BRUCE! BRUCE, IT'S ME...

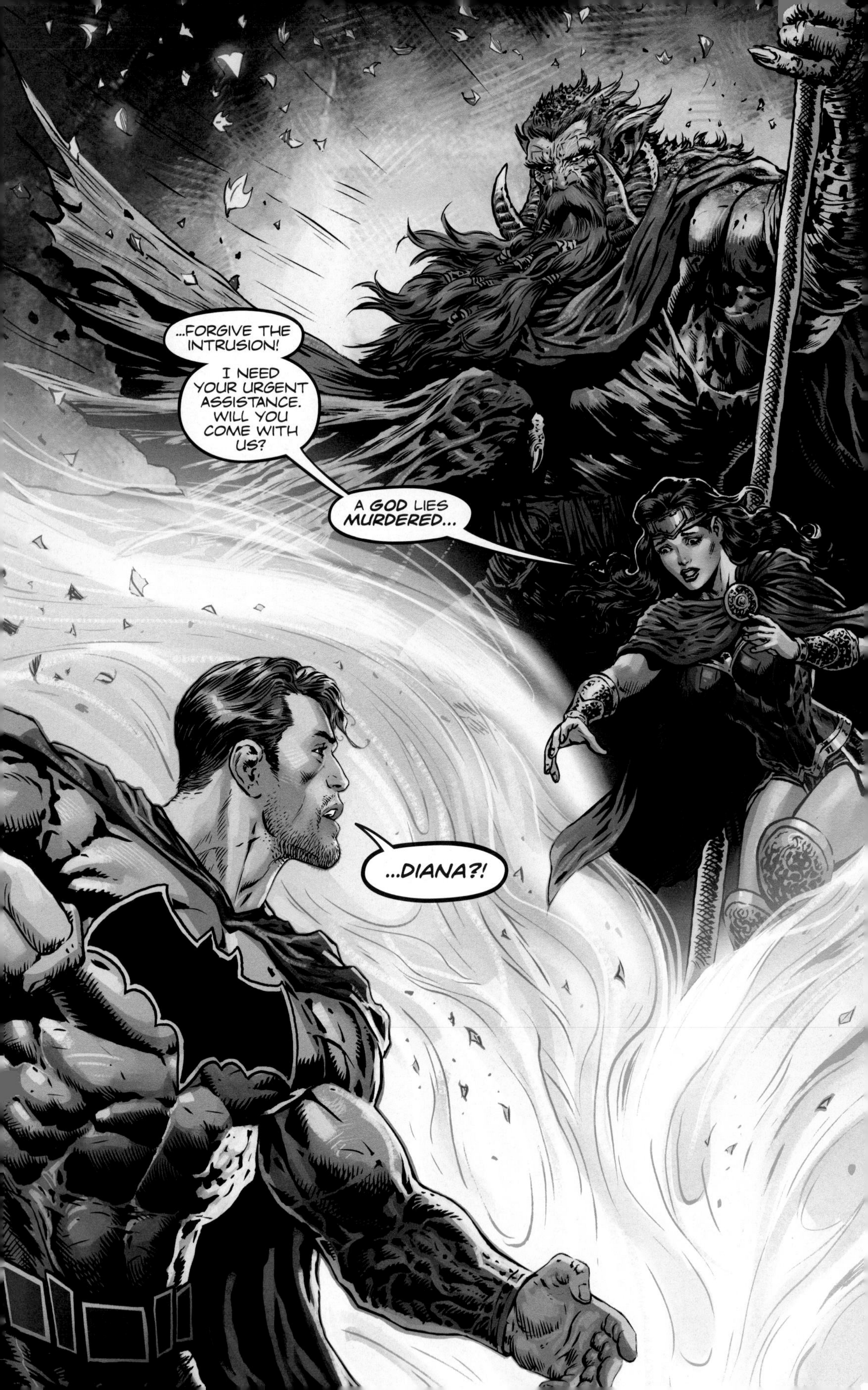
...FORGIVE THE INTRUSION!
I NEED YOUR URGENT ASSISTANCE. WILL YOU COME WITH US?
A **GOD** LIES **MURDERED...**
...DIANA?!

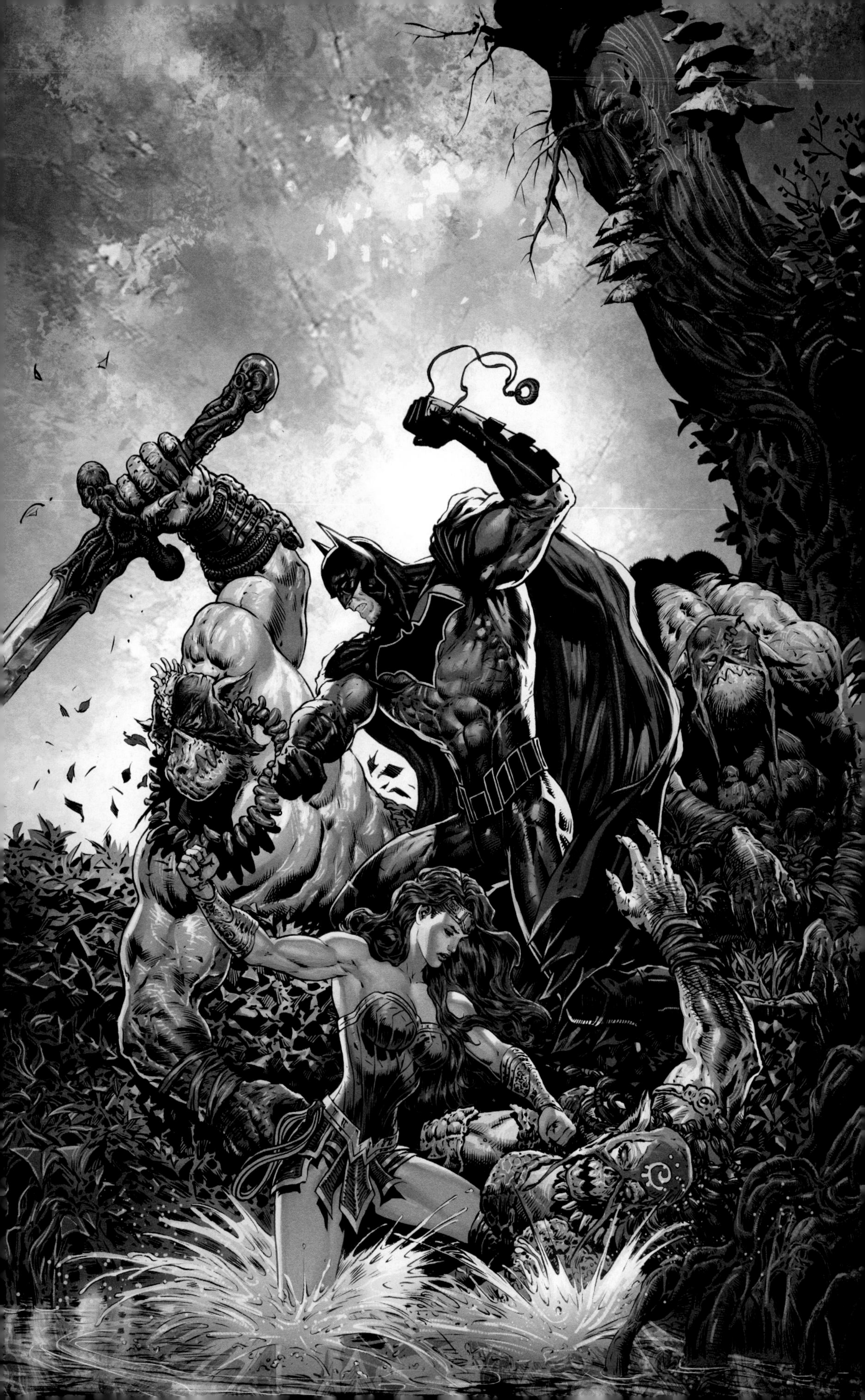

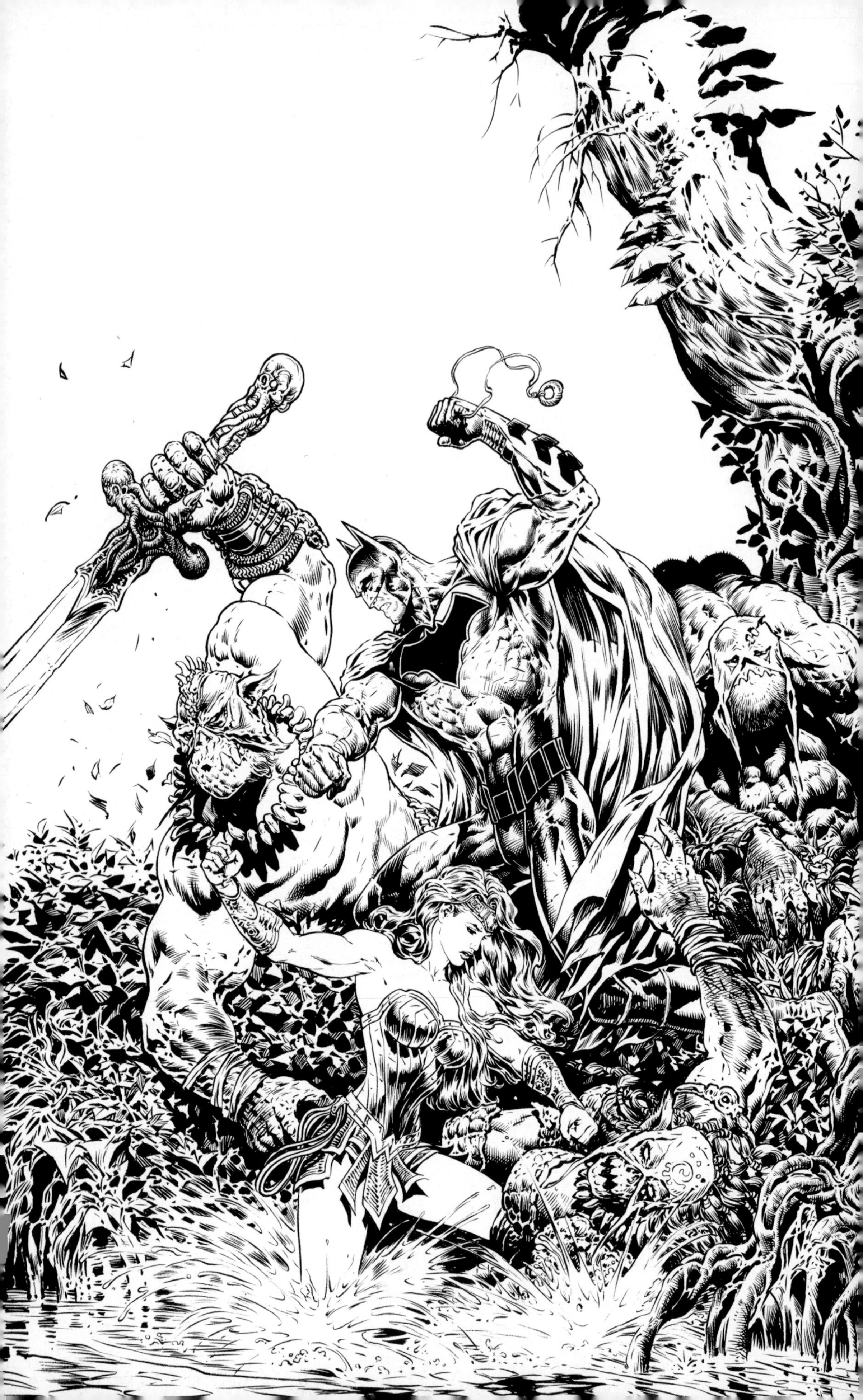

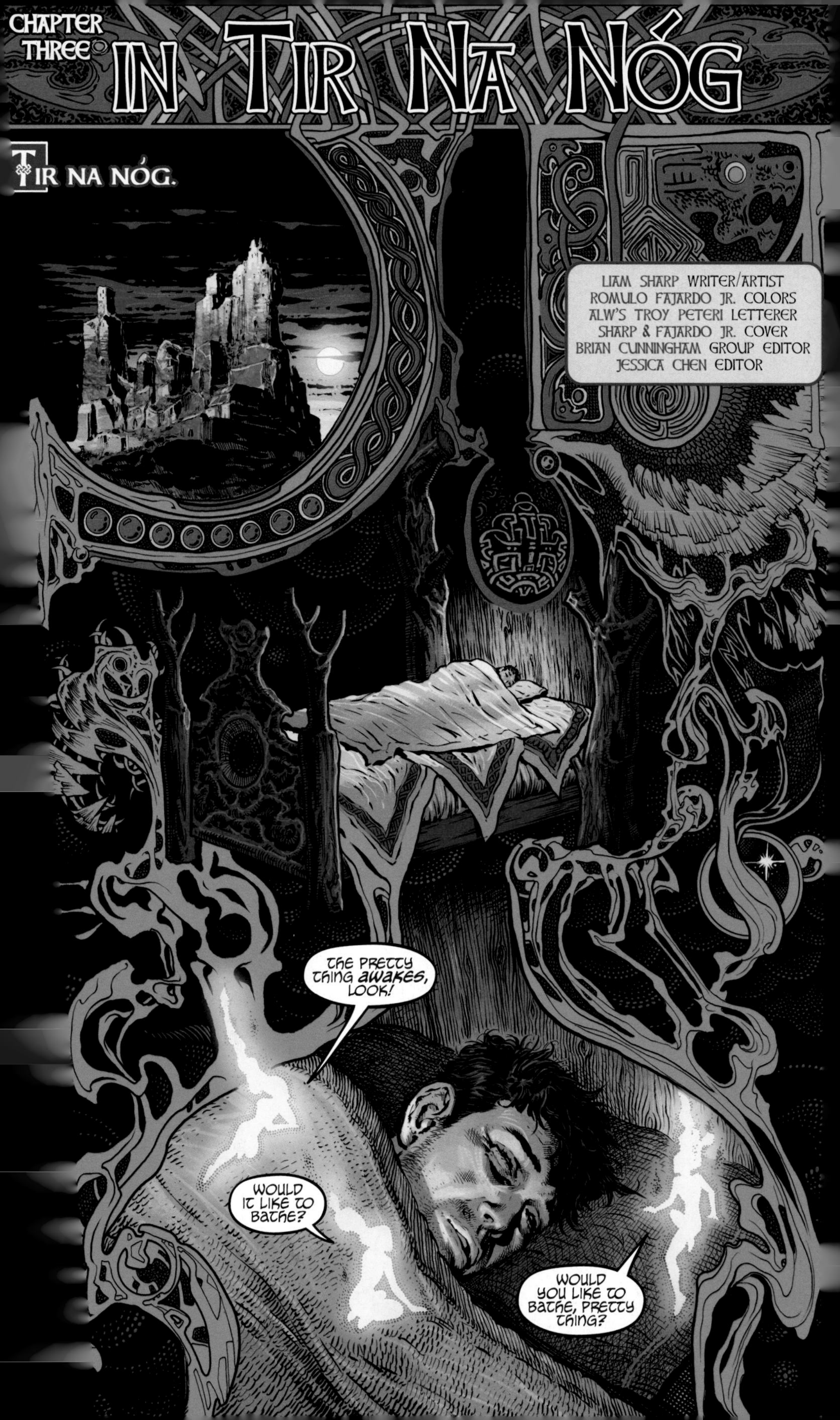
CHAPTER THREE
IN TIR NA NÓG
TIR NA NÓG.
LIAM SHARP WRITER/ARTIST
ROMULO FAJARDO JR. COLORS
ALW'S TROY PETERI LETTERER
SHARP & FAJARDO JR. COVER
BRIAN CUNNINGHAM GROUP EDITOR
JESSICA CHEN EDITOR
THE PRETTY THING AWAKES, LOOK!
WOULD IT LIKE TO BATHE?
WOULD YOU LIKE TO BATHE, PRETTY THING?

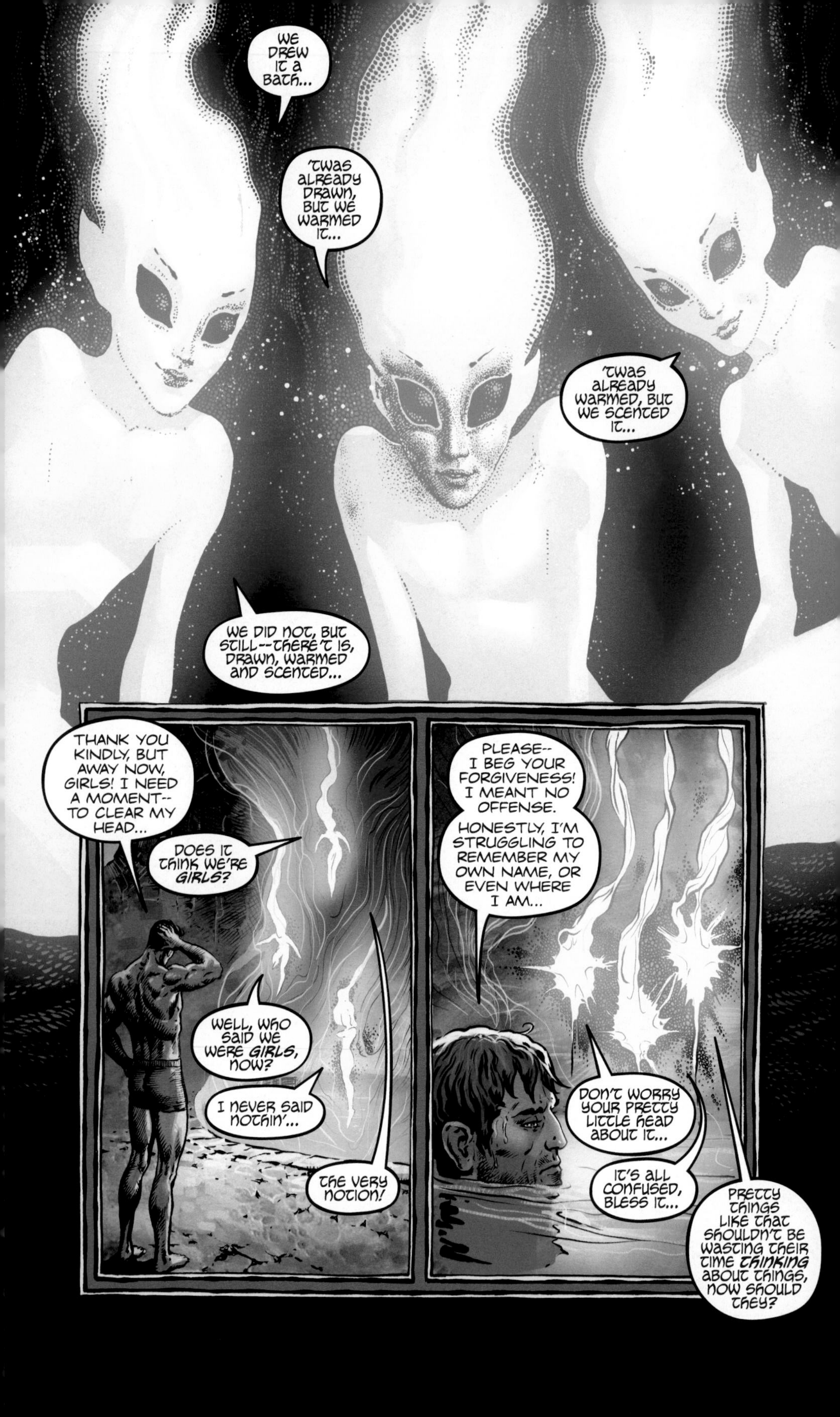
WE DREW IT A BATH...
'TWAS ALREADY DRAWN, BUT WE WARMED IT...
'TWAS ALREADY WARMED, BUT WE SCENTED IT...
WE DID NOT, BUT STILL--THERE'T IS, DRAWN, WARMED AND SCENTED...
THANK YOU KINDLY, BUT AWAY NOW, GIRLS! I NEED A MOMENT-- TO CLEAR MY HEAD...
DOES IT THINK WE'RE *GIRLS?*
WELL, WHO SAID WE WERE *GIRLS*, NOW?
I NEVER SAID NOTHIN'...
THE VERY NOTION!
PLEASE-- I BEG YOUR FORGIVENESS! I MEANT NO OFFENSE.
HONESTLY, I'M STRUGGLING TO REMEMBER MY OWN NAME, OR EVEN WHERE I AM...
DON'T WORRY YOUR PRETTY LITTLE HEAD ABOUT IT...
IT'S ALL CONFUSED, BLESS IT...
PRETTY THINGS LIKE THAT SHOULDN'T BE WASTING THEIR TIME *THINKING* ABOUT THINGS, NOW SHOULD THEY?

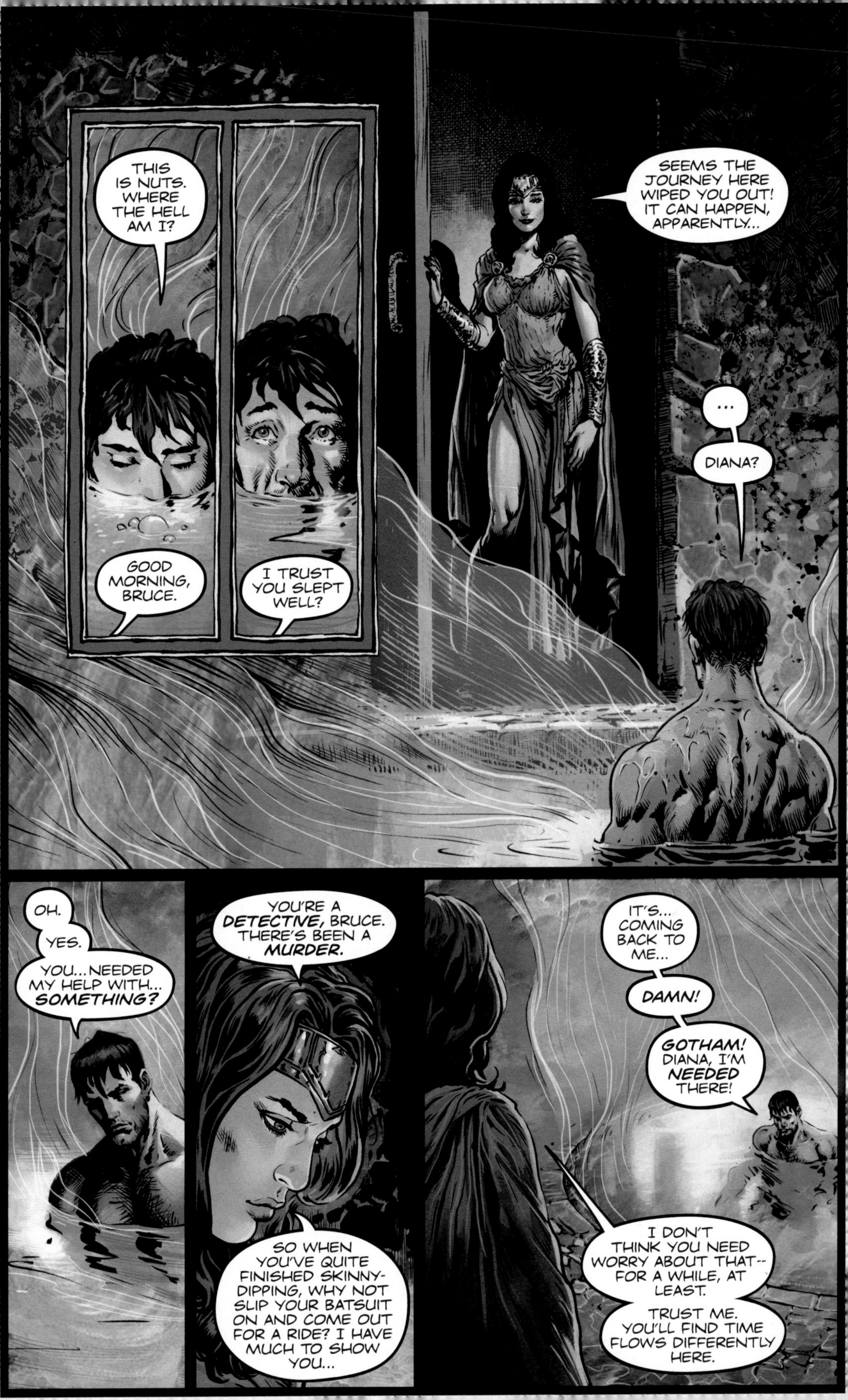
THIS IS NUTS. WHERE THE HELL AM I?
GOOD MORNING, BRUCE.
I TRUST YOU SLEPT WELL?
SEEMS THE JOURNEY HERE WIPED YOU OUT! IT CAN HAPPEN, APPARENTLY...
...
DIANA?
OH.
YES.
YOU...NEEDED MY HELP WITH... SOMETHING?
YOU'RE A DETECTIVE, BRUCE. THERE'S BEEN A MURDER.
SO WHEN YOU'VE QUITE FINISHED SKINNY-DIPPING, WHY NOT SLIP YOUR BATSUIT ON AND COME OUT FOR A RIDE? I HAVE MUCH TO SHOW YOU...
IT'S... COMING BACK TO ME...
DAMN!
GOTHAM! DIANA, I'M NEEDED THERE!
I DON'T THINK YOU NEED WORRY ABOUT THAT-- FOR A WHILE, AT LEAST.
TRUST ME. YOU'LL FIND TIME FLOWS DIFFERENTLY HERE.

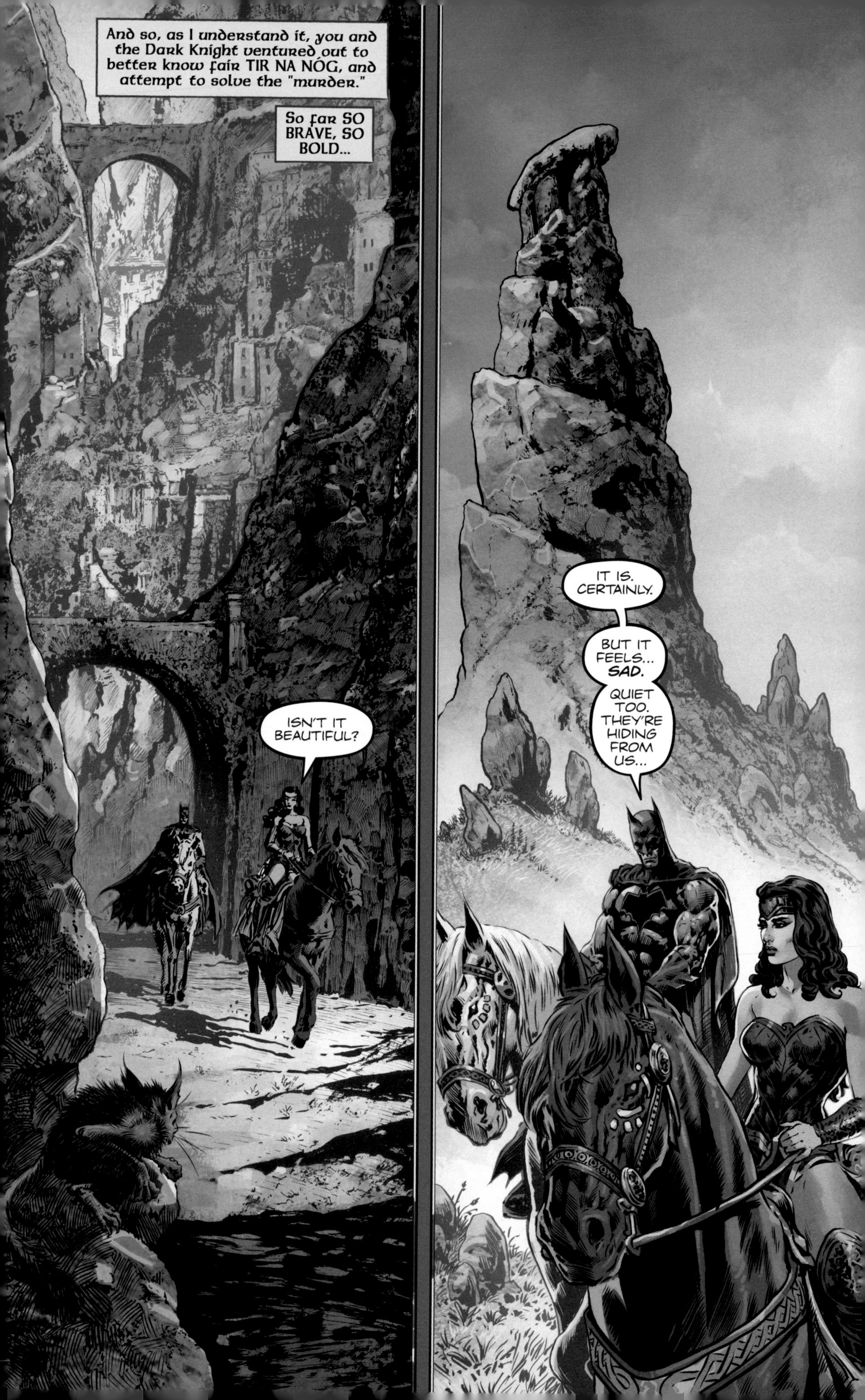
And so, as I understand it, you and the Dark Knight ventured out to better know fair TIR NA NÓG, and attempt to solve the "murder."
So far SO BRAVE, SO BOLD...
ISN'T IT BEAUTIFUL?
IT IS. CERTAINLY.
BUT IT FEELS... SAD.
QUIET TOO. THEY'RE HIDING FROM US...

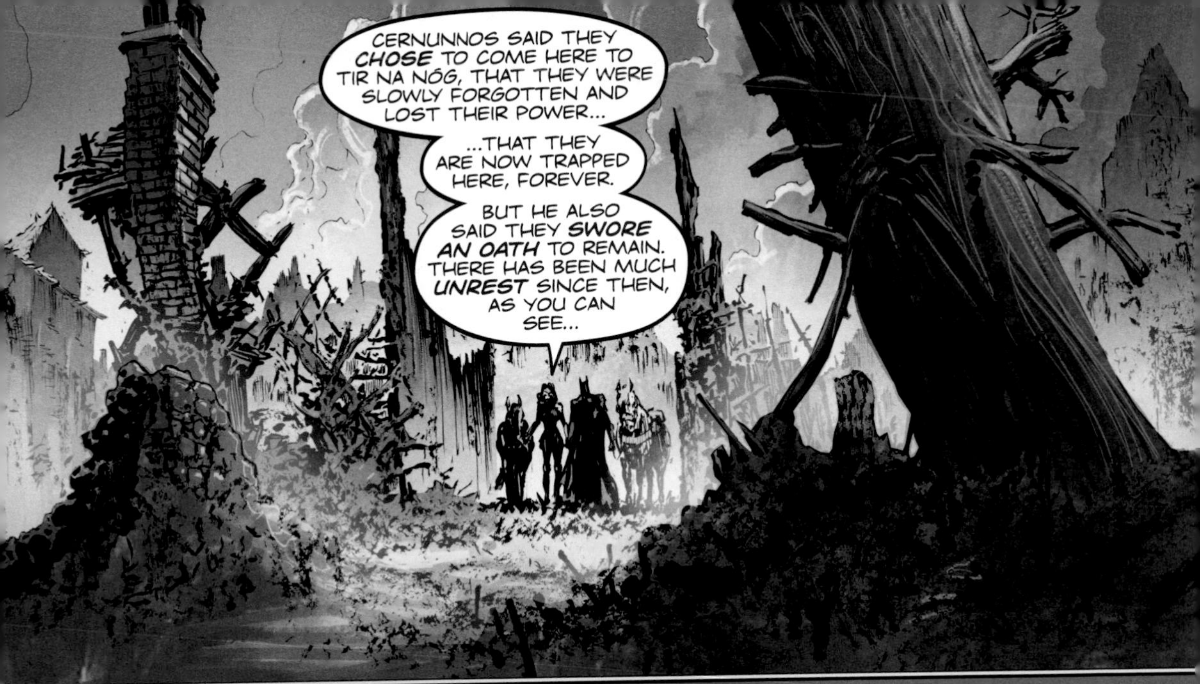
CERNUNNOS SAID THEY CHOSE TO COME HERE TO TIR NA NÓG, THAT THEY WERE SLOWLY FORGOTTEN AND LOST THEIR POWER...
...THAT THEY ARE NOW TRAPPED HERE, FOREVER.
BUT HE ALSO SAID THEY SWORE AN OATH TO REMAIN. THERE HAS BEEN MUCH UNREST SINCE THEN, AS YOU CAN SEE...

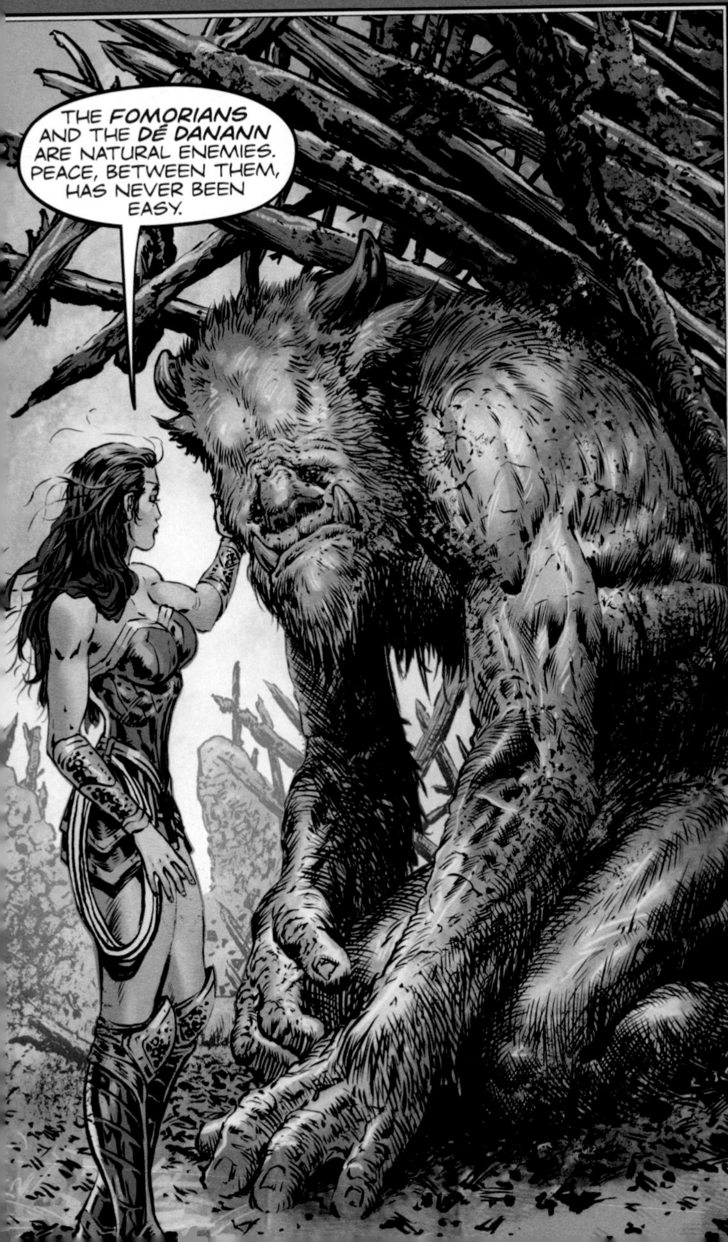
THE FOMORIANS AND THE DÉ DANANN ARE NATURAL ENEMIES. PEACE, BETWEEN THEM, HAS NEVER BEEN EASY.

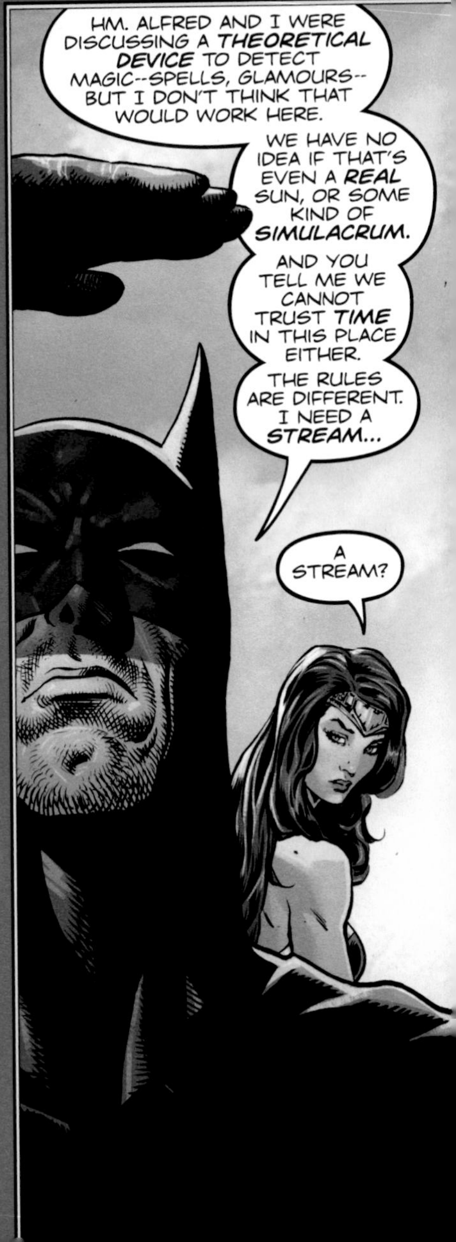
HM. ALFRED AND I WERE DISCUSSING A THEORETICAL DEVICE TO DETECT MAGIC--SPELLS, GLAMOURS--BUT I DON'T THINK THAT WOULD WORK HERE.
WE HAVE NO IDEA IF THAT'S EVEN A REAL SUN, OR SOME KIND OF SIMULACRUM.
AND YOU TELL ME WE CANNOT TRUST TIME IN THIS PLACE EITHER.
THE RULES ARE DIFFERENT. I NEED A STREAM...
A STREAM?

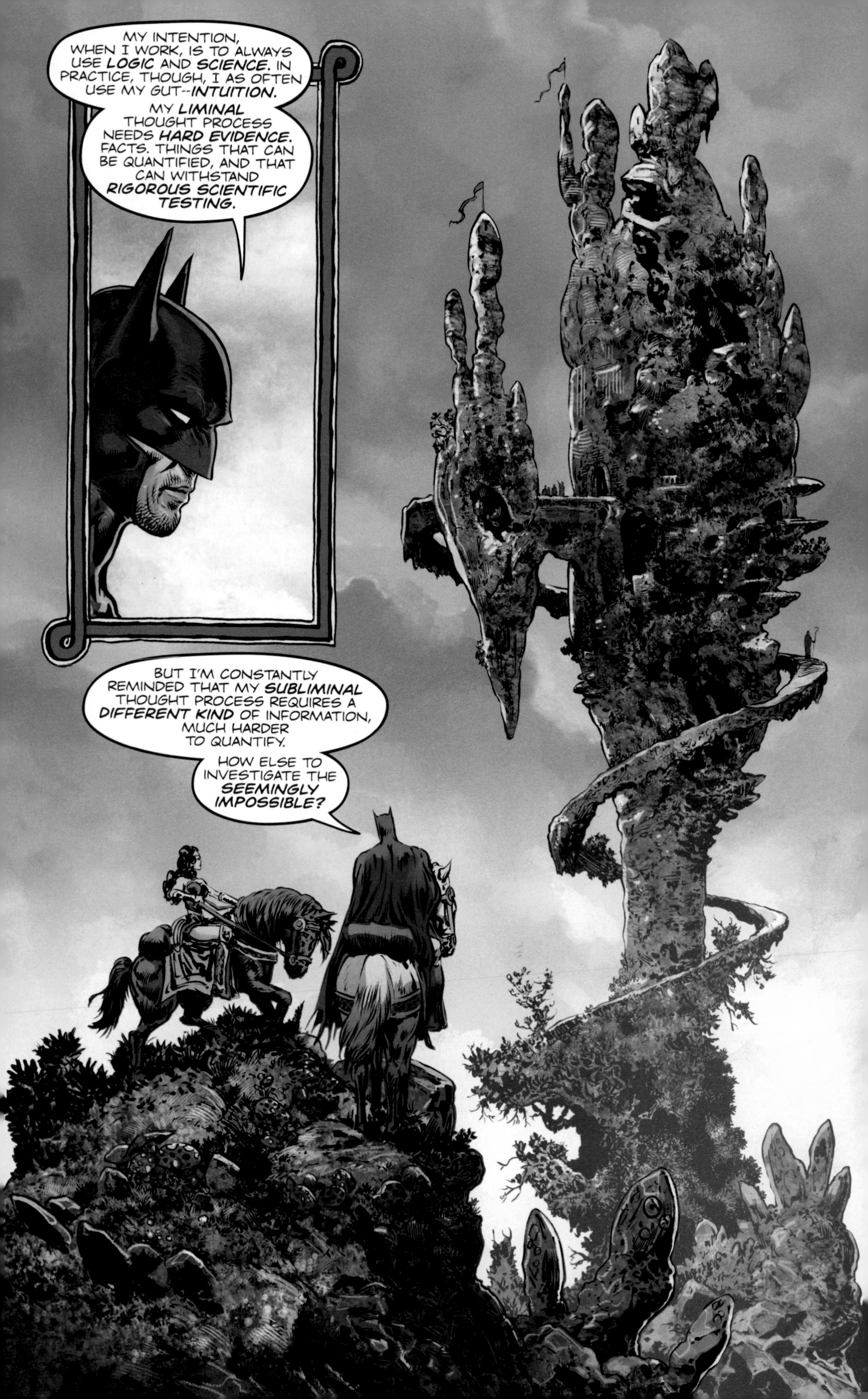
MY INTENTION, WHEN I WORK, IS TO ALWAYS USE LOGIC AND SCIENCE. IN PRACTICE, THOUGH, I AS OFTEN USE MY GUT--INTUITION.
MY LIMINAL THOUGHT PROCESS NEEDS HARD EVIDENCE. FACTS. THINGS THAT CAN BE QUANTIFIED, AND THAT CAN WITHSTAND RIGOROUS SCIENTIFIC TESTING.
BUT I'M CONSTANTLY REMINDED THAT MY SUBLIMINAL THOUGHT PROCESS REQUIRES A DIFFERENT KIND OF INFORMATION, MUCH HARDER TO QUANTIFY.
HOW ELSE TO INVESTIGATE THE SEEMINGLY IMPOSSIBLE?

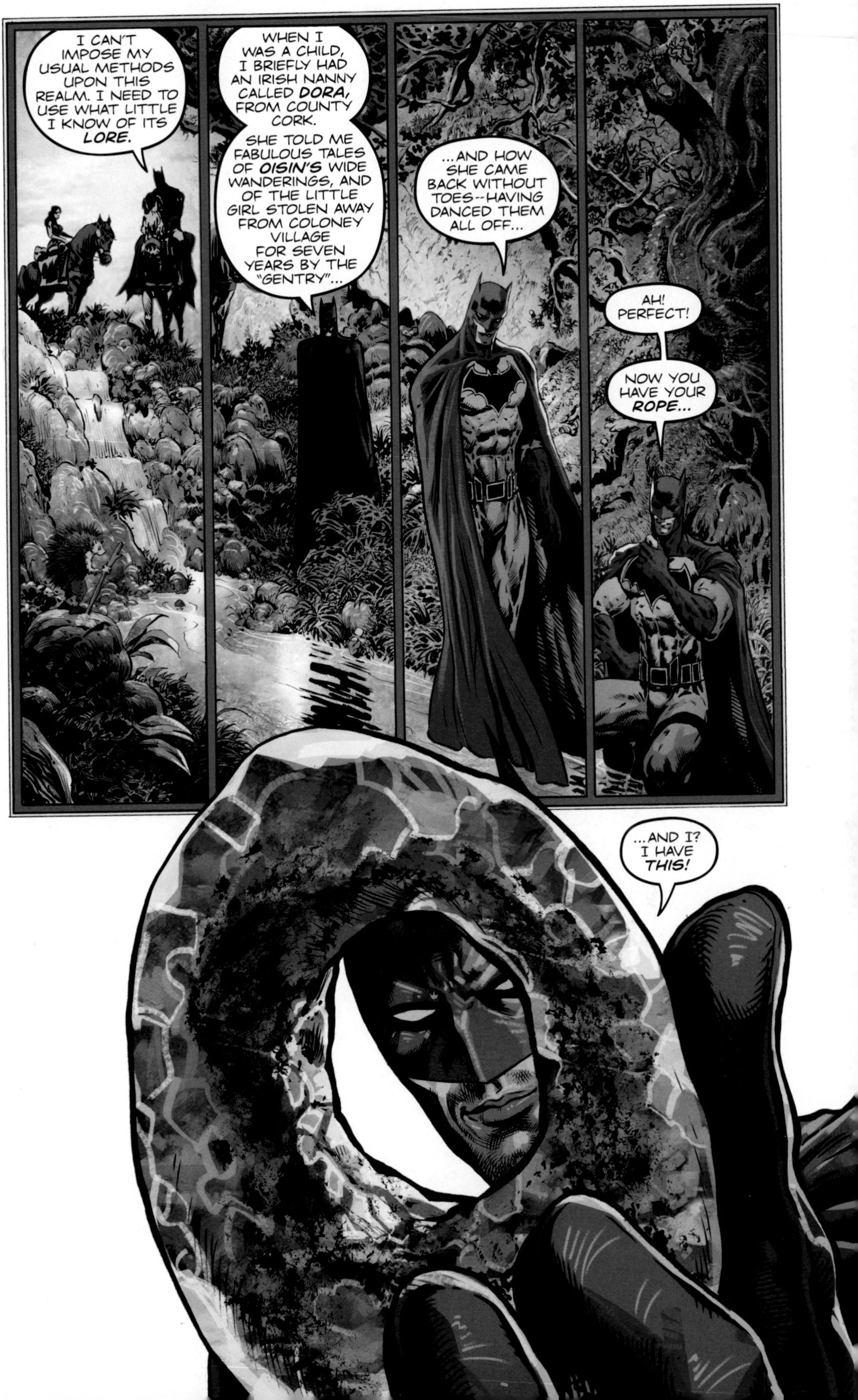
I CAN'T IMPOSE MY USUAL METHODS UPON THIS REALM. I NEED TO USE WHAT LITTLE I KNOW OF ITS LORE.
WHEN I WAS A CHILD, I BRIEFLY HAD AN IRISH NANNY CALLED DORA, FROM COUNTY CORK.
SHE TOLD ME FABULOUS TALES OF OISIN'S WIDE WANDERINGS, AND OF THE LITTLE GIRL STOLEN AWAY FROM COLONEY VILLAGE FOR SEVEN YEARS BY THE "GENTRY"...
...AND HOW SHE CAME BACK WITHOUT TOES--HAVING DANCED THEM ALL OFF...
AH! PERFECT!
NOW YOU HAVE YOUR ROPE...
...AND I? I HAVE THIS!

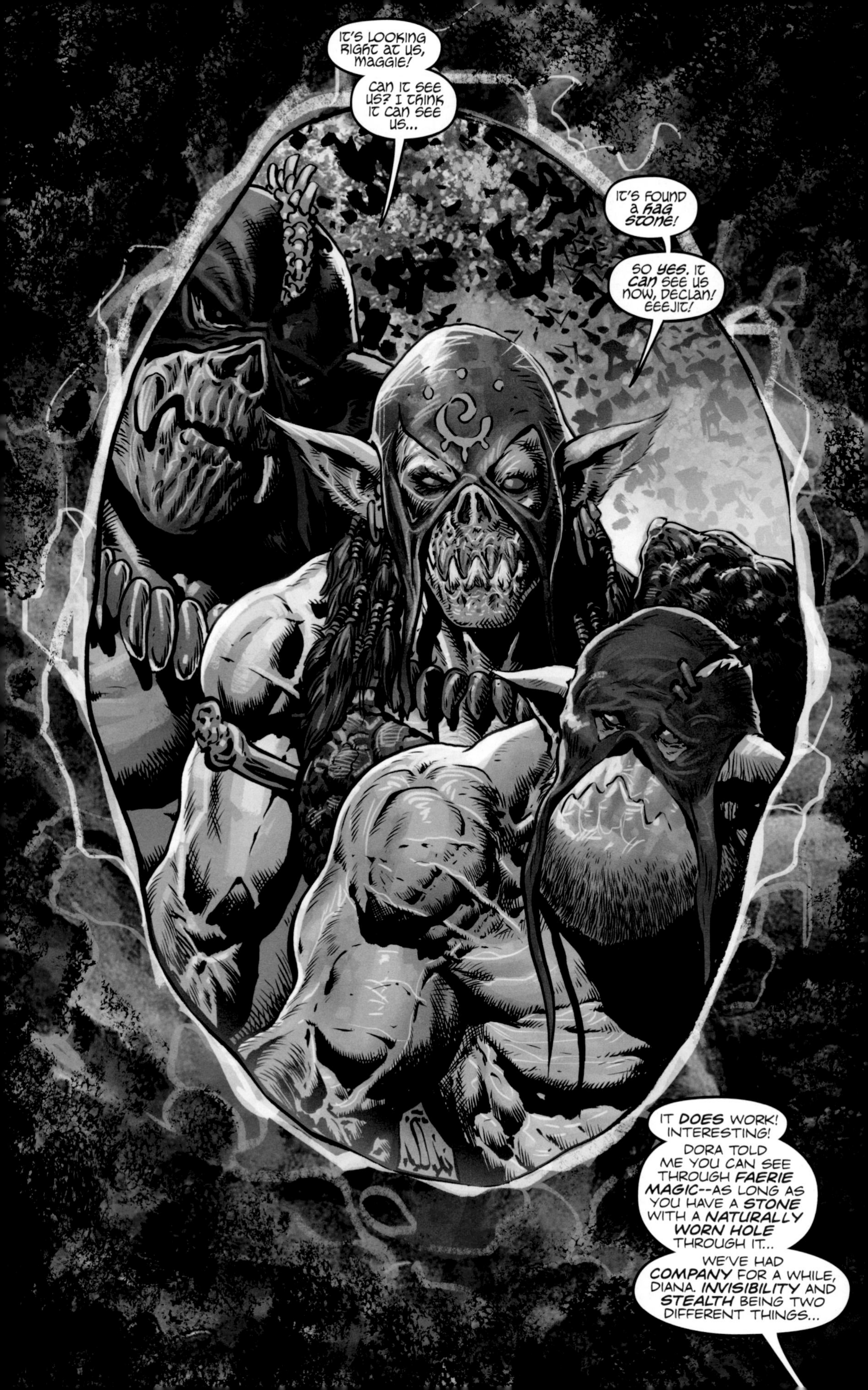
IT'S LOOKING RIGHT AT US, MAGGIE!
CAN IT SEE US? I THINK IT CAN SEE US...
IT'S FOUND A HAG STONE!
SO YES. IT CAN SEE US NOW, DECLAN! EEEJIT!
IT DOES WORK! INTERESTING!
DORA TOLD ME YOU CAN SEE THROUGH FAERIE MAGIC--AS LONG AS YOU HAVE A STONE WITH A NATURALLY WORN HOLE THROUGH IT...
WE'VE HAD COMPANY FOR A WHILE, DIANA. INVISIBILITY AND STEALTH BEING TWO DIFFERENT THINGS...

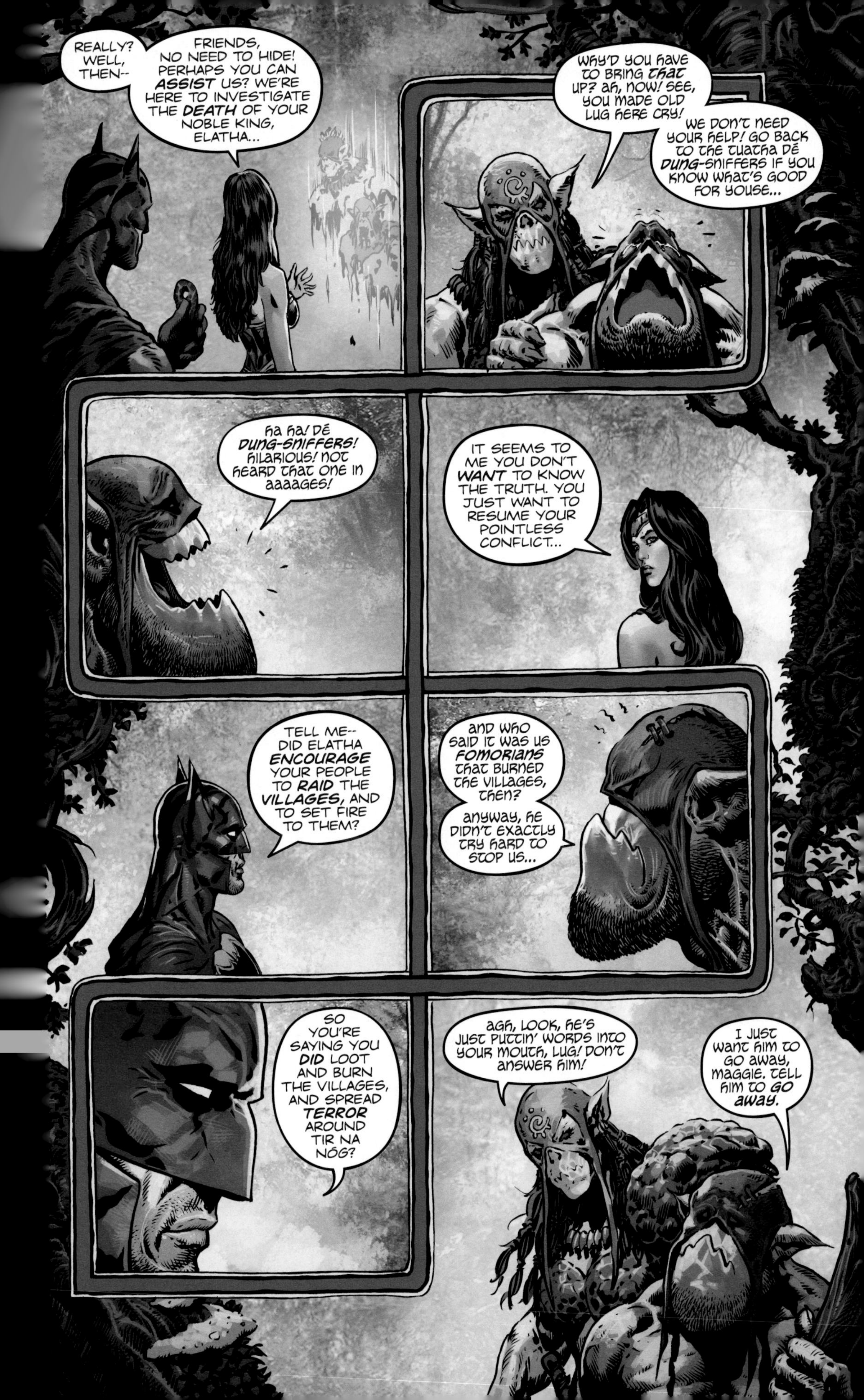
REALLY? WELL, THEN--
FRIENDS, NO NEED TO HIDE! PERHAPS YOU CAN ASSIST US? WE'RE HERE TO INVESTIGATE THE DEATH OF YOUR NOBLE KING, ELATHA...
WHY'D YOU HAVE TO BRING THAT UP? AH, NOW! SEE, YOU MADE OLD LUG HERE CRY!
WE DON'T NEED YOUR HELP! GO BACK TO THE TUATHA DÉ DUNG-SNIFFERS IF YOU KNOW WHAT'S GOOD FOR YOUSE...
HA HA! DÉ DUNG-SNIFFERS! HILARIOUS! NOT HEARD THAT ONE IN AAAAGES!
IT SEEMS TO ME YOU DON'T WANT TO KNOW THE TRUTH. YOU JUST WANT TO RESUME YOUR POINTLESS CONFLICT...
TELL ME-- DID ELATHA ENCOURAGE YOUR PEOPLE TO RAID THE VILLAGES, AND TO SET FIRE TO THEM?
AND WHO SAID IT WAS US FOMORIANS THAT BURNED THE VILLAGES, THEN?
ANYWAY, HE DIDN'T EXACTLY TRY HARD TO STOP US...
SO YOU'RE SAYING YOU DID LOOT AND BURN THE VILLAGES, AND SPREAD TERROR AROUND TIR NA NÓG?
AGH, LOOK, HE'S JUST PUTTIN' WORDS INTO YOUR MOUTH, LUG! DON'T ANSWER HIM!
I JUST WANT HIM TO GO AWAY, MAGGIE. TELL HIM TO GO AWAY.

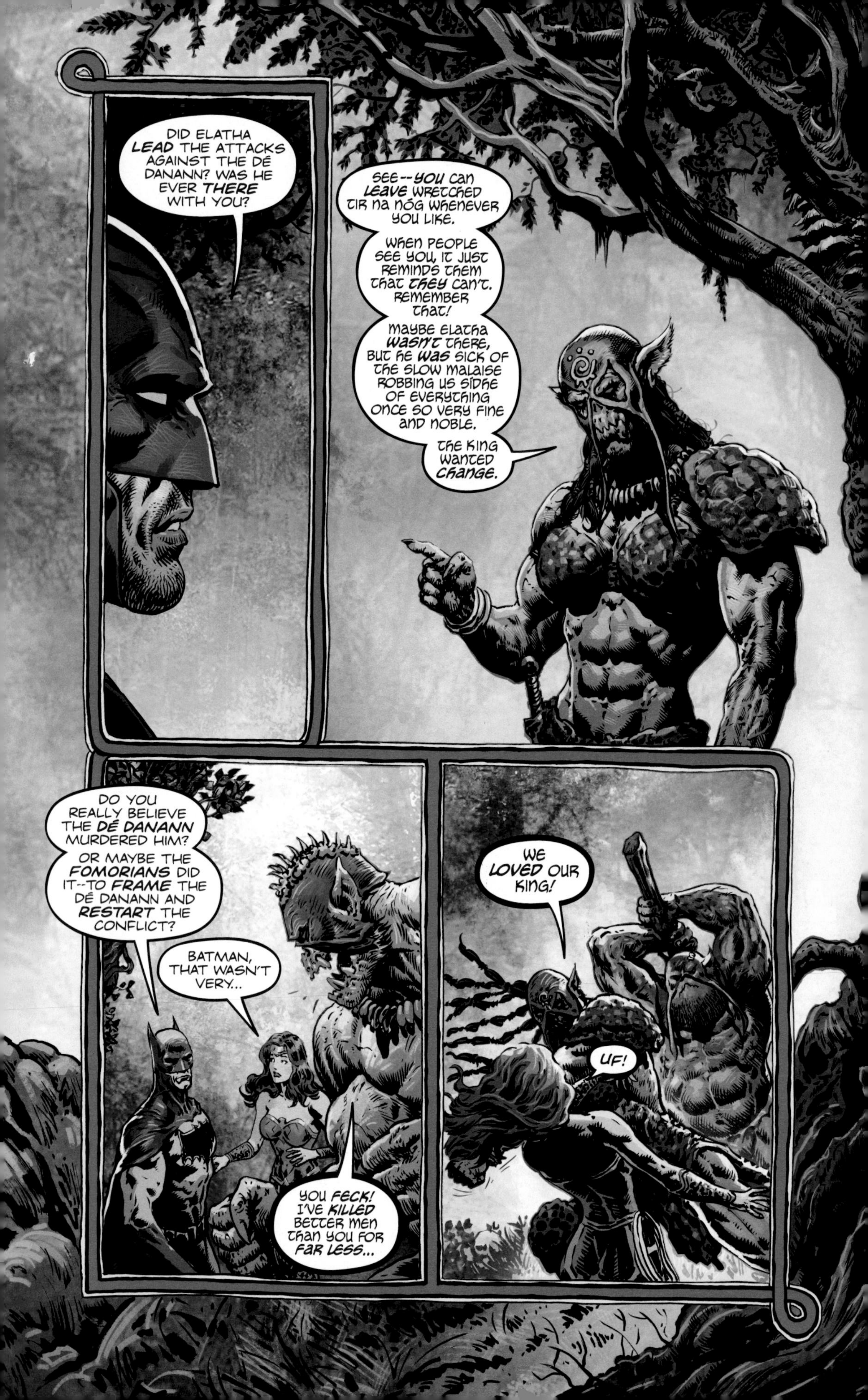
DID ELATHA LEAD THE ATTACKS AGAINST THE DÉ DANANN? WAS HE EVER THERE WITH YOU?
SEE--YOU CAN LEAVE WRETCHED TIR NA NÓG WHENEVER YOU LIKE.
WHEN PEOPLE SEE YOU, IT JUST REMINDS THEM THAT THEY CAN'T. REMEMBER THAT!
MAYBE ELATHA WASN'T THERE, BUT HE WAS SICK OF THE SLOW MALAISE ROBBING US SIDHE OF EVERYTHING ONCE SO VERY FINE AND NOBLE.
THE KING WANTED CHANGE.
DO YOU REALLY BELIEVE THE DÉ DANANN MURDERED HIM?
OR MAYBE THE FOMORIANS DID IT--TO FRAME THE DÉ DANANN AND RESTART THE CONFLICT?
BATMAN, THAT WASN'T VERY...
YOU FECK! I'VE KILLED BETTER MEN THAN YOU FOR FAR LESS...
WE LOVED OUR KING!
UF!

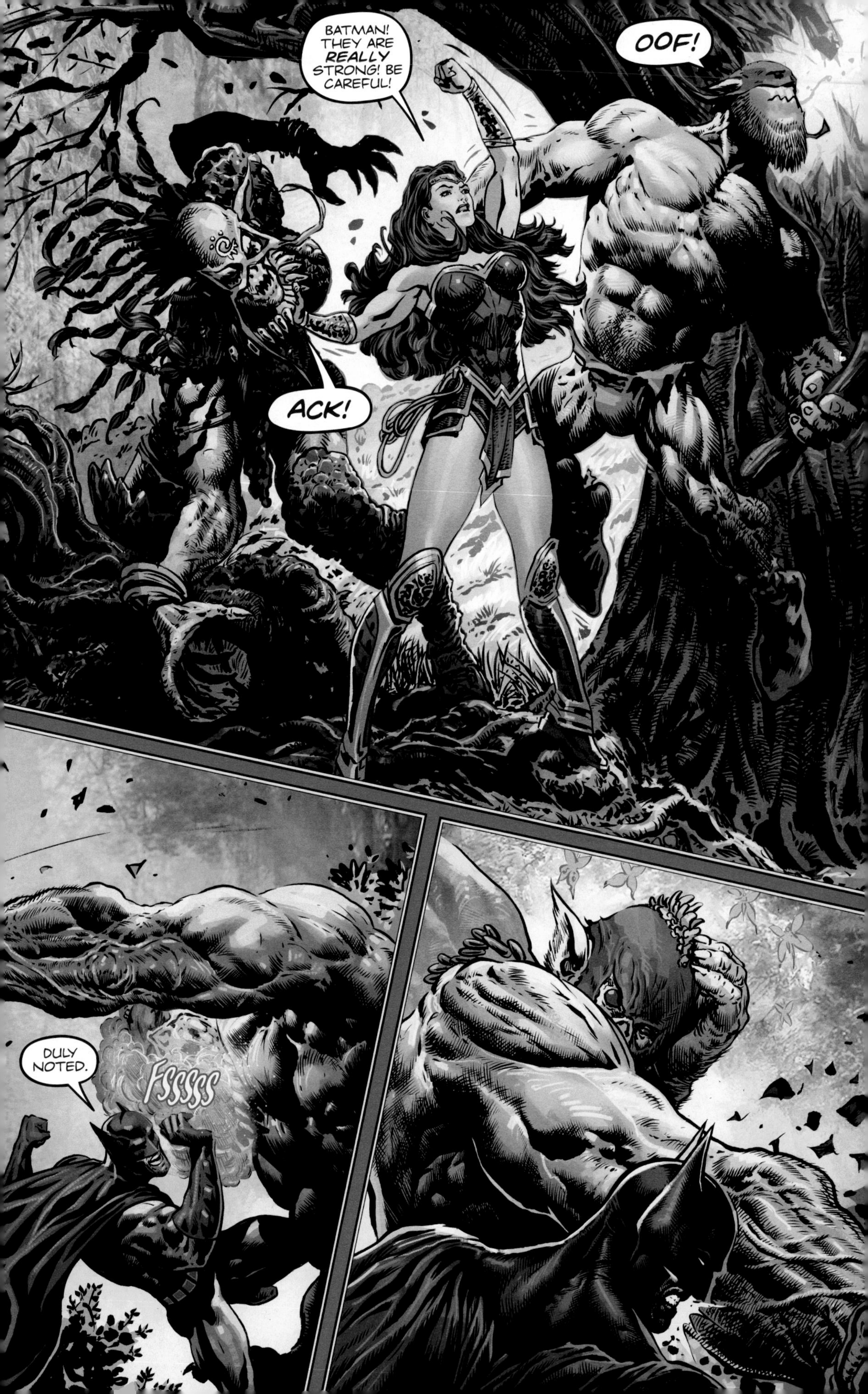
BATMAN! THEY ARE REALLY STRONG! BE CAREFUL!
OOF!
ACK!
DULY NOTED.
FSSSSS

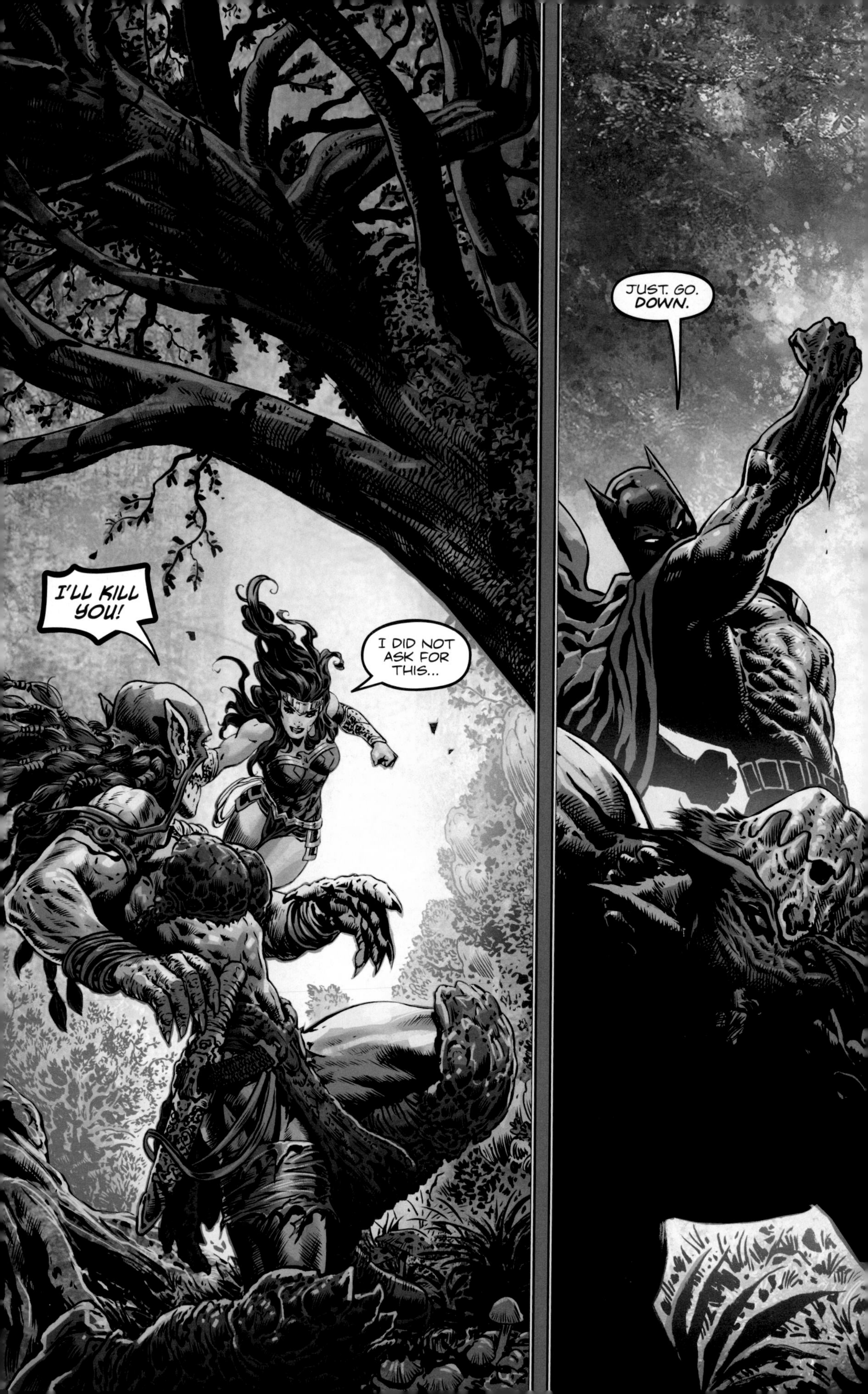
I'LL KILL YOU!
I DID NOT ASK FOR THIS...
JUST. GO. DOWN.

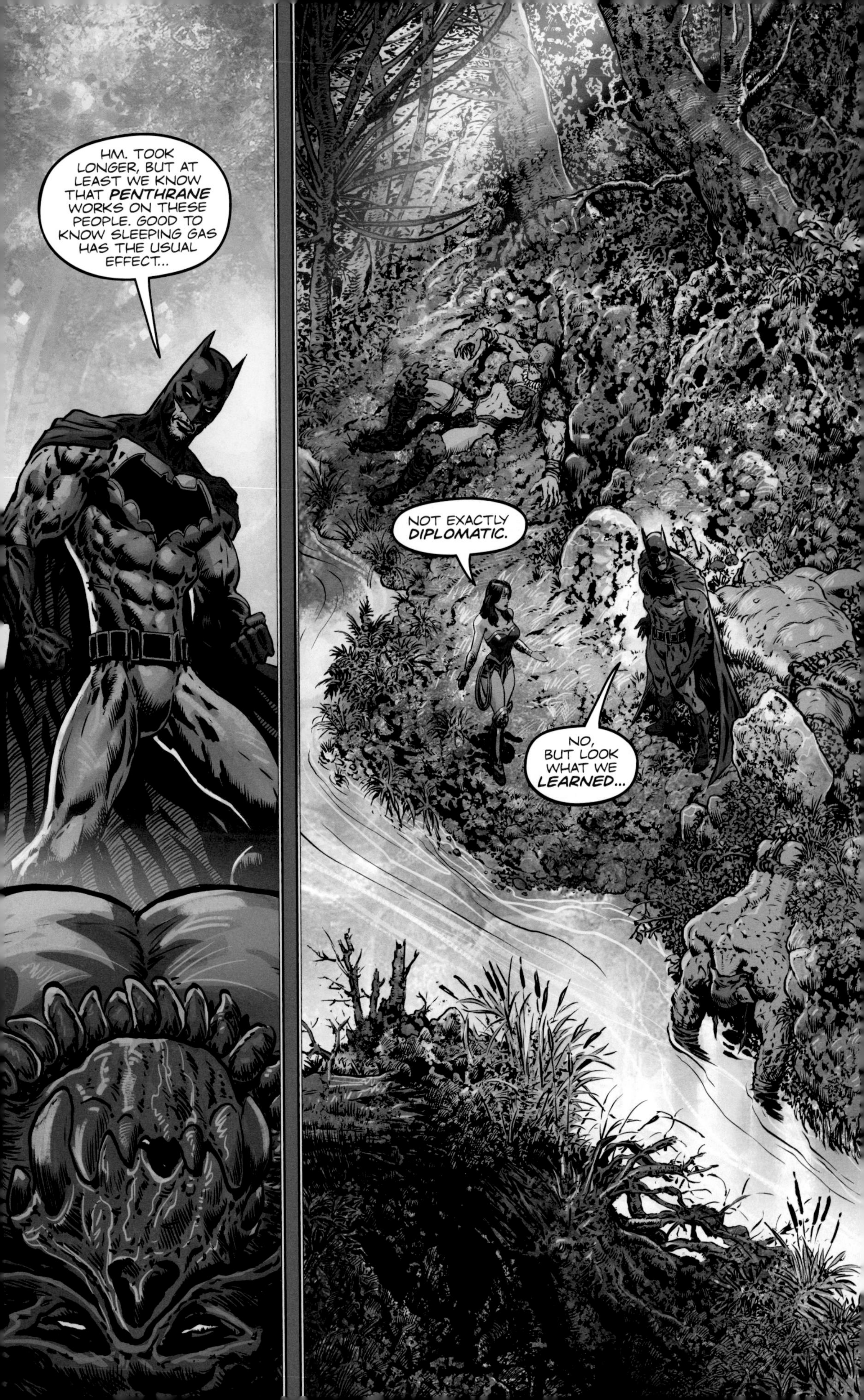
HM. TOOK LONGER, BUT AT LEAST WE KNOW THAT PENTHRANE WORKS ON THESE PEOPLE. GOOD TO KNOW SLEEPING GAS HAS THE USUAL EFFECT...
NOT EXACTLY DIPLOMATIC.
NO, BUT LOOK WHAT WE LEARNED...

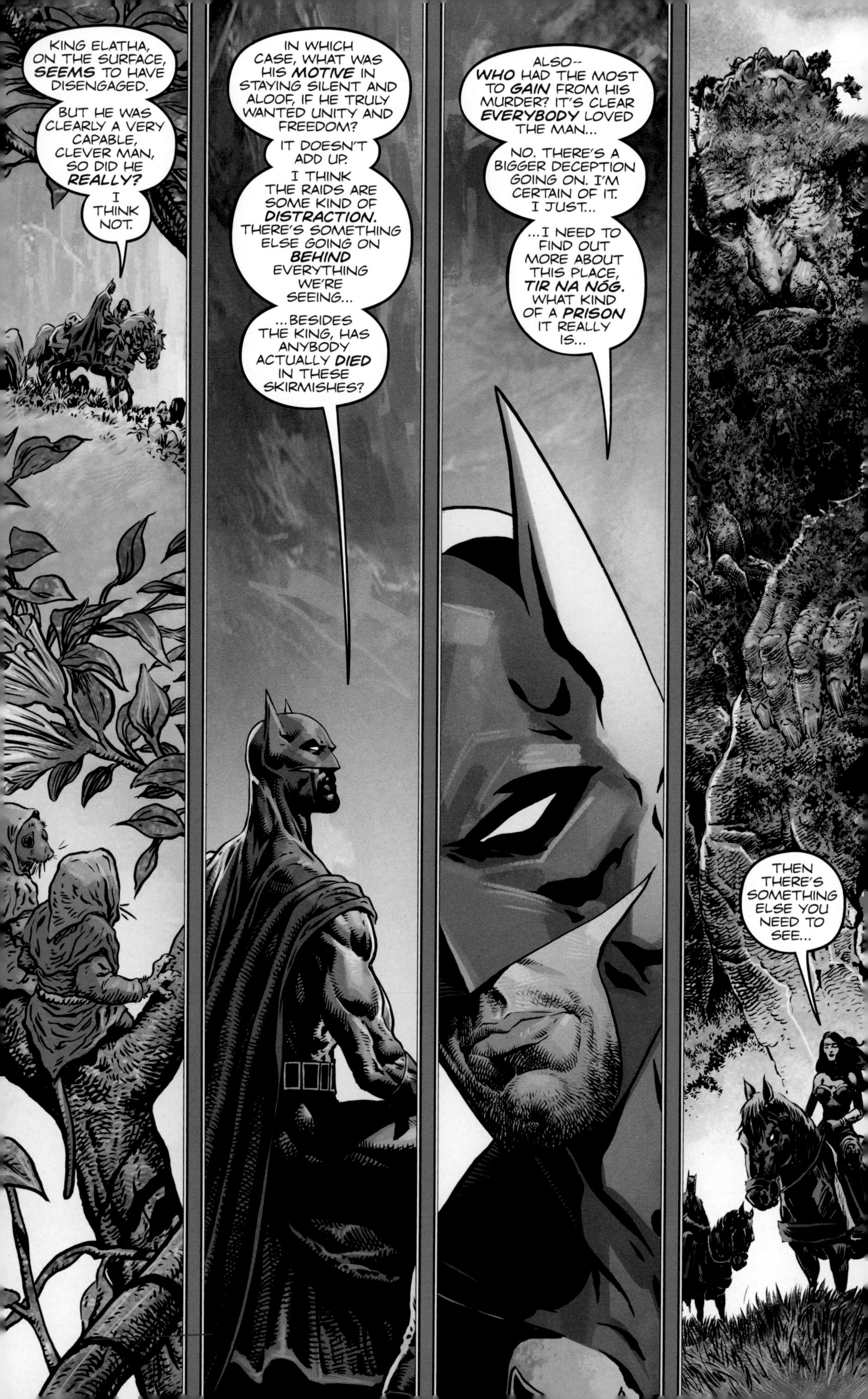
KING ELATHA, ON THE SURFACE, SEEMS TO HAVE DISENGAGED.
BUT HE WAS CLEARLY A VERY CAPABLE, CLEVER MAN, SO DID HE REALLY?
I THINK NOT.
IN WHICH CASE, WHAT WAS HIS MOTIVE IN STAYING SILENT AND ALOOF, IF HE TRULY WANTED UNITY AND FREEDOM?
IT DOESN'T ADD UP.
I THINK THE RAIDS ARE SOME KIND OF DISTRACTION. THERE'S SOMETHING ELSE GOING ON BEHIND EVERYTHING WE'RE SEEING...
...BESIDES THE KING, HAS ANYBODY ACTUALLY DIED IN THESE SKIRMISHES?
ALSO-- WHO HAD THE MOST TO GAIN FROM HIS MURDER? IT'S CLEAR EVERYBODY LOVED THE MAN...
NO. THERE'S A BIGGER DECEPTION GOING ON. I'M CERTAIN OF IT. I JUST...
...I NEED TO FIND OUT MORE ABOUT THIS PLACE, TIR NA NÓG. WHAT KIND OF A PRISON IT REALLY IS...
THEN THERE'S SOMETHING ELSE YOU NEED TO SEE...

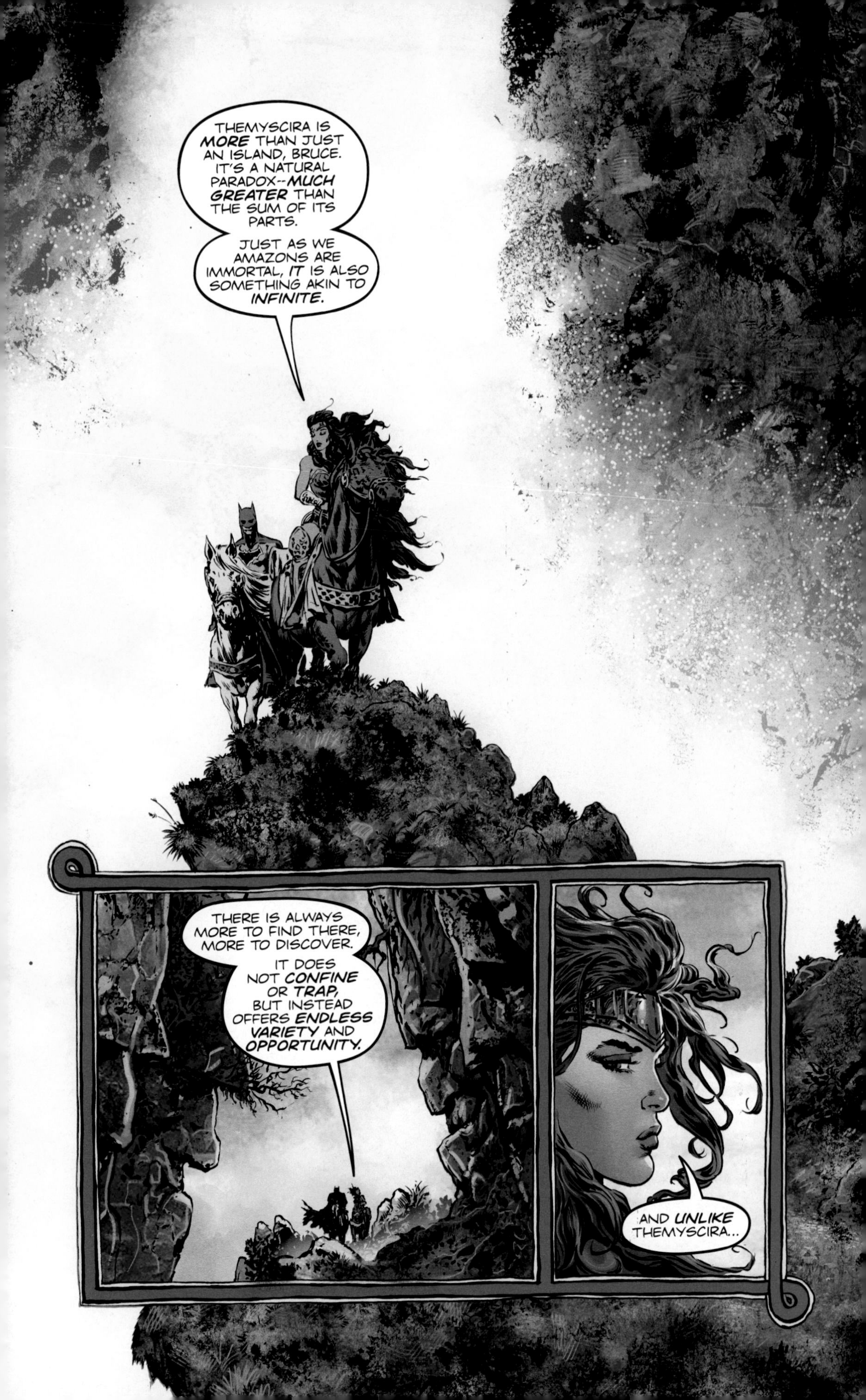
THEMYSCIRA IS MORE THAN JUST AN ISLAND, BRUCE. IT'S A NATURAL PARADOX--MUCH GREATER THAN THE SUM OF ITS PARTS.
JUST AS WE AMAZONS ARE IMMORTAL, IT IS ALSO SOMETHING AKIN TO INFINITE.
THERE IS ALWAYS MORE TO FIND THERE, MORE TO DISCOVER.
IT DOES NOT CONFINE OR TRAP, BUT INSTEAD OFFERS ENDLESS VARIETY AND OPPORTUNITY.
AND UNLIKE THEMYSCIRA...

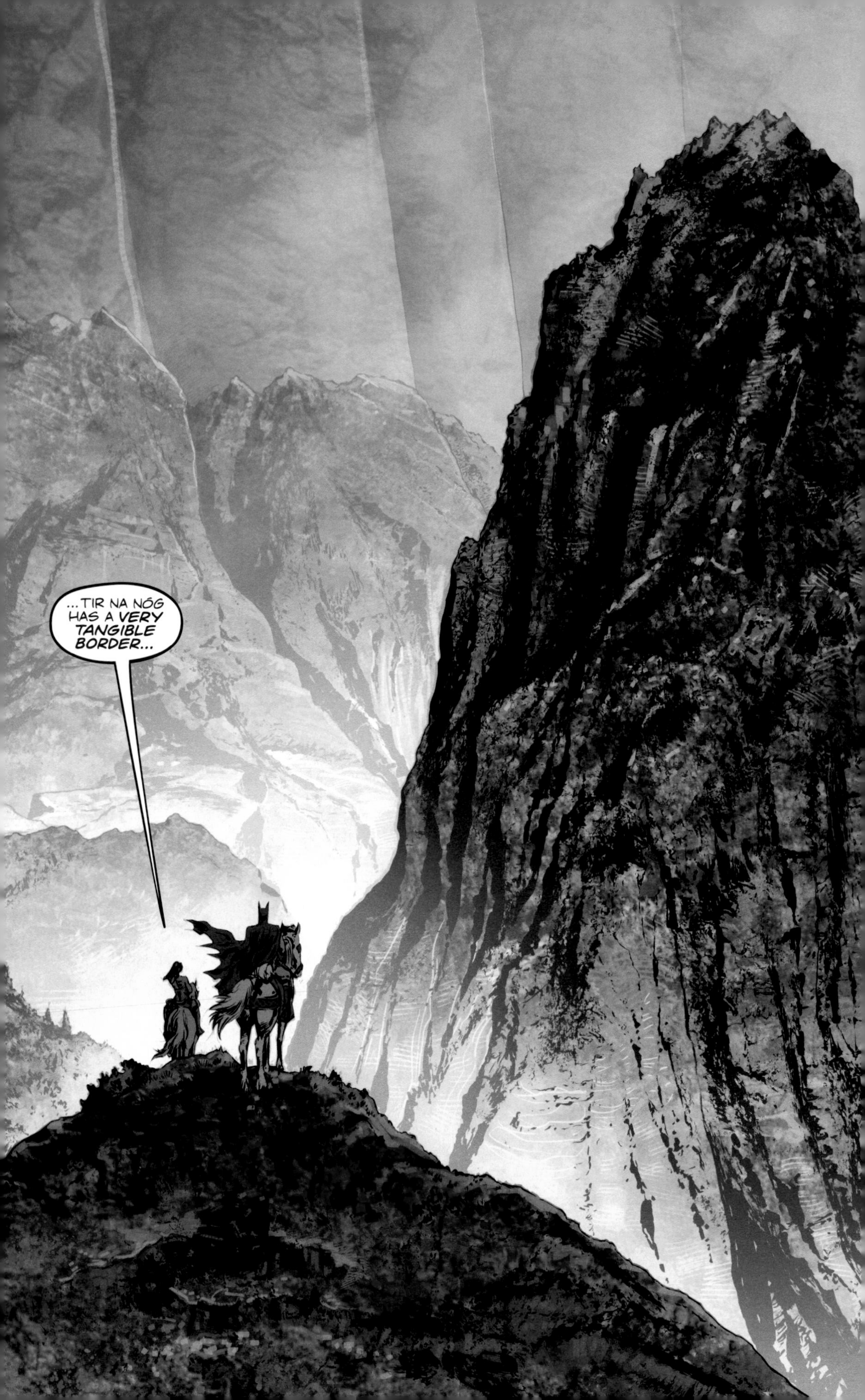
...TIR NA NÓG HAS A VERY TANGIBLE BORDER...

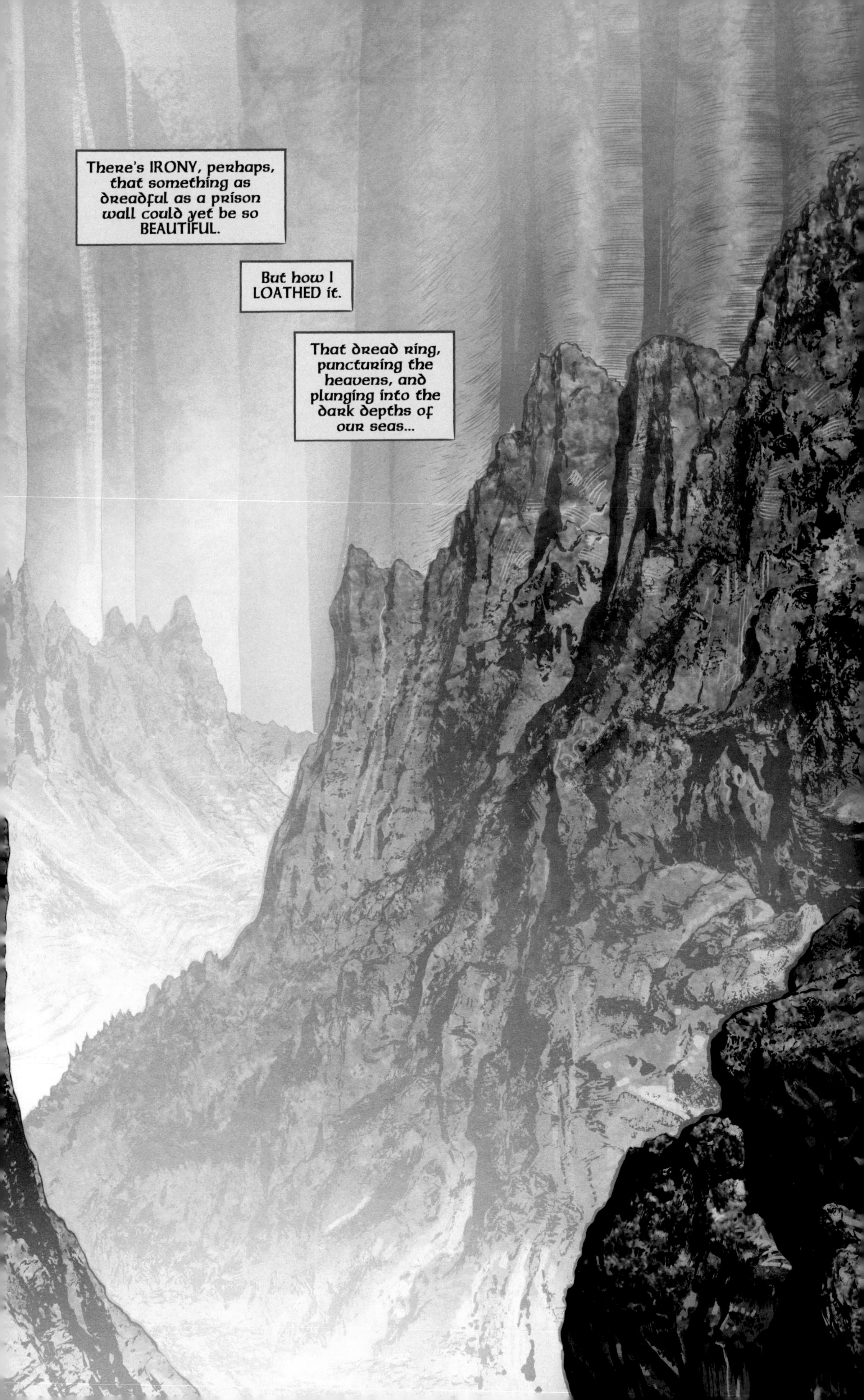
There's IRONY, perhaps, that something as dreadful as a prison wall could yet be so BEAUTIFUL.
But how I LOATHED it.
That dread ring, puncturing the heavens, and plunging into the dark depths of our seas...

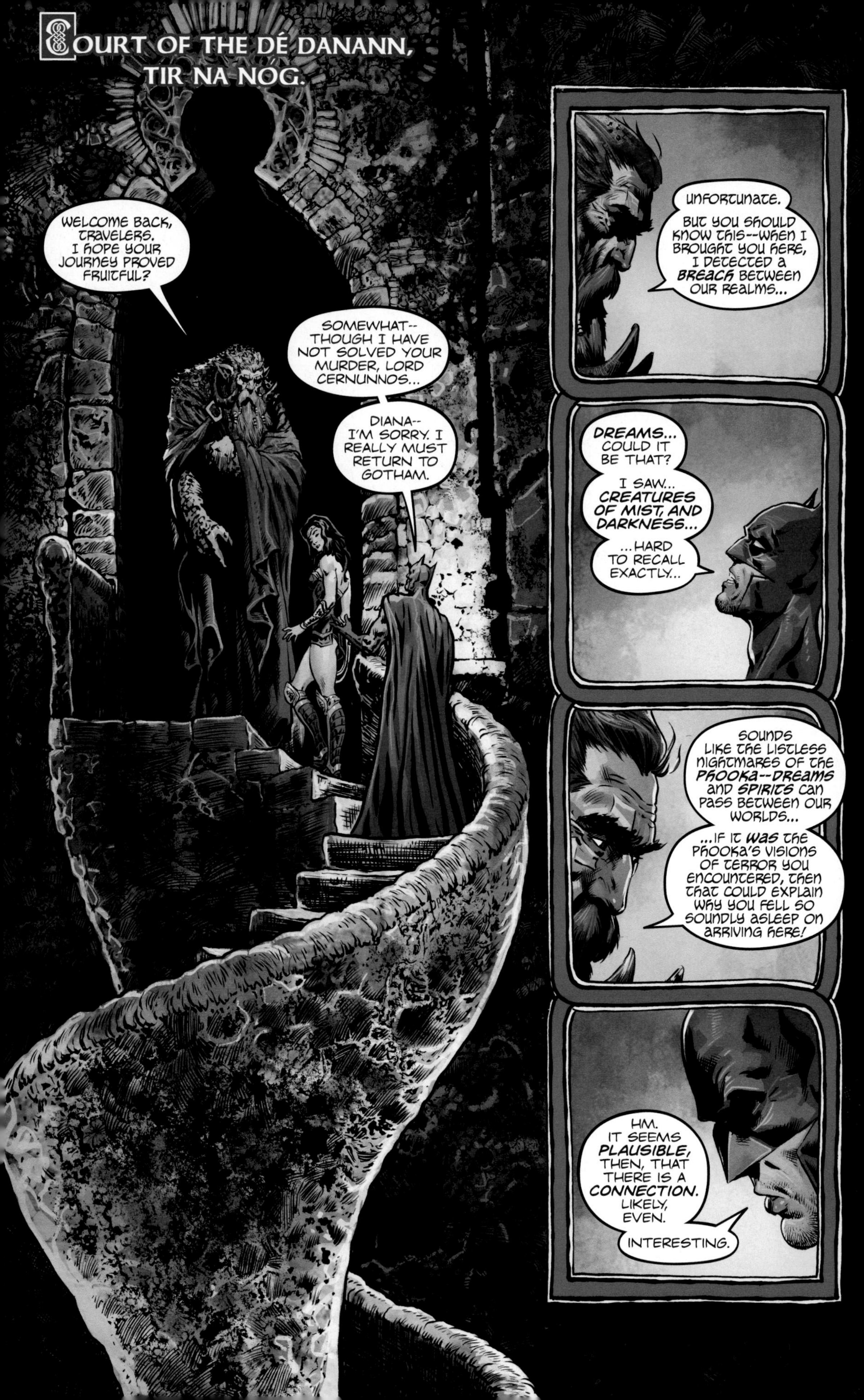
COURT OF THE DÉ DANANN, TIR NA NÓG.
WELCOME BACK, TRAVELERS. I HOPE YOUR JOURNEY PROVED FRUITFUL?
SOMEWHAT-- THOUGH I HAVE NOT SOLVED YOUR MURDER, LORD CERNUNNOS...
DIANA-- I'M SORRY. I REALLY MUST RETURN TO GOTHAM.
UNFORTUNATE.
BUT YOU SHOULD KNOW THIS--WHEN I BROUGHT YOU HERE, I DETECTED A BREACH BETWEEN OUR REALMS...
DREAMS... COULD IT BE THAT?
I SAW... CREATURES OF MIST, AND DARKNESS...
...HARD TO RECALL EXACTLY...
SOUNDS LIKE THE LISTLESS NIGHTMARES OF THE PHOOKA--DREAMS AND SPIRITS CAN PASS BETWEEN OUR WORLDS...
...IF IT WAS THE PHOOKA'S VISIONS OF TERROR YOU ENCOUNTERED, THEN THAT COULD EXPLAIN WHY YOU FELL SO SOUNDLY ASLEEP ON ARRIVING HERE!
HM. IT SEEMS PLAUSIBLE, THEN, THAT THERE IS A CONNECTION. LIKELY, EVEN.
INTERESTING.

AND WHAT CAN YOU TELL US ABOUT *THE WALL...*

WHAT IS THERE TO TELL, OTHER THAN IT SIMPLY *IS?*

A GLAMOUR HAS FOGGED OUR COLLECTIVE MEMORIES, BUT...

...THERE ARE SOME STORIES THAT SAY WE WERE NOT SIMPLY *FORGOTTEN,* AND THAT WE SEALED OURSELVES IN HERE WITH OUR *DARKEST ENEMIES...*SO THAT THE WORLD MIGHT HAVE *DONE WITH THEM.*

BUT NONE KNOW FOR SURE, AS WE FOOLISHLY CAST SPELLS OF FORGETFULNESS-- THE BETTER TO DEAL WITH THIS SELF-INFLICTED IMPRISONMENT...

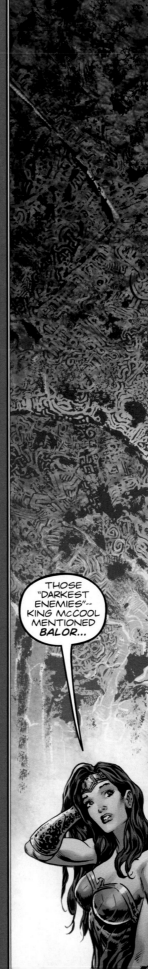

THOSE "DARKEST ENEMIES"-- KING MCCOOL MENTIONED *BALOR...*

HE OF THE *EVIL EYE?*

PERHAPS--IT IS SOMETIMES SAID SO--BUT THAT'S ALL JUST *ORAL TRADITION.*

NONE AMONGST US TRULY *RECALLS* THOSE FIERCE BATTLES--FIGHT THEM THOUGH WE SURELY DID!

WE EVEN TALK OF OUR KINFOLK, THE *FIR BOLG,* AS THOUGH THEY WERE *MONSTERS*--

--BUT WE DO NOT *KNOW* THAT THEY *WERE,* FOR WE DO NOT REMEMBER--NOT EVEN KING MCCOOL, WHO VANQUISHED THEM BENEATH THE SEA!

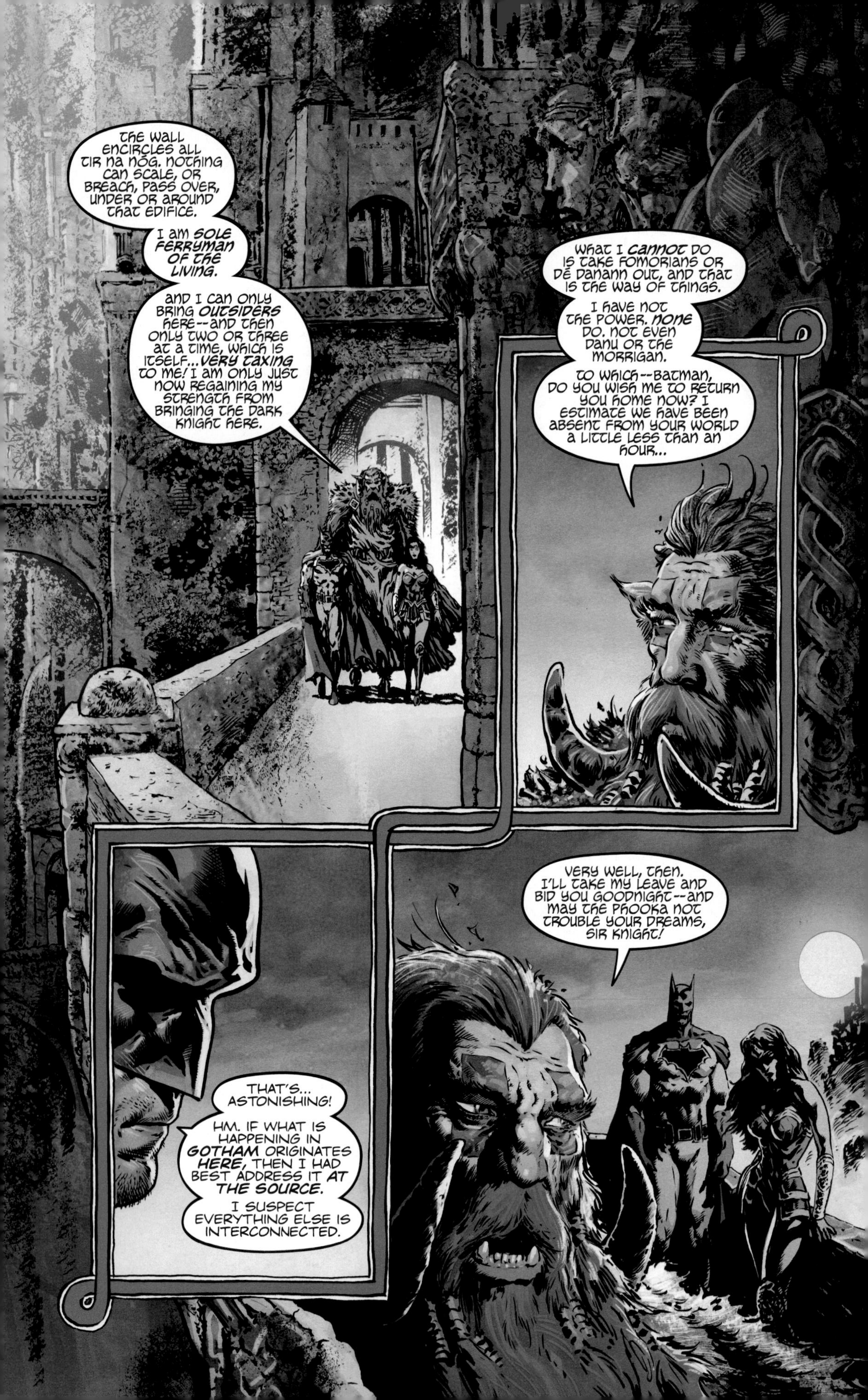
THE WALL ENCIRCLES ALL TIR NA NÓG. NOTHING CAN SCALE, OR BREACH, PASS OVER, UNDER OR AROUND THAT EDIFICE.
I AM SOLE FERRYMAN OF THE LIVING.
AND I CAN ONLY BRING OUTSIDERS HERE--AND THEN ONLY TWO OR THREE AT A TIME, WHICH IS ITSELF...VERY TAXING TO ME! I AM ONLY JUST NOW REGAINING MY STRENGTH FROM BRINGING THE DARK KNIGHT HERE.
WHAT I CANNOT DO IS TAKE FOMORIANS OR DÉ DANANN OUT, AND THAT IS THE WAY OF THINGS.
I HAVE NOT THE POWER. NONE DO. NOT EVEN DANU OR THE MORRIGAN.
TO WHICH--BATMAN, DO YOU WISH ME TO RETURN YOU HOME NOW? I ESTIMATE WE HAVE BEEN ABSENT FROM YOUR WORLD A LITTLE LESS THAN AN HOUR...
THAT'S... ASTONISHING!
HM. IF WHAT IS HAPPENING IN GOTHAM ORIGINATES HERE, THEN I HAD BEST ADDRESS IT AT THE SOURCE.
I SUSPECT EVERYTHING ELSE IS INTERCONNECTED.
VERY WELL, THEN. I'LL TAKE MY LEAVE AND BID YOU GOODNIGHT--AND MAY THE PHOOKA NOT TROUBLE YOUR DREAMS, SIR KNIGHT!

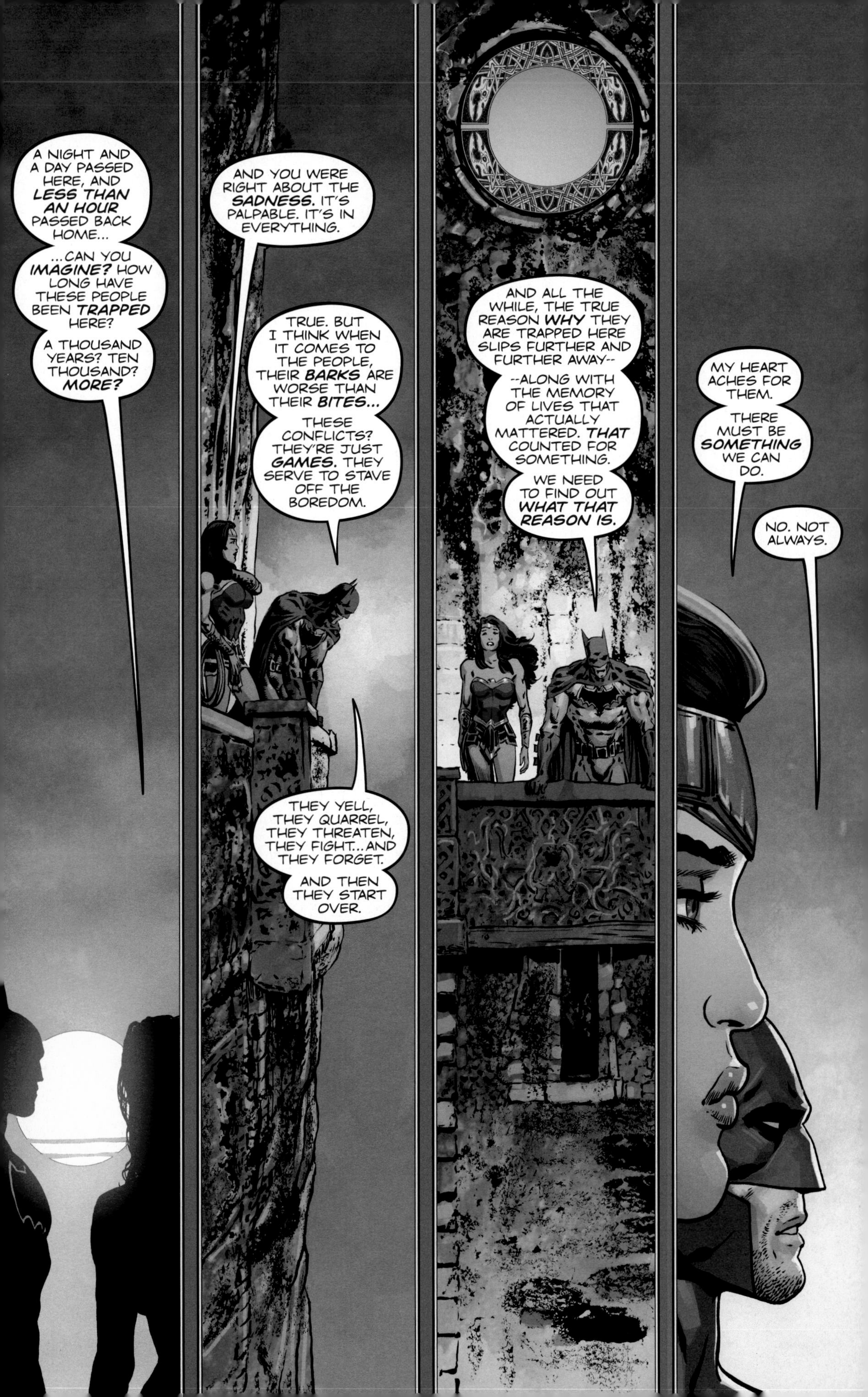
A NIGHT AND A DAY PASSED HERE, AND LESS THAN AN HOUR PASSED BACK HOME...
...CAN YOU IMAGINE? HOW LONG HAVE THESE PEOPLE BEEN TRAPPED HERE?
A THOUSAND YEARS? TEN THOUSAND? MORE?
AND YOU WERE RIGHT ABOUT THE SADNESS. IT'S PALPABLE. IT'S IN EVERYTHING.
TRUE. BUT I THINK WHEN IT COMES TO THE PEOPLE, THEIR BARKS ARE WORSE THAN THEIR BITES...
THESE CONFLICTS? THEY'RE JUST GAMES. THEY SERVE TO STAVE OFF THE BOREDOM.
THEY YELL, THEY QUARREL, THEY THREATEN, THEY FIGHT...AND THEY FORGET.
AND THEN THEY START OVER.
AND ALL THE WHILE, THE TRUE REASON WHY THEY ARE TRAPPED HERE SLIPS FURTHER AND FURTHER AWAY--
--ALONG WITH THE MEMORY OF LIVES THAT ACTUALLY MATTERED. THAT COUNTED FOR SOMETHING.
WE NEED TO FIND OUT WHAT THAT REASON IS.
MY HEART ACHES FOR THEM.
THERE MUST BE SOMETHING WE CAN DO.
NO. NOT ALWAYS.

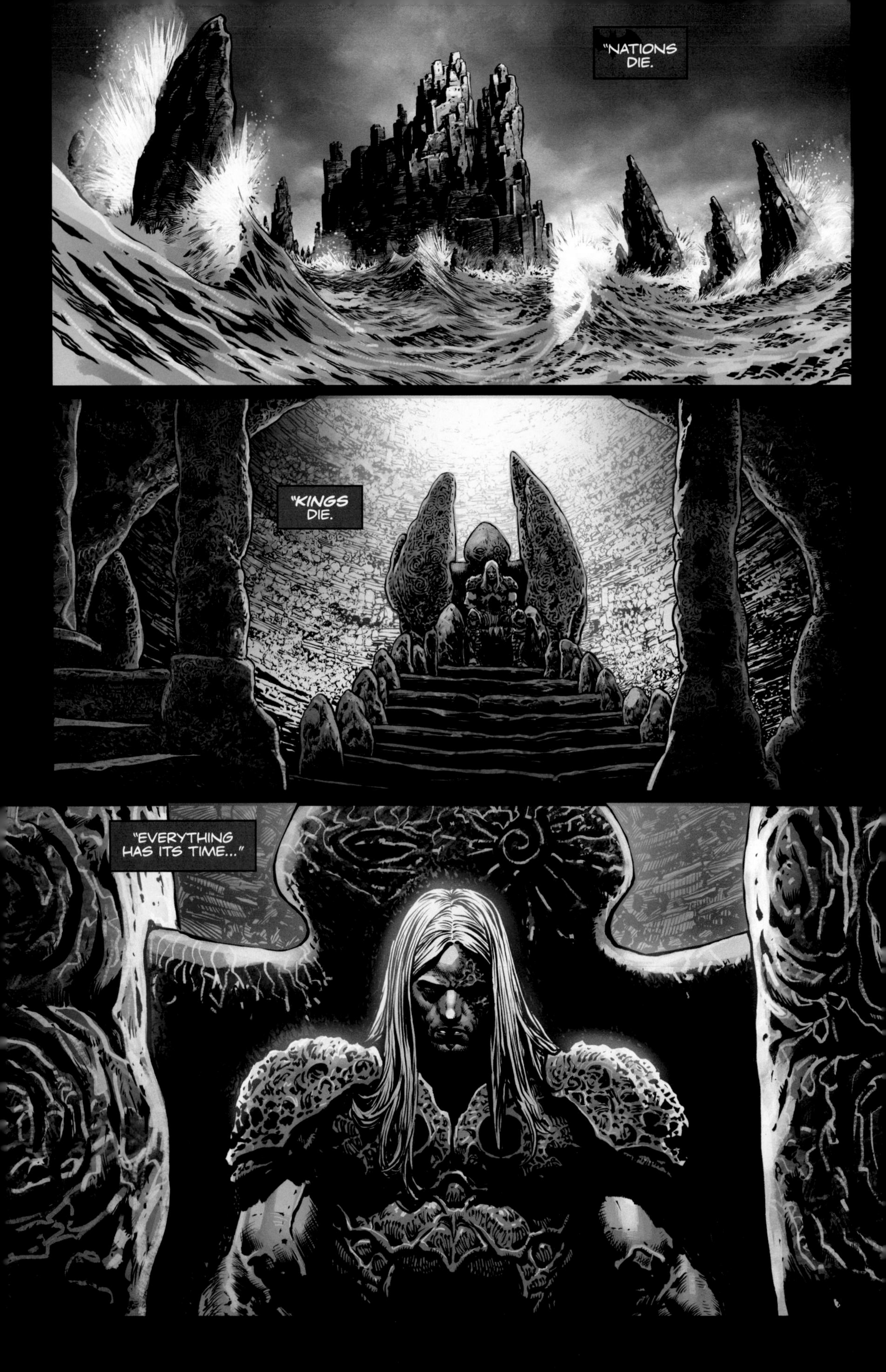
"NATIONS DIE.
"KINGS DIE.
"EVERYTHING HAS ITS TIME..."

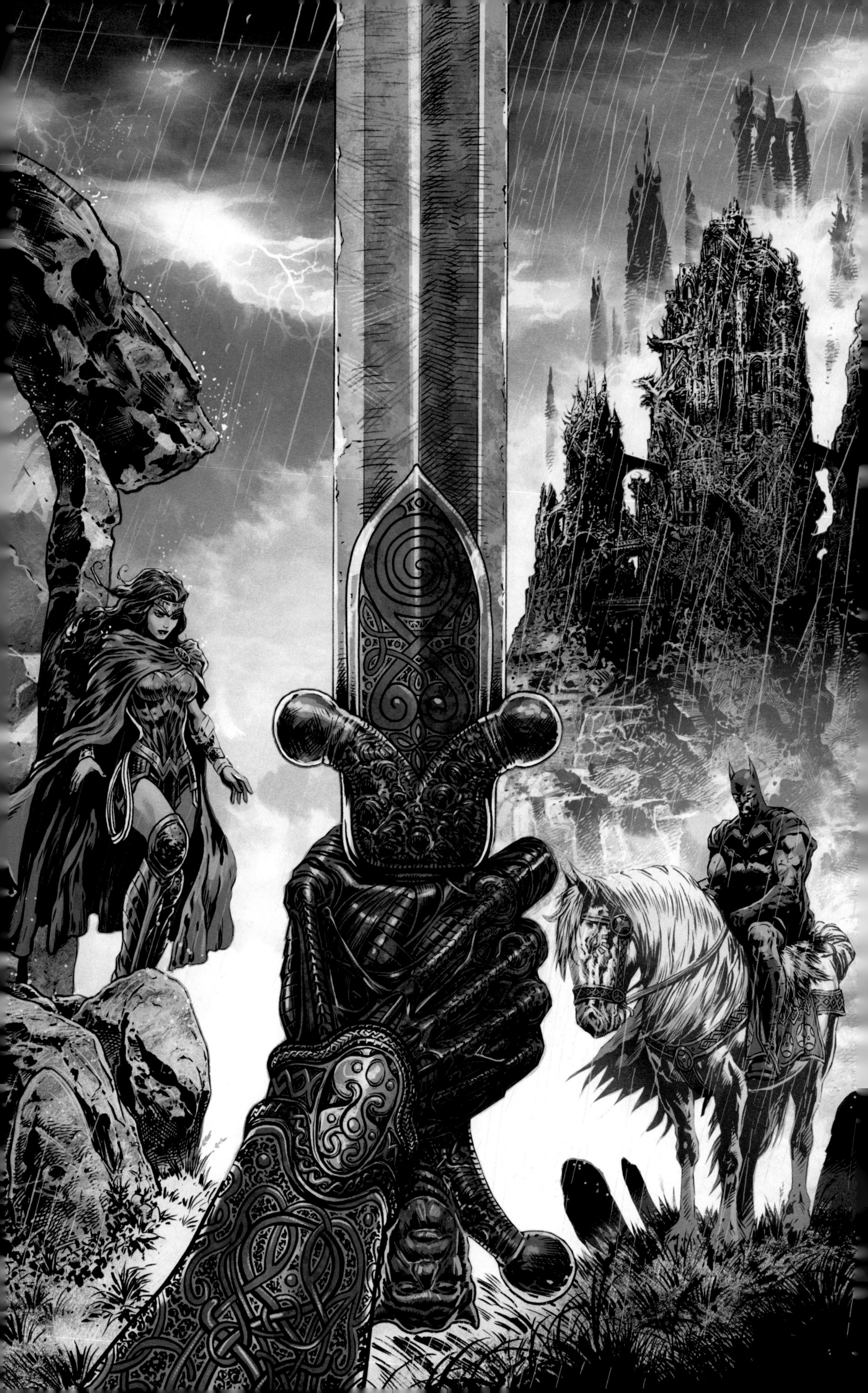

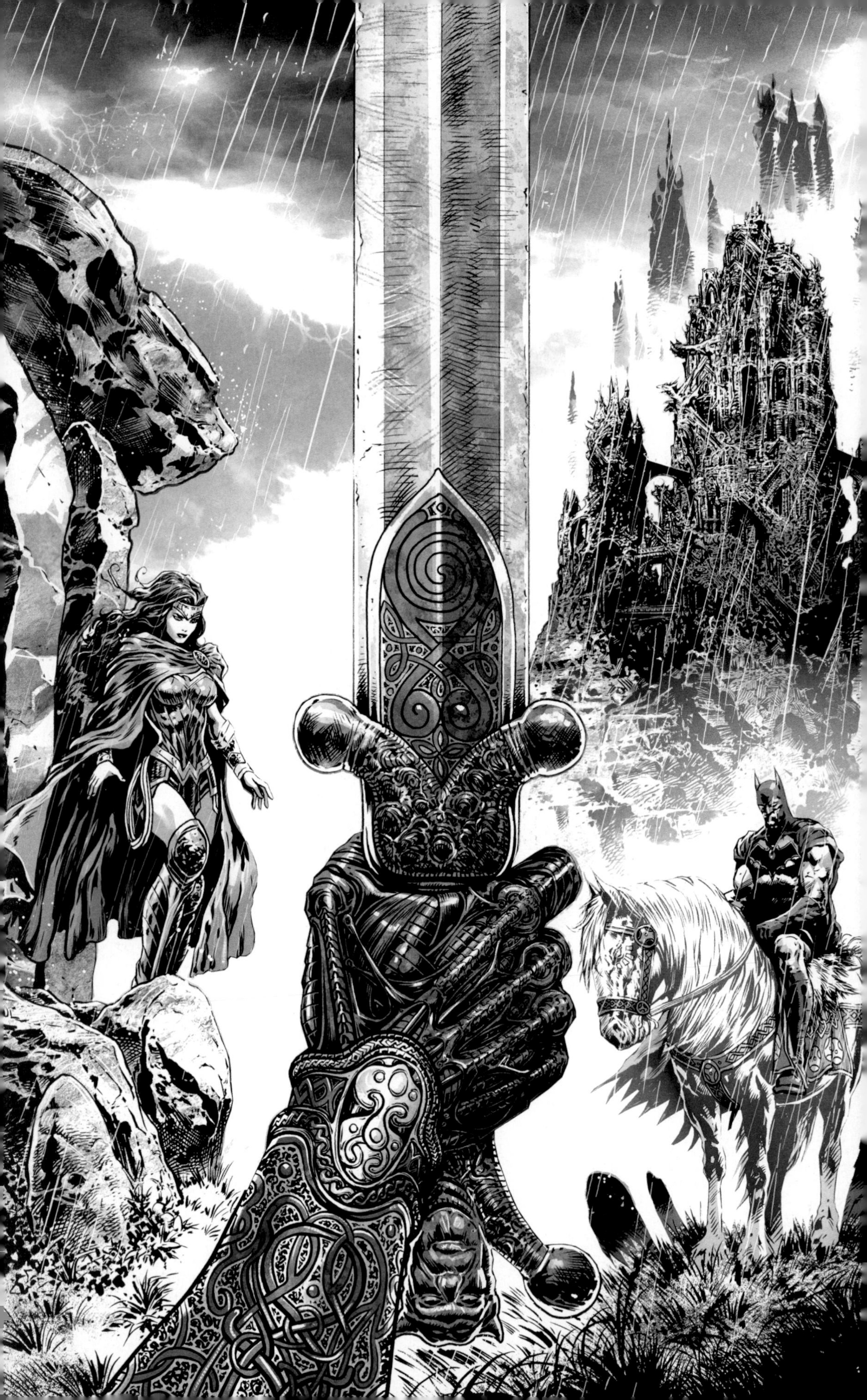

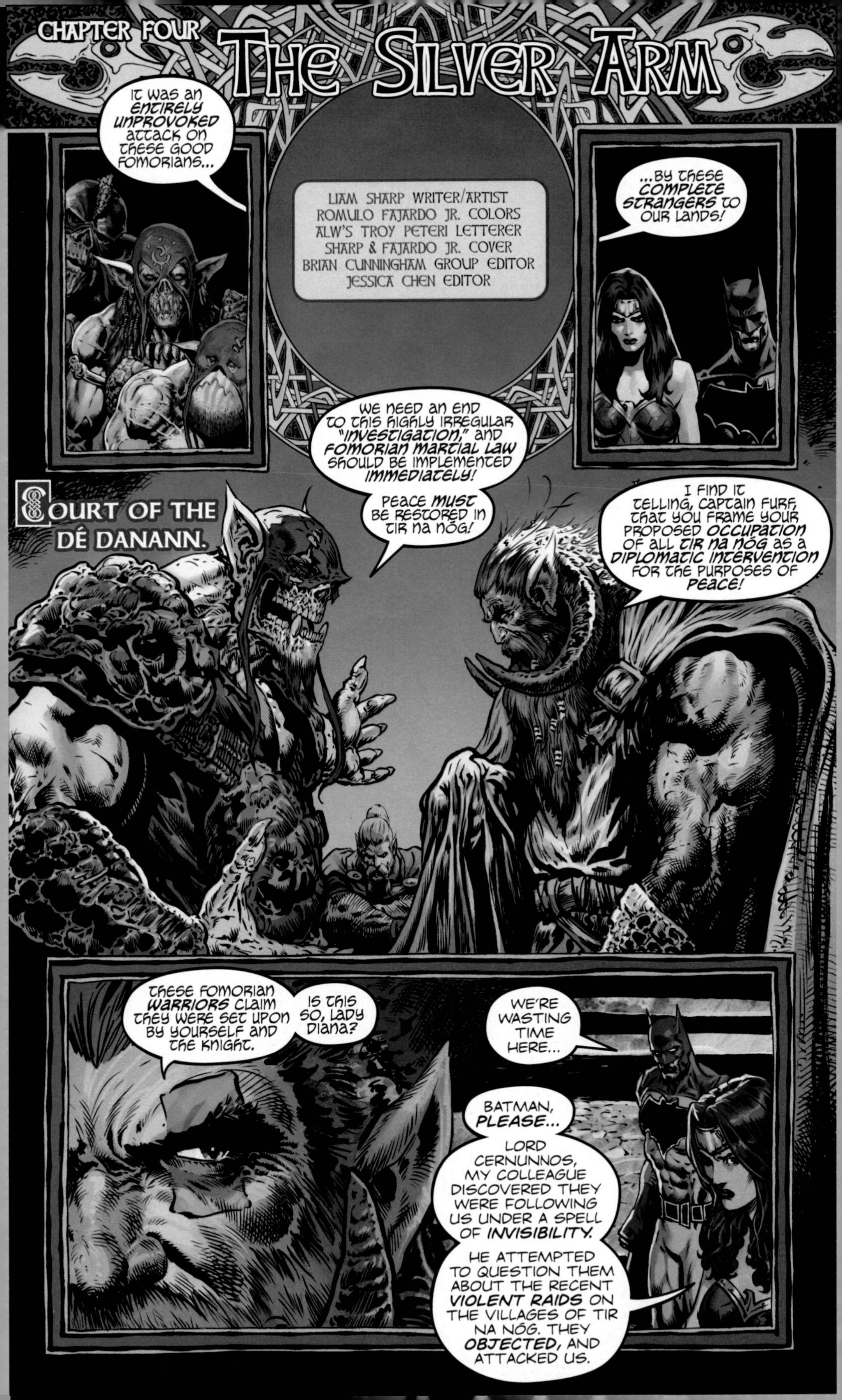
CHAPTER FOUR
THE SILVER ARM
IT WAS AN ENTIRELY UNPROVOKED ATTACK ON THESE GOOD FOMORIANS...
LIAM SHARP WRITER/ARTIST
ROMULO FAJARDO JR. COLORS
ALW'S TROY PETERI LETTERER
SHARP & FAJARDO JR. COVER
BRIAN CUNNINGHAM GROUP EDITOR
JESSICA CHEN EDITOR
...BY THESE COMPLETE STRANGERS TO OUR LANDS!
COURT OF THE DÉ DANANN.
WE NEED AN END TO THIS HIGHLY IRREGULAR "INVESTIGATION," AND FOMORIAN MARTIAL LAW SHOULD BE IMPLEMENTED IMMEDIATELY!
PEACE MUST BE RESTORED IN TIR NA NÓG!
I FIND IT TELLING, CAPTAIN FURF, THAT YOU FRAME YOUR PROPOSED OCCUPATION OF ALL TIR NA NÓG AS A DIPLOMATIC INTERVENTION FOR THE PURPOSES OF PEACE!
THESE FOMORIAN WARRIORS CLAIM THEY WERE SET UPON BY YOURSELF AND THE KNIGHT.
IS THIS SO, LADY DIANA?
WE'RE WASTING TIME HERE...
BATMAN, PLEASE...
LORD CERNUNNOS, MY COLLEAGUE DISCOVERED THEY WERE FOLLOWING US UNDER A SPELL OF INVISIBILITY.
HE ATTEMPTED TO QUESTION THEM ABOUT THE RECENT VIOLENT RAIDS ON THE VILLAGES OF TIR NA NÓG. THEY OBJECTED, AND ATTACKED US.

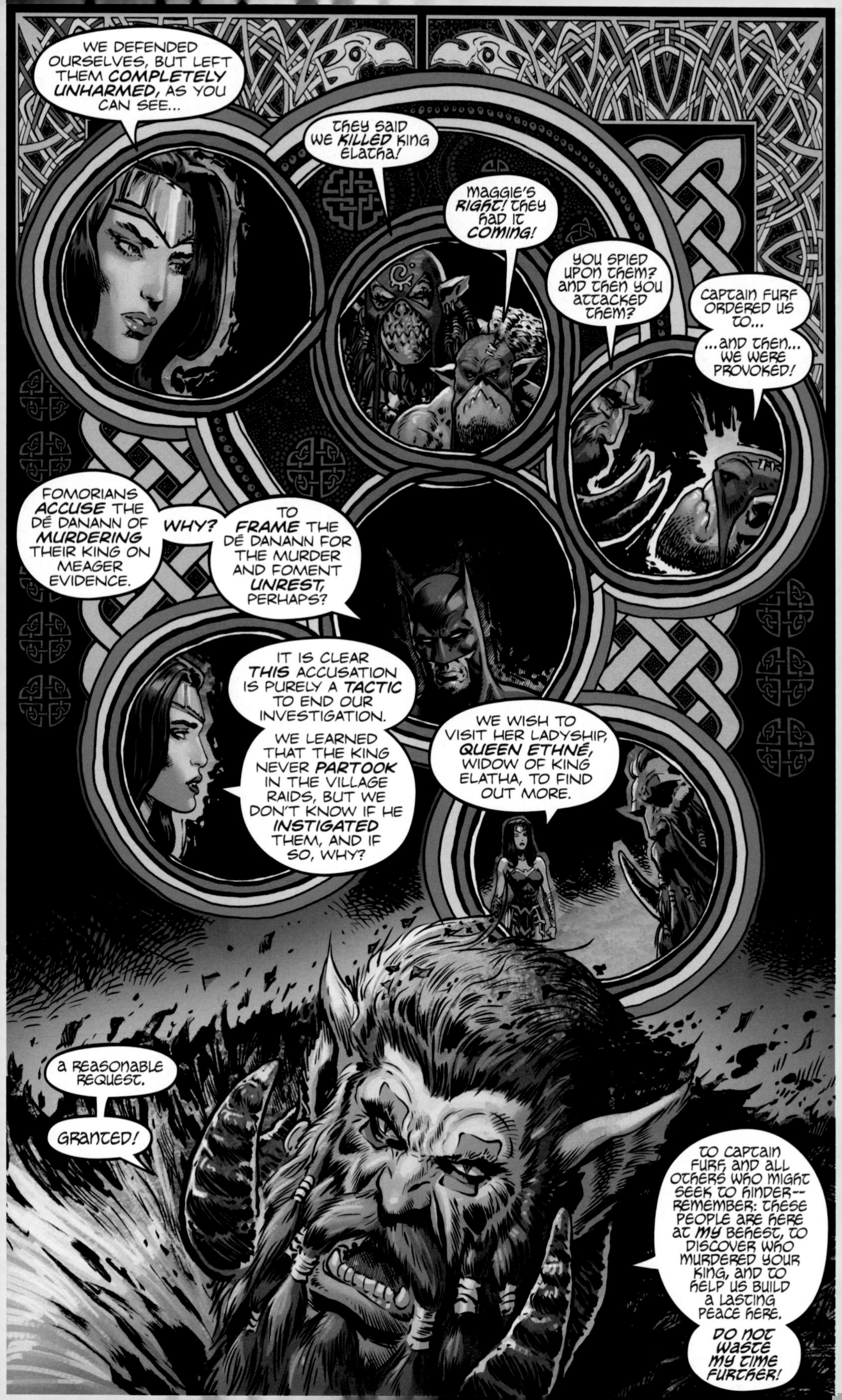
WE DEFENDED OURSELVES, BUT LEFT THEM COMPLETELY UNHARMED, AS YOU CAN SEE...
THEY SAID WE KILLED KING ELATHA!
MAGGIE'S RIGHT! THEY HAD IT COMING!
YOU SPIED UPON THEM? AND THEN YOU ATTACKED THEM?
CAPTAIN FURF ORDERED US TO...
...AND THEN... WE WERE PROVOKED!
FOMORIANS ACCUSE THE DÉ DANANN OF MURDERING THEIR KING ON MEAGER EVIDENCE.
WHY?
TO FRAME THE DÉ DANANN FOR THE MURDER AND FOMENT UNREST, PERHAPS?
IT IS CLEAR THIS ACCUSATION IS PURELY A TACTIC TO END OUR INVESTIGATION.
WE LEARNED THAT THE KING NEVER PARTOOK IN THE VILLAGE RAIDS, BUT WE DON'T KNOW IF HE INSTIGATED THEM, AND IF SO, WHY?
WE WISH TO VISIT HER LADYSHIP, QUEEN ETHNÉ, WIDOW OF KING ELATHA, TO FIND OUT MORE.
A REASONABLE REQUEST.
GRANTED!
TO CAPTAIN FURF, AND ALL OTHERS WHO MIGHT SEEK TO HINDER-- REMEMBER: THESE PEOPLE ARE HERE AT MY BEHEST, TO DISCOVER WHO MURDERED YOUR KING, AND TO HELP US BUILD A LASTING PEACE HERE.
DO NOT WASTE MY TIME FURTHER!

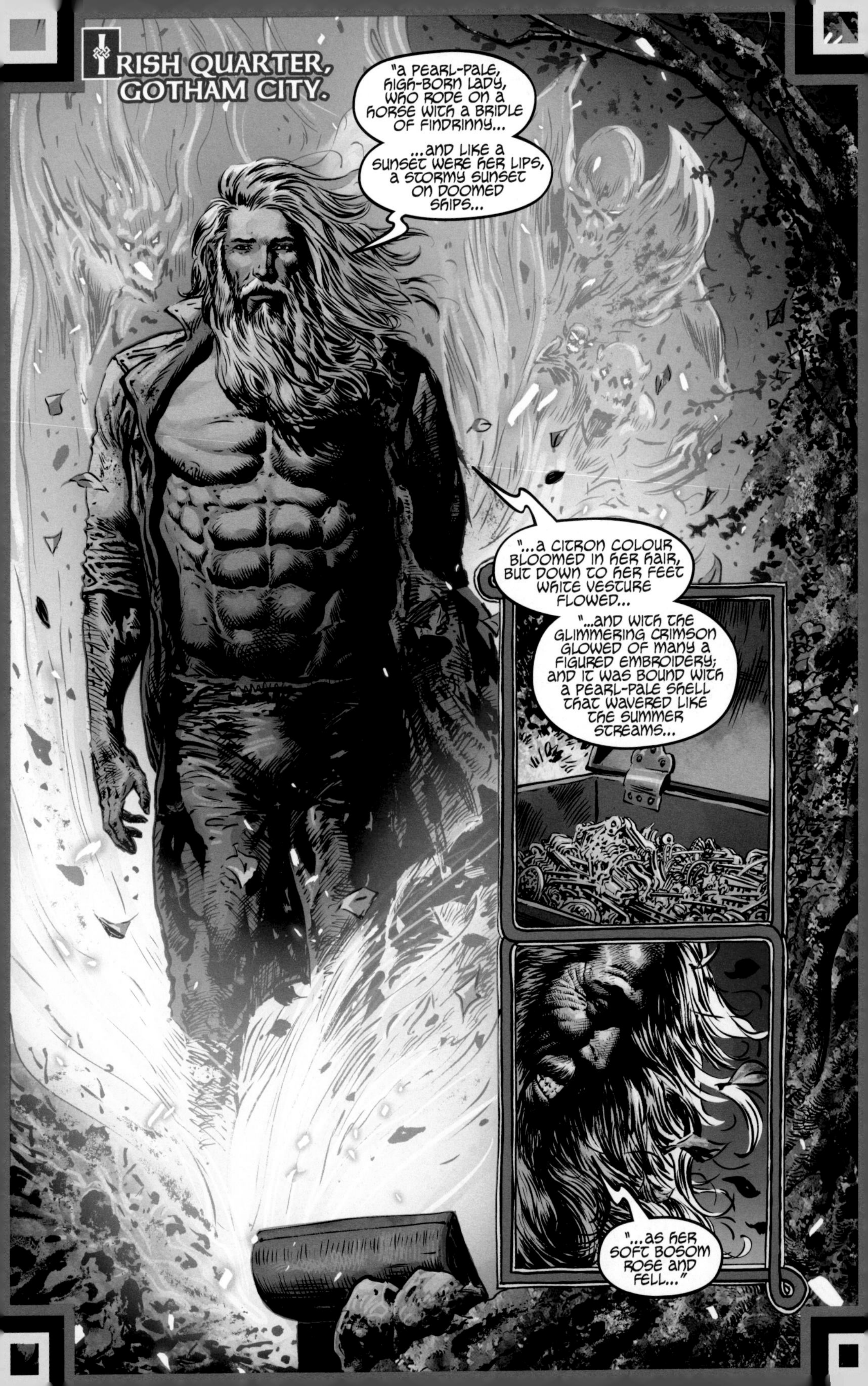
IRISH QUARTER, GOTHAM CITY.
"a PEARL-PALE, HIGH-BORN LADY, WHO RODE ON A HORSE WITH A BRIDLE OF FINDRINNY...
...AND LIKE A SUNSET WERE HER LIPS, A STORMY SUNSET ON DOOMED SHIPS...
"...A CITRON COLOUR BLOOMED IN HER HAIR, BUT DOWN TO HER FEET WHITE VESTURE FLOWED...
"...AND WITH THE GLIMMERING CRIMSON GLOWED OF MANY A FIGURED EMBROIDERY; AND IT WAS BOUND WITH A PEARL-PALE SHELL THAT WAVERED LIKE THE SUMMER STREAMS...
"...AS HER SOFT BOSOM ROSE AND FELL..."

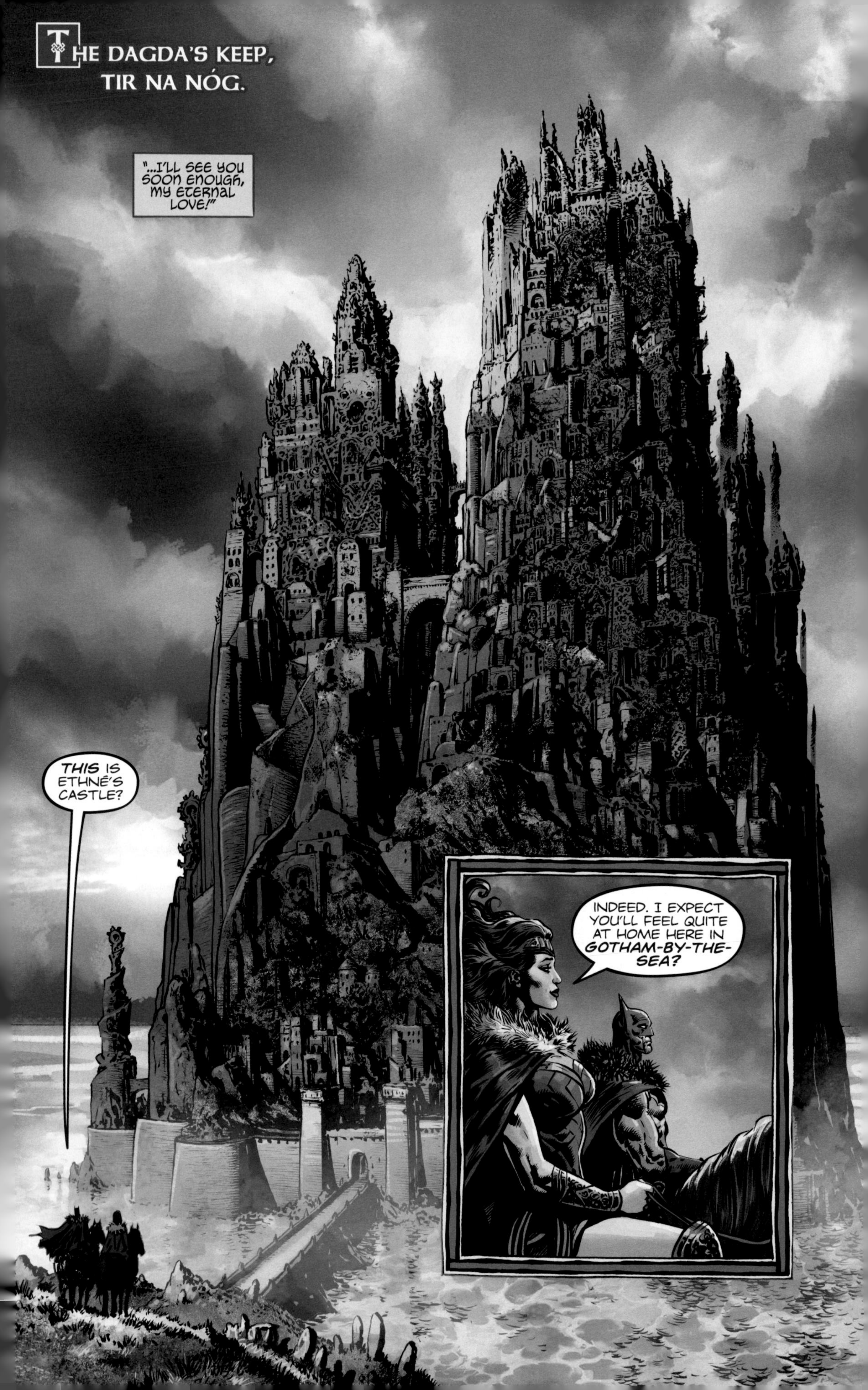
THE DAGDA'S KEEP, TIR NA NÓG.
"...I'LL SEE YOU SOON ENOUGH, MY ETERNAL LOVE!"
THIS IS ETHNÉ'S CASTLE?
INDEED. I EXPECT YOU'LL FEEL QUITE AT HOME HERE IN GOTHAM-BY-THE-SEA?

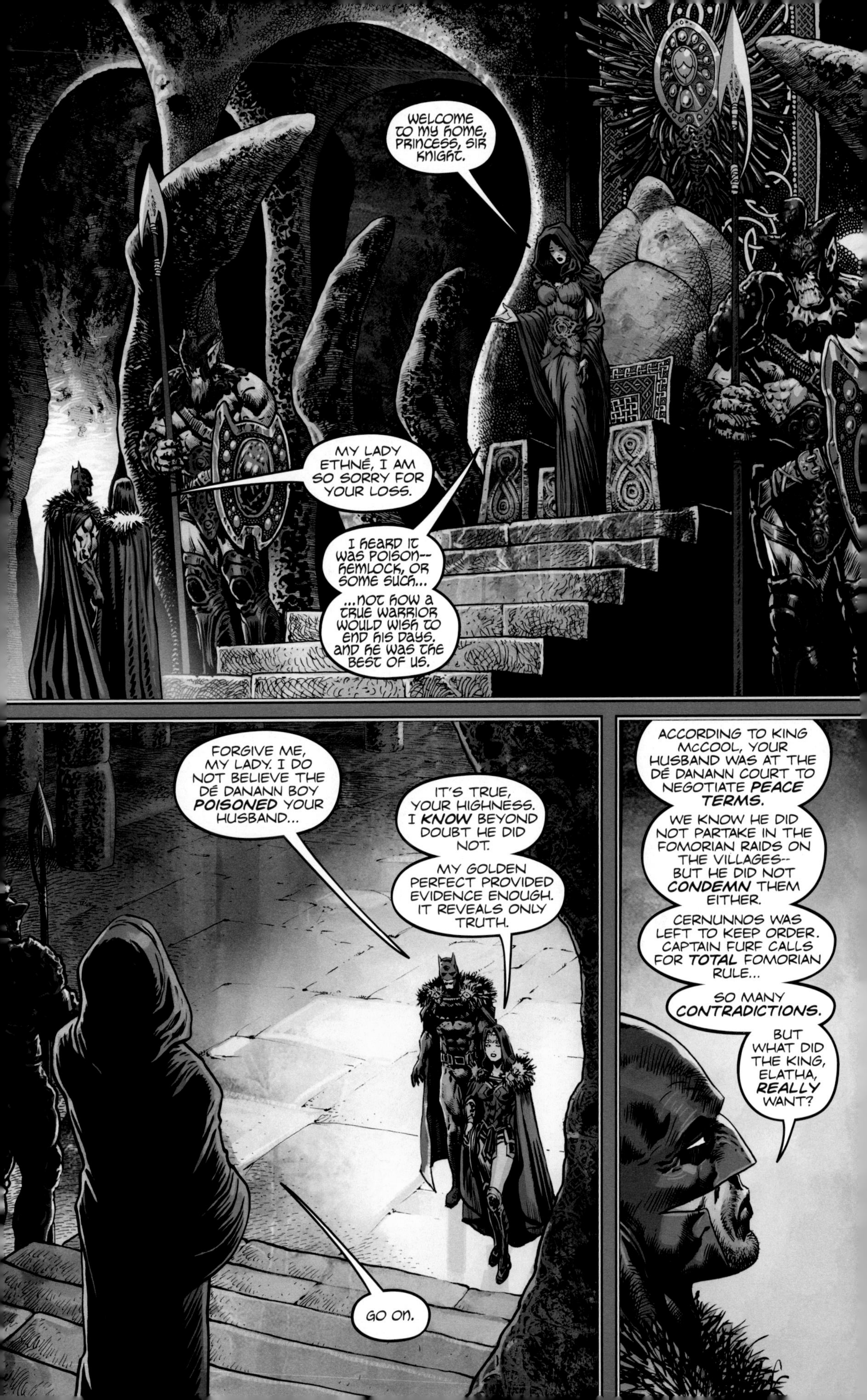

WELCOME TO MY HOME, PRINCESS, SIR KNIGHT.
MY LADY ETHNÉ, I AM SO SORRY FOR YOUR LOSS.
I HEARD IT WAS POISON-- HEMLOCK, OR SOME SUCH...
...NOT HOW A TRUE WARRIOR WOULD WISH TO END HIS DAYS, AND HE WAS THE BEST OF US.
FORGIVE ME, MY LADY. I DO NOT BELIEVE THE DÉ DANANN BOY **POISONED** YOUR HUSBAND...
IT'S TRUE, YOUR HIGHNESS. I **KNOW** BEYOND DOUBT HE DID NOT.
MY GOLDEN PERFECT PROVIDED EVIDENCE ENOUGH. IT REVEALS ONLY TRUTH.
GO ON.
ACCORDING TO KING McCOOL, YOUR HUSBAND WAS AT THE DÉ DANANN COURT TO NEGOTIATE **PEACE TERMS.**
WE KNOW HE DID NOT PARTAKE IN THE FOMORIAN RAIDS ON THE VILLAGES-- BUT HE DID NOT **CONDEMN** THEM EITHER.
CERNUNNOS WAS LEFT TO KEEP ORDER. CAPTAIN FURF CALLS FOR **TOTAL** FOMORIAN RULE...
SO MANY **CONTRADICTIONS.**
BUT WHAT DID THE KING, ELATHA, **REALLY** WANT?

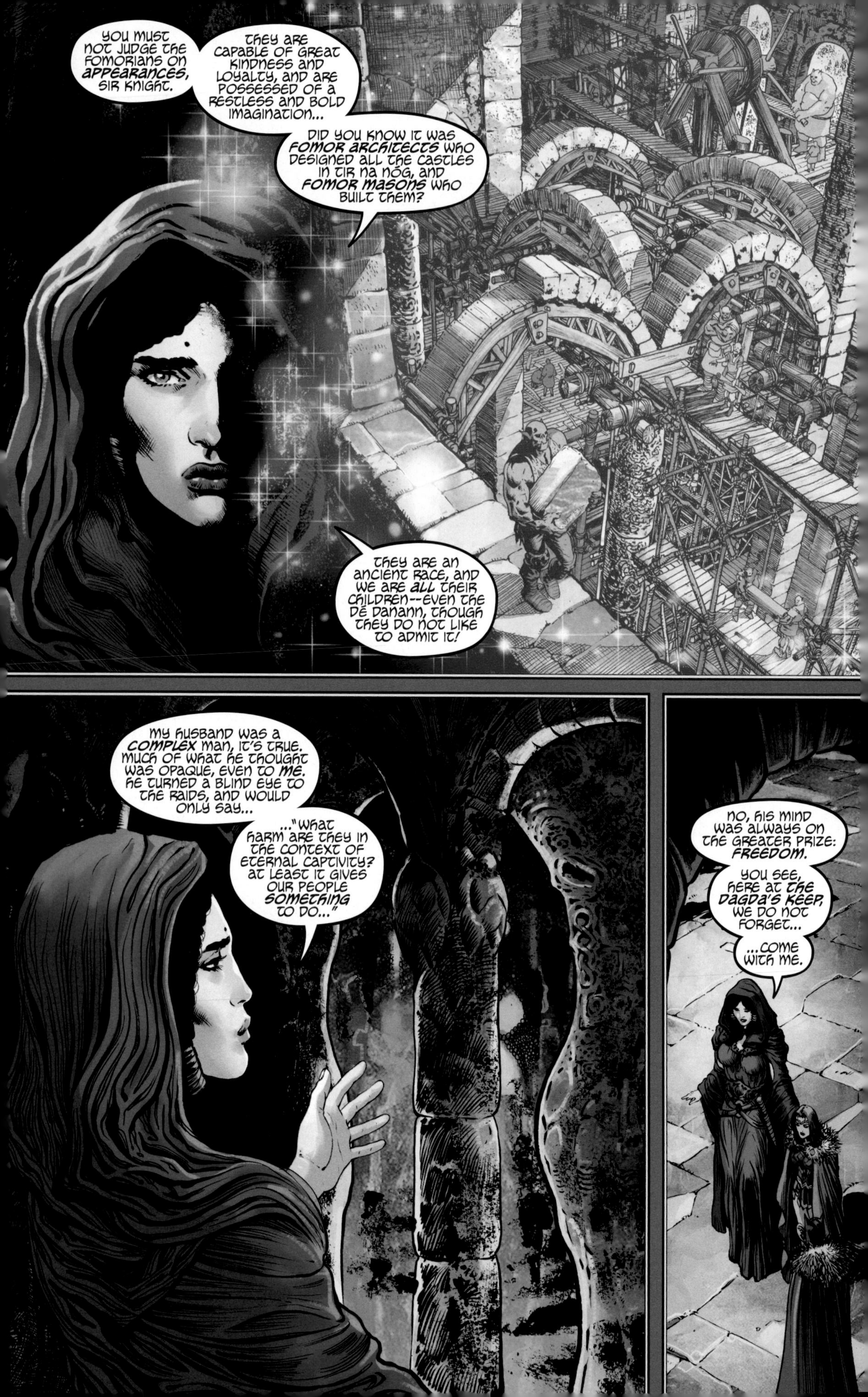

YOU MUST NOT JUDGE THE FOMORIANS ON APPEARANCES, SIR KNIGHT.
THEY ARE CAPABLE OF GREAT KINDNESS AND LOYALTY, AND ARE POSSESSED OF A RESTLESS AND BOLD IMAGINATION...
DID YOU KNOW IT WAS FOMOR ARCHITECTS WHO DESIGNED ALL THE CASTLES IN TIR NA NÓG, AND FOMOR MASONS WHO BUILT THEM?
THEY ARE AN ANCIENT RACE, AND WE ARE ALL THEIR CHILDREN--EVEN THE DÉ DANANN, THOUGH THEY DO NOT LIKE TO ADMIT IT!
MY HUSBAND WAS A COMPLEX MAN, IT'S TRUE. MUCH OF WHAT HE THOUGHT WAS OPAQUE, EVEN TO ME. HE TURNED A BLIND EYE TO THE RAIDS, AND WOULD ONLY SAY...
..."WHAT HARM ARE THEY IN THE CONTEXT OF ETERNAL CAPTIVITY? AT LEAST IT GIVES OUR PEOPLE SOMETHING TO DO..."
NO, HIS MIND WAS ALWAYS ON THE GREATER PRIZE: FREEDOM.
YOU SEE, HERE AT THE DAGDA'S KEEP, WE DO NOT FORGET...
...COME WITH ME.

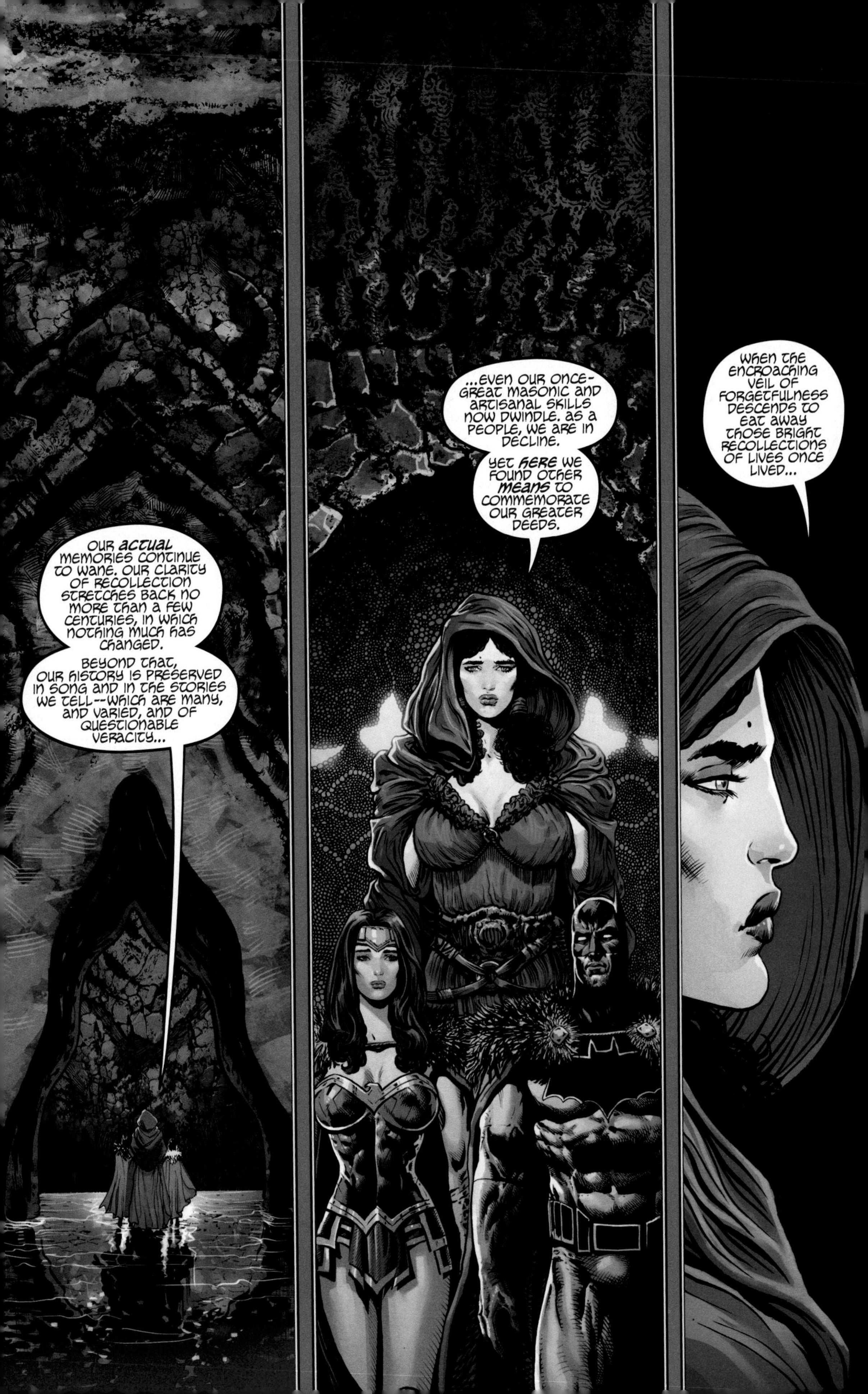
OUR ACTUAL MEMORIES CONTINUE TO WANE. OUR CLARITY OF RECOLLECTION STRETCHES BACK NO MORE THAN A FEW CENTURIES, IN WHICH NOTHING MUCH HAS CHANGED.
BEYOND THAT, OUR HISTORY IS PRESERVED IN SONG AND IN THE STORIES WE TELL--WHICH ARE MANY, AND VARIED, AND OF QUESTIONABLE VERACITY...
...EVEN OUR ONCE-GREAT MASONIC AND ARTISANAL SKILLS NOW DWINDLE. AS A PEOPLE, WE ARE IN DECLINE.
YET HERE WE FOUND OTHER MEANS TO COMMEMORATE OUR GREATER DEEDS.
WHEN THE ENCROACHING VEIL OF FORGETFULNESS DESCENDS TO EAT AWAY THOSE BRIGHT RECOLLECTIONS OF LIVES ONCE LIVED...

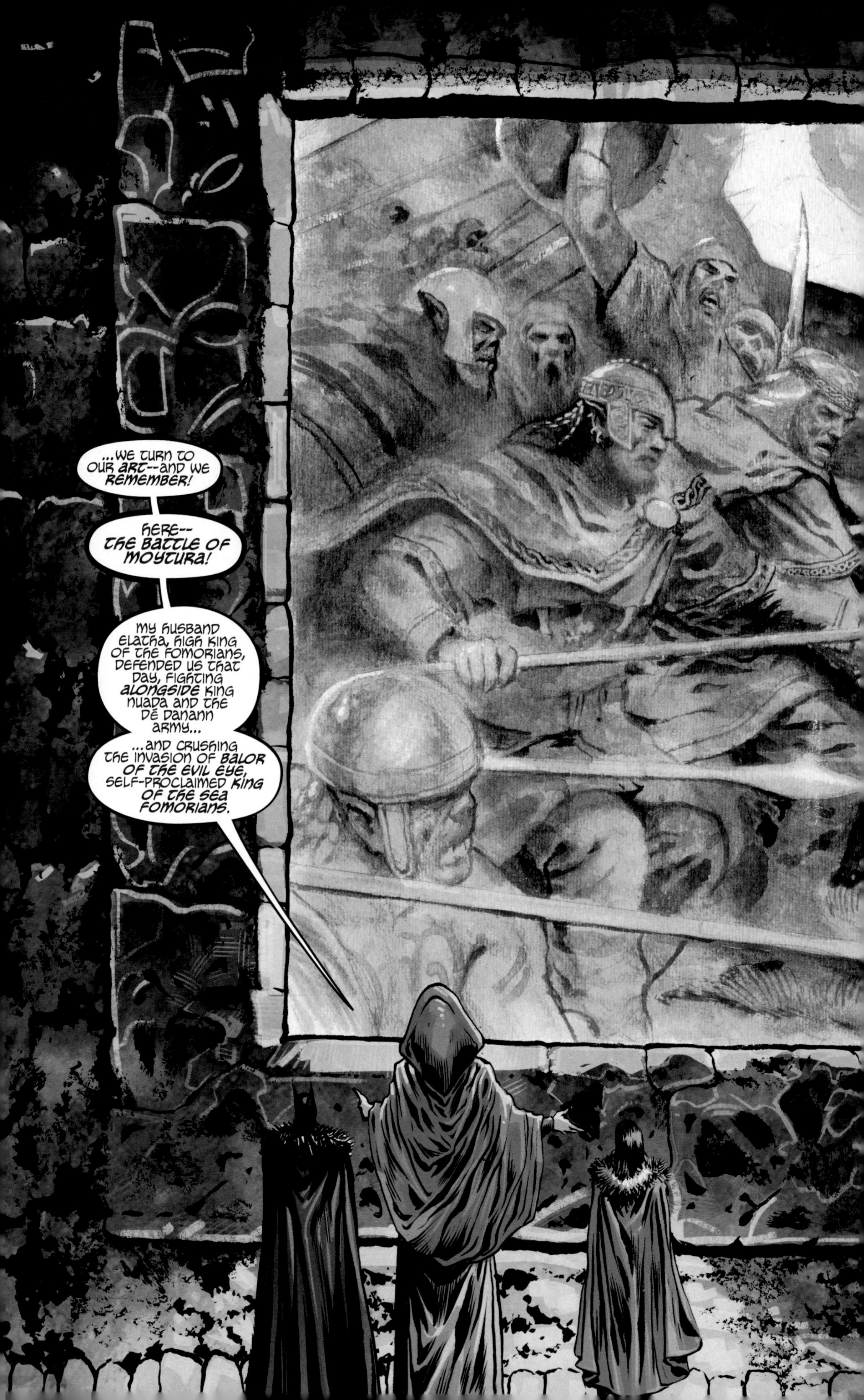
...WE TURN TO OUR ART--AND WE REMEMBER!
HERE-- THE BATTLE OF MOYTURA!
MY HUSBAND ELATHA, HIGH KING OF THE FOMORIANS, DEFENDED US THAT DAY, FIGHTING ALONGSIDE KING NUADA AND THE DÉ DANANN ARMY...
...AND CRUSHING THE INVASION OF BALOR OF THE EVIL EYE, SELF-PROCLAIMED KING OF THE SEA FOMORIANS.

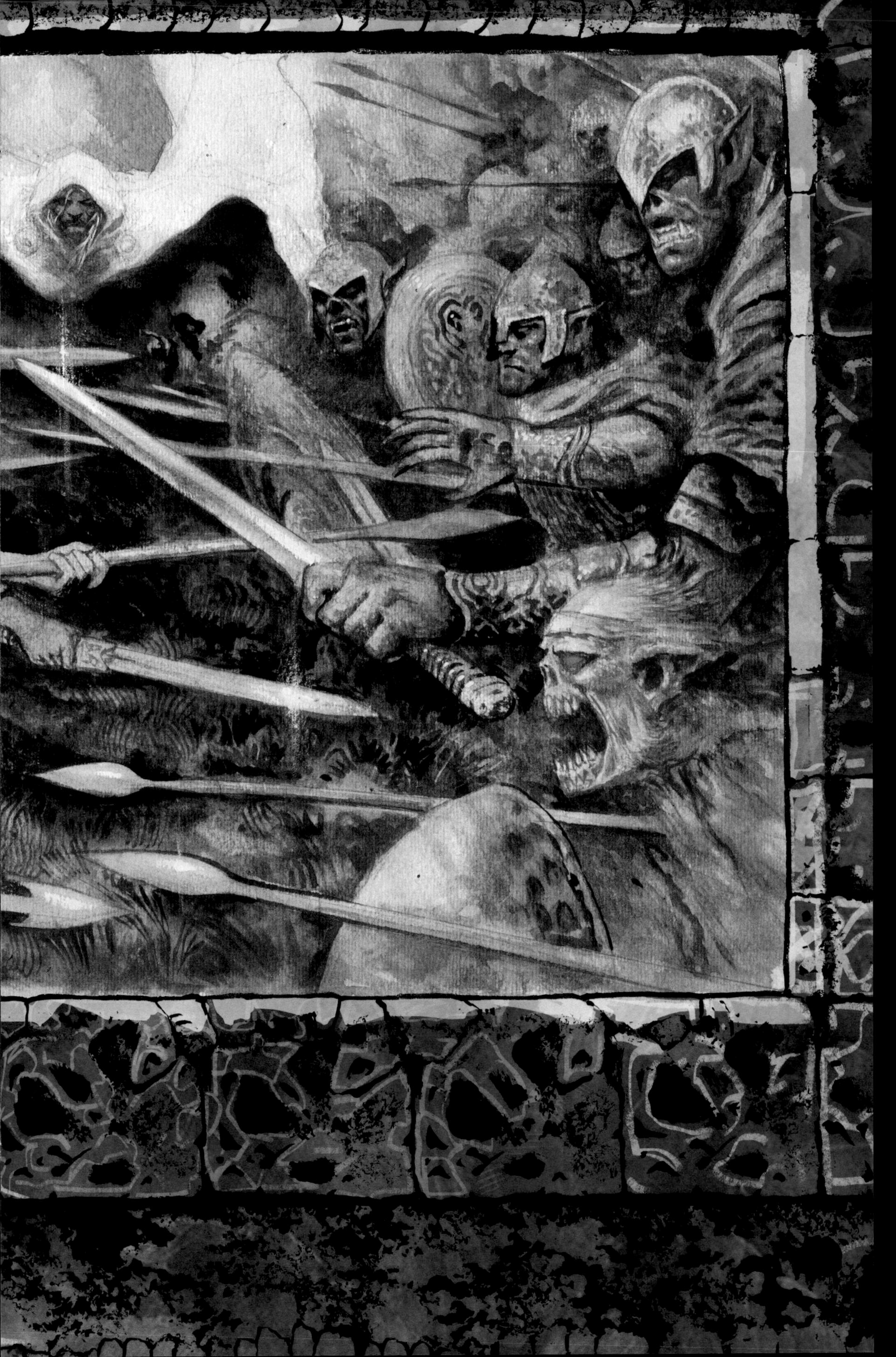

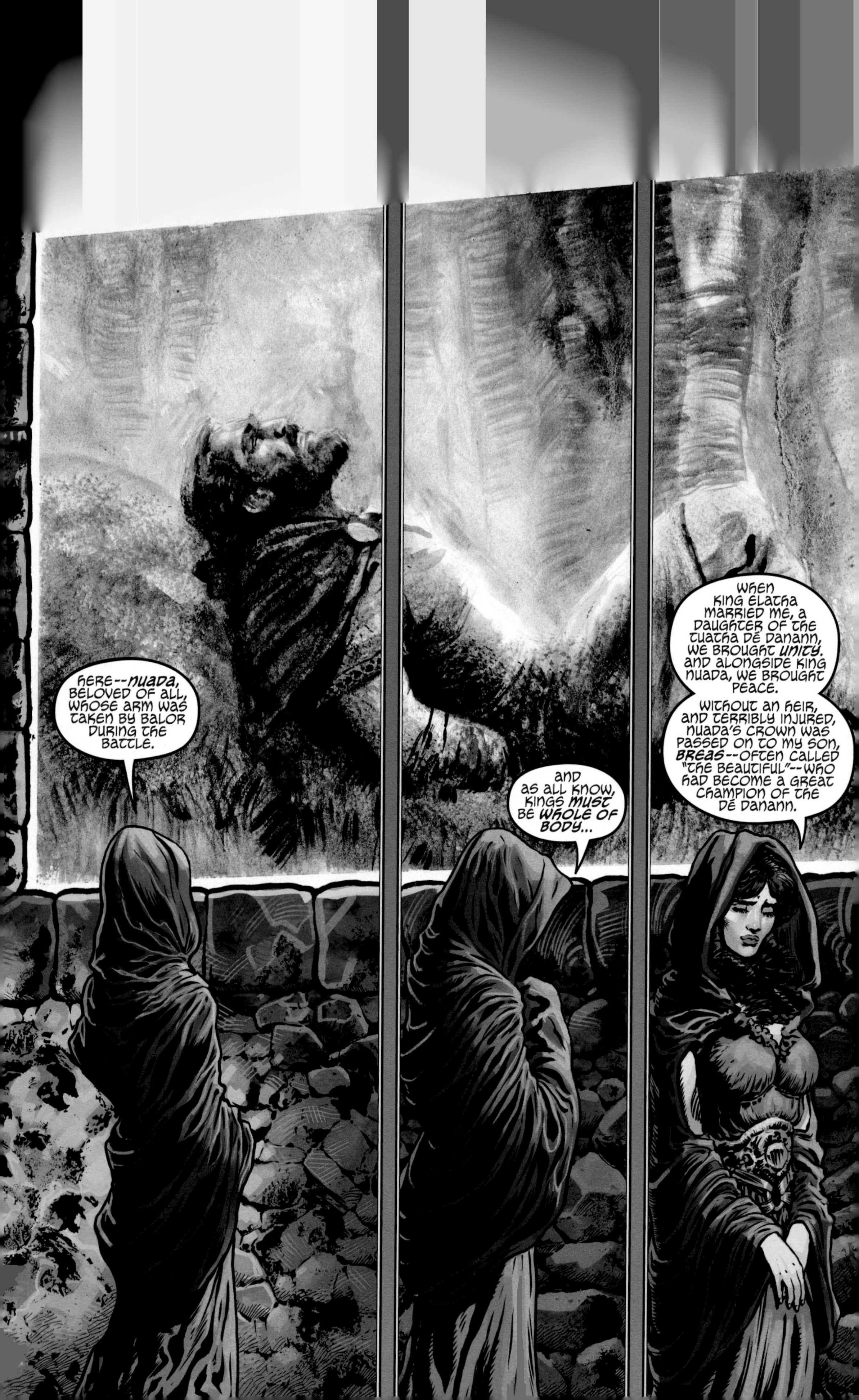
HERE--NUADA, BELOVED OF ALL, WHOSE ARM WAS TAKEN BY BALOR DURING THE BATTLE.
AND AS ALL KNOW, KINGS MUST BE WHOLE OF BODY...
WHEN KING ELATHA MARRIED ME, A DAUGHTER OF THE TUATHA DÉ DANANN, WE BROUGHT UNITY. AND ALONGSIDE KING NUADA, WE BROUGHT PEACE.
WITHOUT AN HEIR, AND TERRIBLY INJURED, NUADA'S CROWN WAS PASSED ON TO MY SON, BREAS--OFTEN CALLED "THE BEAUTIFUL"--WHO HAD BECOME A GREAT CHAMPION OF THE DÉ DANANN.

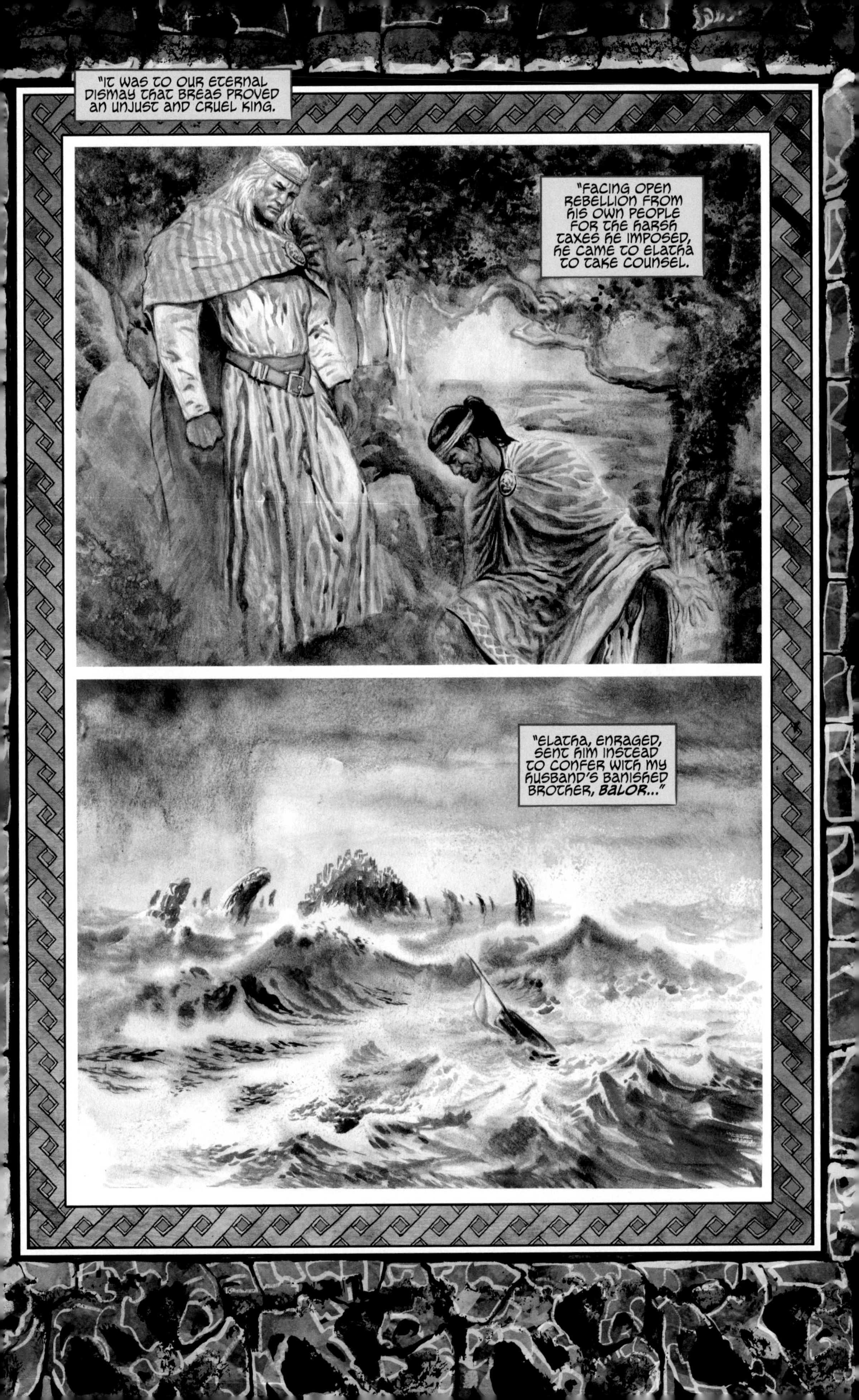
"IT WAS TO OUR ETERNAL DISMAY THAT BREAS PROVED AN UNJUST AND CRUEL KING.
"FACING OPEN REBELLION FROM HIS OWN PEOPLE FOR THE HARSH TAXES HE IMPOSED, HE CAME TO ELATHA TO TAKE COUNSEL.
"ELATHA, ENRAGED, SENT HIM INSTEAD TO CONFER WITH MY HUSBAND'S BANISHED BROTHER, *BALOR*..."

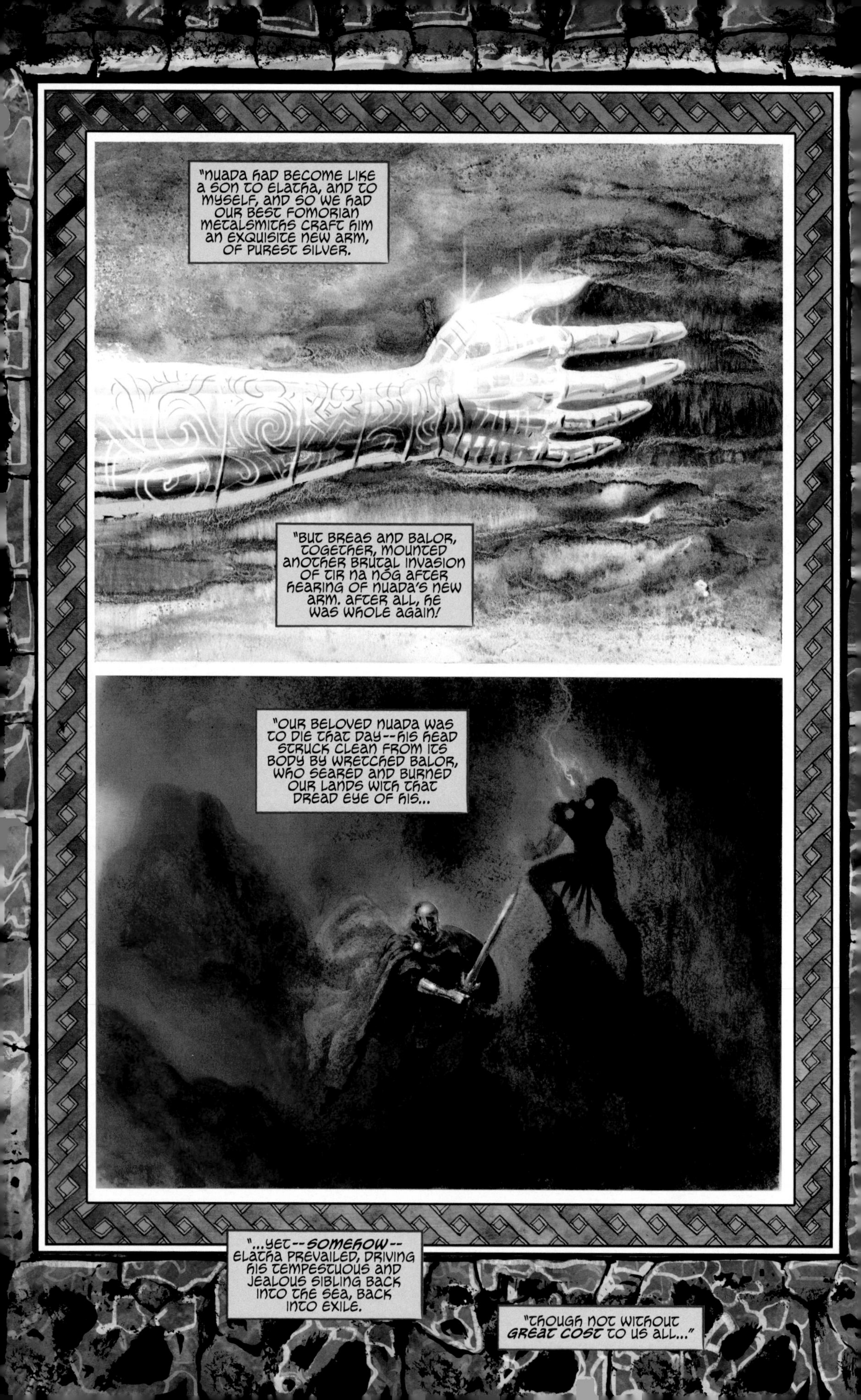
"NUADA HAD BECOME LIKE A SON TO ELATHA, AND TO MYSELF, AND SO WE HAD OUR BEST FOMORIAN METALSMITHS CRAFT HIM AN EXQUISITE NEW ARM, OF PUREST SILVER.
"BUT BREAS AND BALOR, TOGETHER, MOUNTED ANOTHER BRUTAL INVASION OF TIR NA NÓG AFTER HEARING OF NUADA'S NEW ARM. AFTER ALL, HE WAS WHOLE AGAIN!
"OUR BELOVED NUADA WAS TO DIE THAT DAY--HIS HEAD STRUCK CLEAN FROM ITS BODY BY WRETCHED BALOR, WHO SEARED AND BURNED OUR LANDS WITH THAT DREAD EYE OF HIS...
"...YET--SOMEHOW--ELATHA PREVAILED, DRIVING HIS TEMPESTUOUS AND JEALOUS SIBLING BACK INTO THE SEA, BACK INTO EXILE.
"THOUGH NOT WITHOUT GREAT COST TO US ALL..."

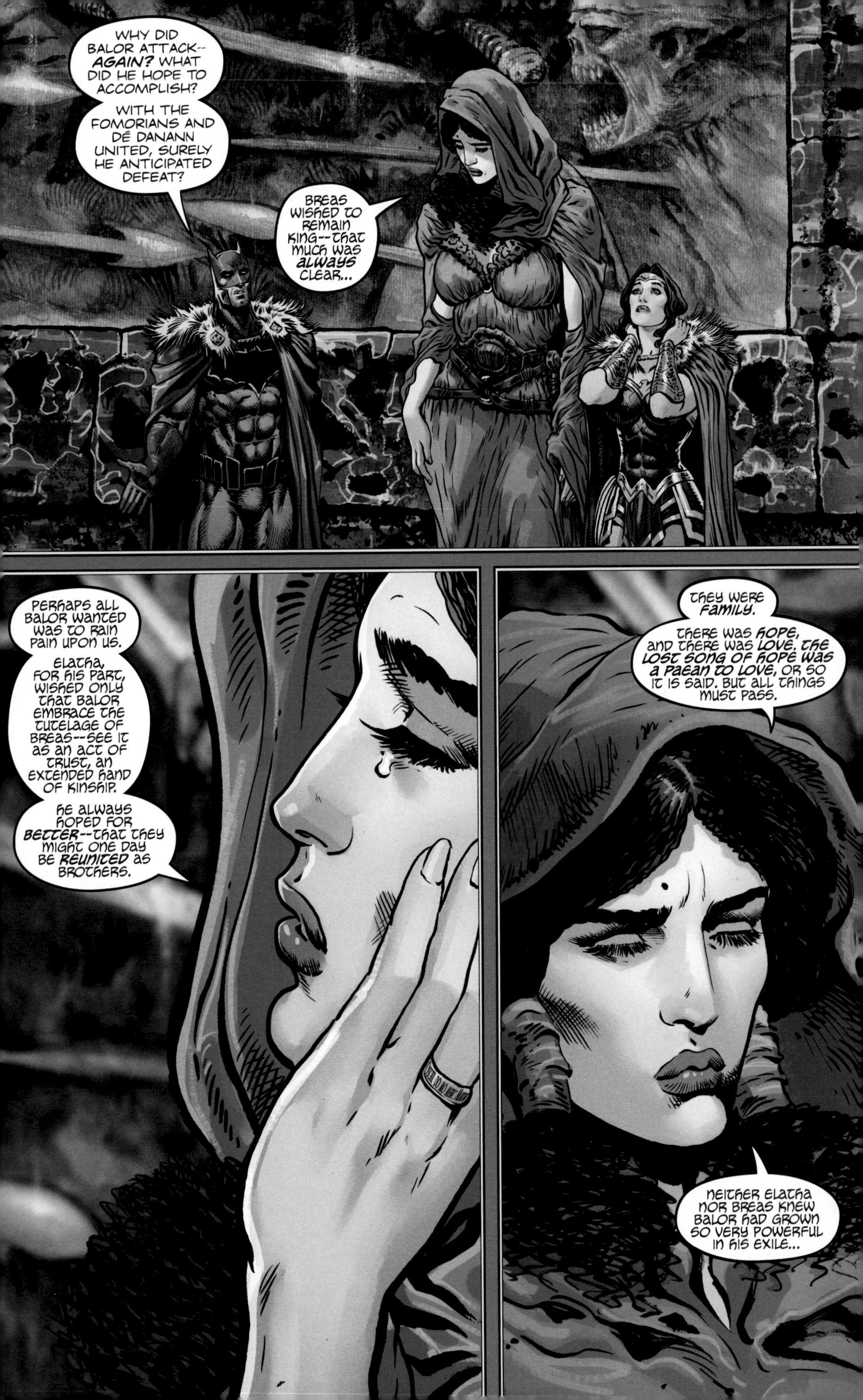
WHY DID BALOR ATTACK-- AGAIN? WHAT DID HE HOPE TO ACCOMPLISH?
WITH THE FOMORIANS AND DÉ DANANN UNITED, SURELY HE ANTICIPATED DEFEAT?
BREAS WISHED TO REMAIN KING--THAT MUCH WAS ALWAYS CLEAR...
PERHAPS ALL BALOR WANTED WAS TO RAIN PAIN UPON US.
ELATHA, FOR HIS PART, WISHED ONLY THAT BALOR EMBRACE THE TUTELAGE OF BREAS--SEE IT AS AN ACT OF TRUST, AN EXTENDED HAND OF KINSHIP.
HE ALWAYS HOPED FOR BETTER--THAT THEY MIGHT ONE DAY BE REUNITED AS BROTHERS.
THEY WERE FAMILY.
THERE WAS HOPE, AND THERE WAS LOVE. THE LOST SONG OF HOPE WAS A PAEAN TO LOVE, OR SO IT IS SAID. BUT ALL THINGS MUST PASS.
NEITHER ELATHA NOR BREAS KNEW BALOR HAD GROWN SO VERY POWERFUL IN HIS EXILE...

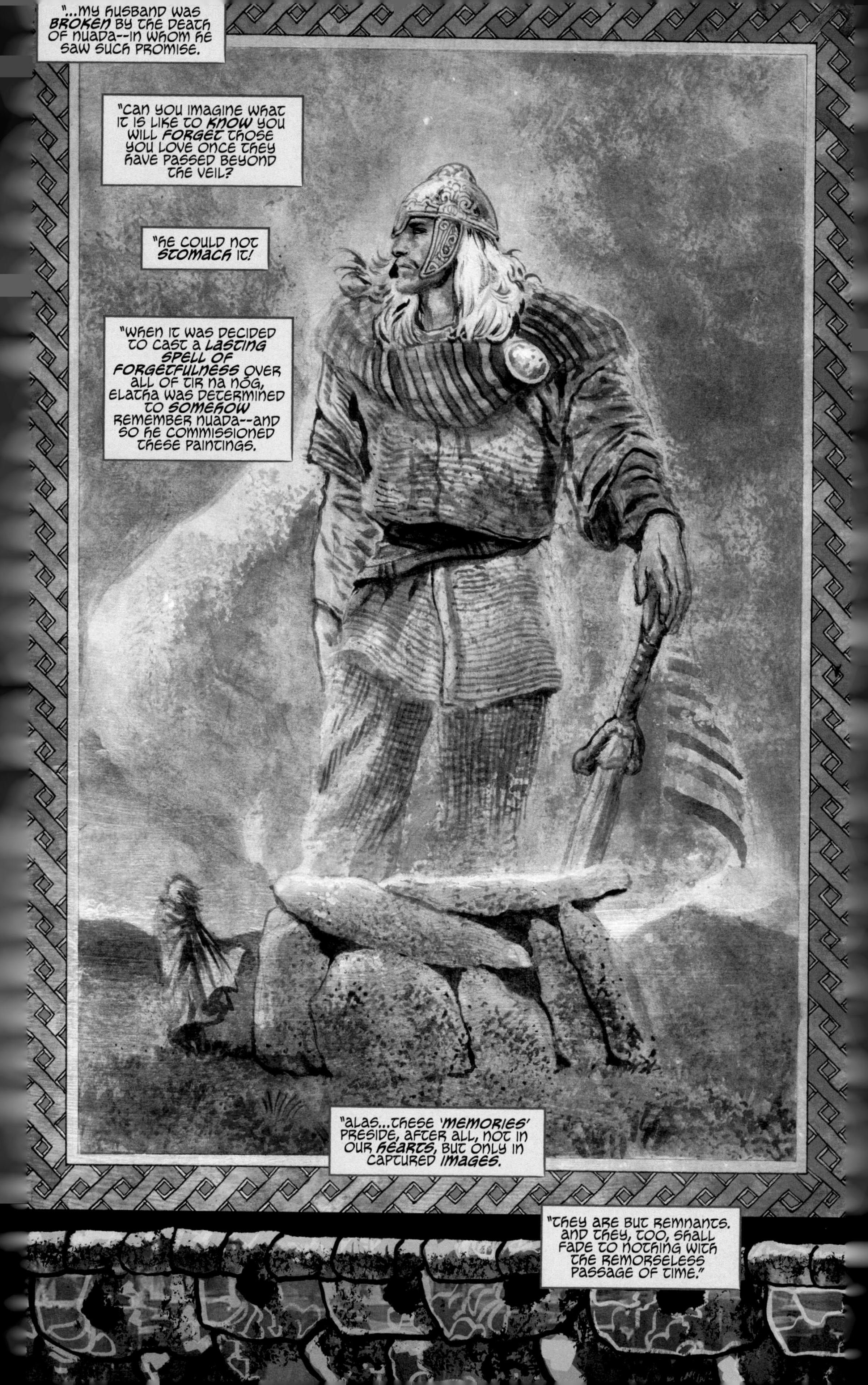
"...MY HUSBAND WAS BROKEN BY THE DEATH OF NUADA--IN WHOM HE SAW SUCH PROMISE.
"CAN YOU IMAGINE WHAT IT IS LIKE TO KNOW YOU WILL FORGET THOSE YOU LOVE ONCE THEY HAVE PASSED BEYOND THE VEIL?
"HE COULD NOT STOMACH IT!
"WHEN IT WAS DECIDED TO CAST A LASTING SPELL OF FORGETFULNESS OVER ALL OF TIR NA NOG, ELATHA WAS DETERMINED TO SOMEHOW REMEMBER NUADA--AND SO HE COMMISSIONED THESE PAINTINGS.
"ALAS...THESE 'MEMORIES' PRESIDE, AFTER ALL, NOT IN OUR HEARTS, BUT ONLY IN CAPTURED IMAGES.
"THEY ARE BUT REMNANTS. AND THEY, TOO, SHALL FADE TO NOTHING WITH THE REMORSELESS PASSAGE OF TIME."

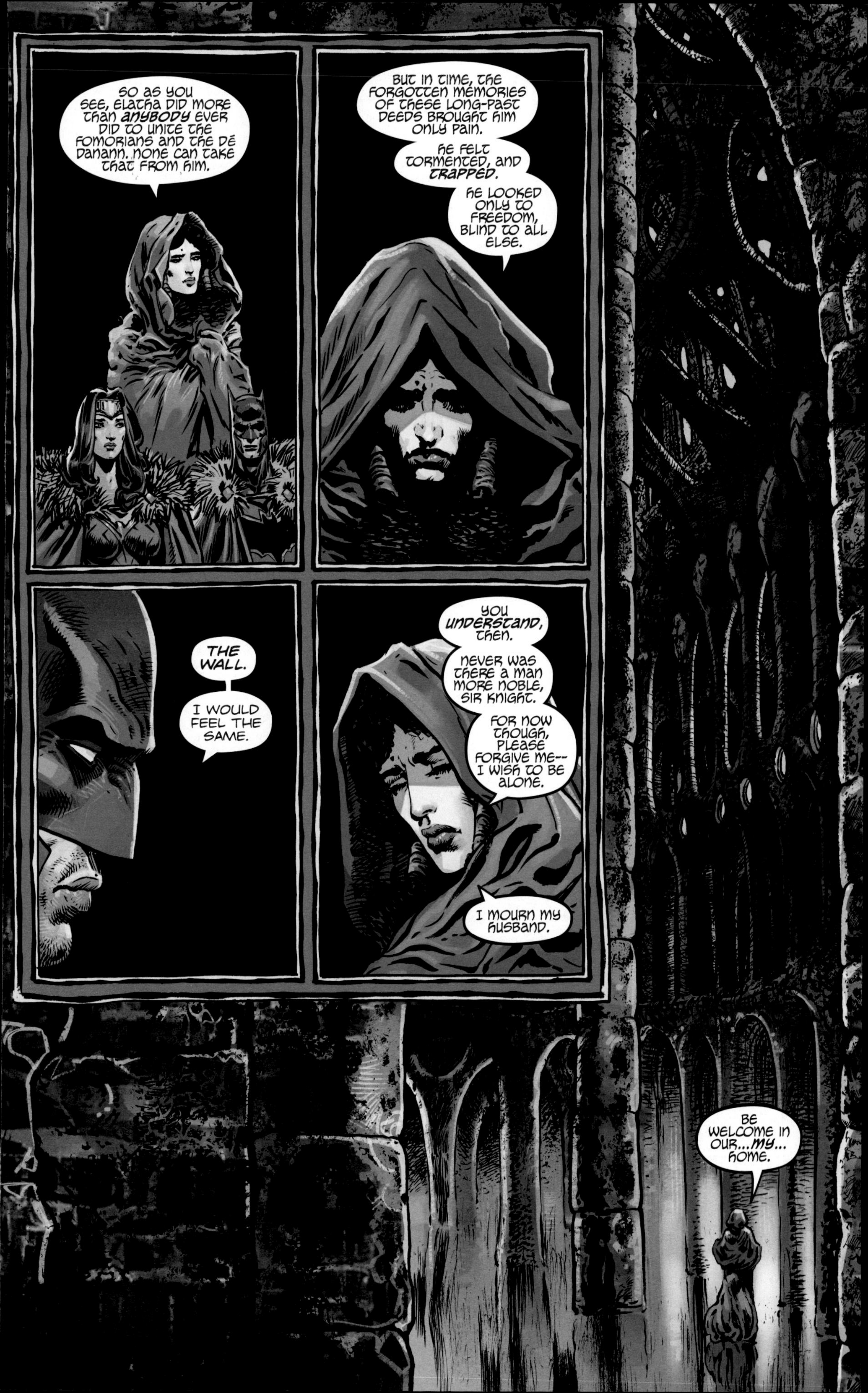

SO AS YOU SEE, ELATHA DID MORE THAN ANYBODY EVER DID TO UNITE THE FOMORIANS AND THE DÉ DANANN. NONE CAN TAKE THAT FROM HIM.
BUT IN TIME, THE FORGOTTEN MEMORIES OF THESE LONG-PAST DEEDS BROUGHT HIM ONLY PAIN.
HE FELT TORMENTED, AND TRAPPED.
HE LOOKED ONLY TO FREEDOM, BLIND TO ALL ELSE.
THE WALL.
I WOULD FEEL THE SAME.
YOU UNDERSTAND, THEN.
NEVER WAS THERE A MAN MORE NOBLE, SIR KNIGHT.
FOR NOW THOUGH, PLEASE FORGIVE ME-- I WISH TO BE ALONE.
I MOURN MY HUSBAND.
BE WELCOME IN OUR...MY... HOME.

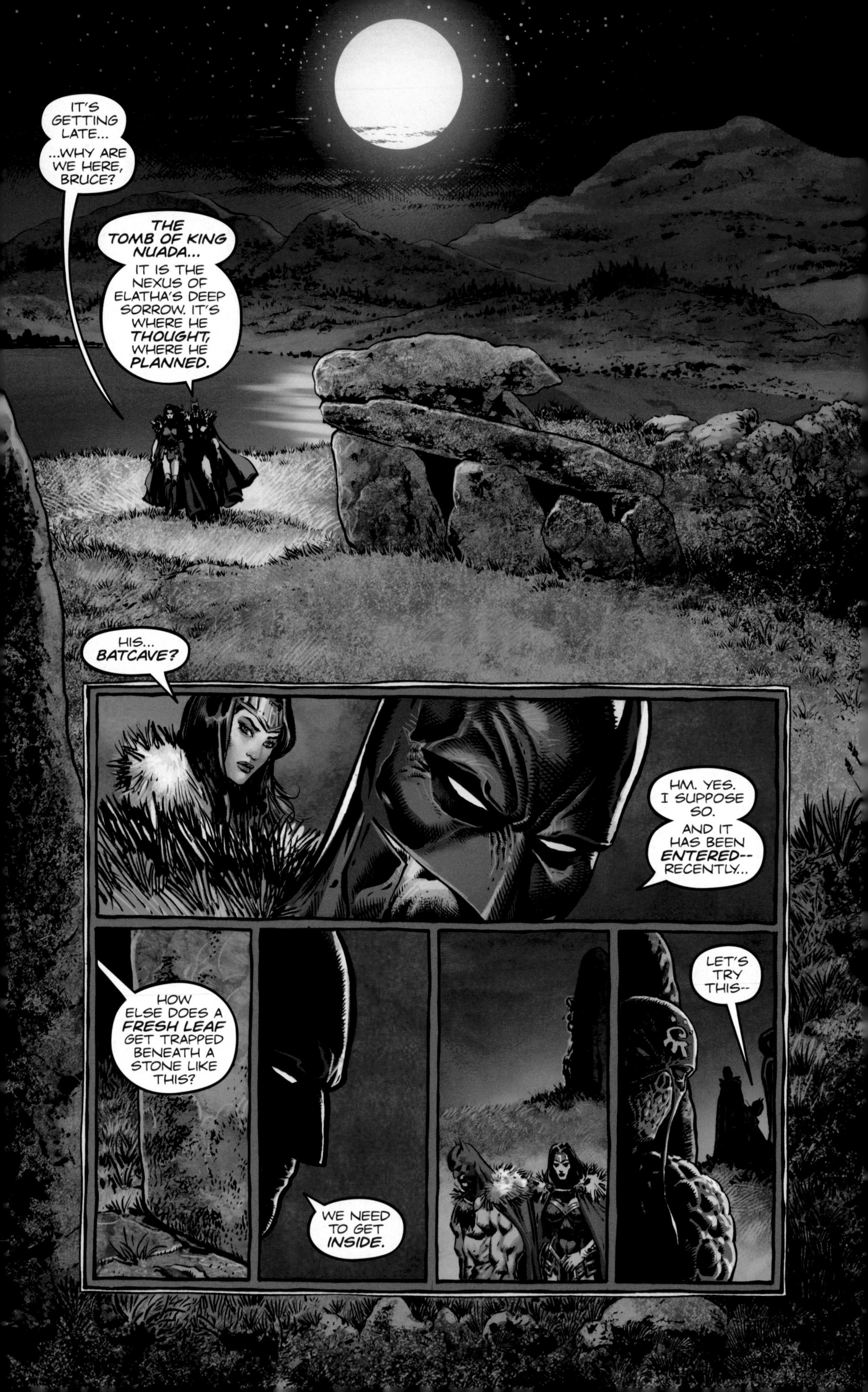

IT'S GETTING LATE...
...WHY ARE WE HERE, BRUCE?
THE TOMB OF KING NUADA...
IT IS THE NEXUS OF ELATHA'S DEEP SORROW. IT'S WHERE HE THOUGHT, WHERE HE PLANNED.
HIS... BATCAVE?
HM. YES. I SUPPOSE SO.
AND IT HAS BEEN ENTERED-- RECENTLY...
HOW ELSE DOES A FRESH LEAF GET TRAPPED BENEATH A STONE LIKE THIS?
WE NEED TO GET INSIDE.
LET'S TRY THIS--

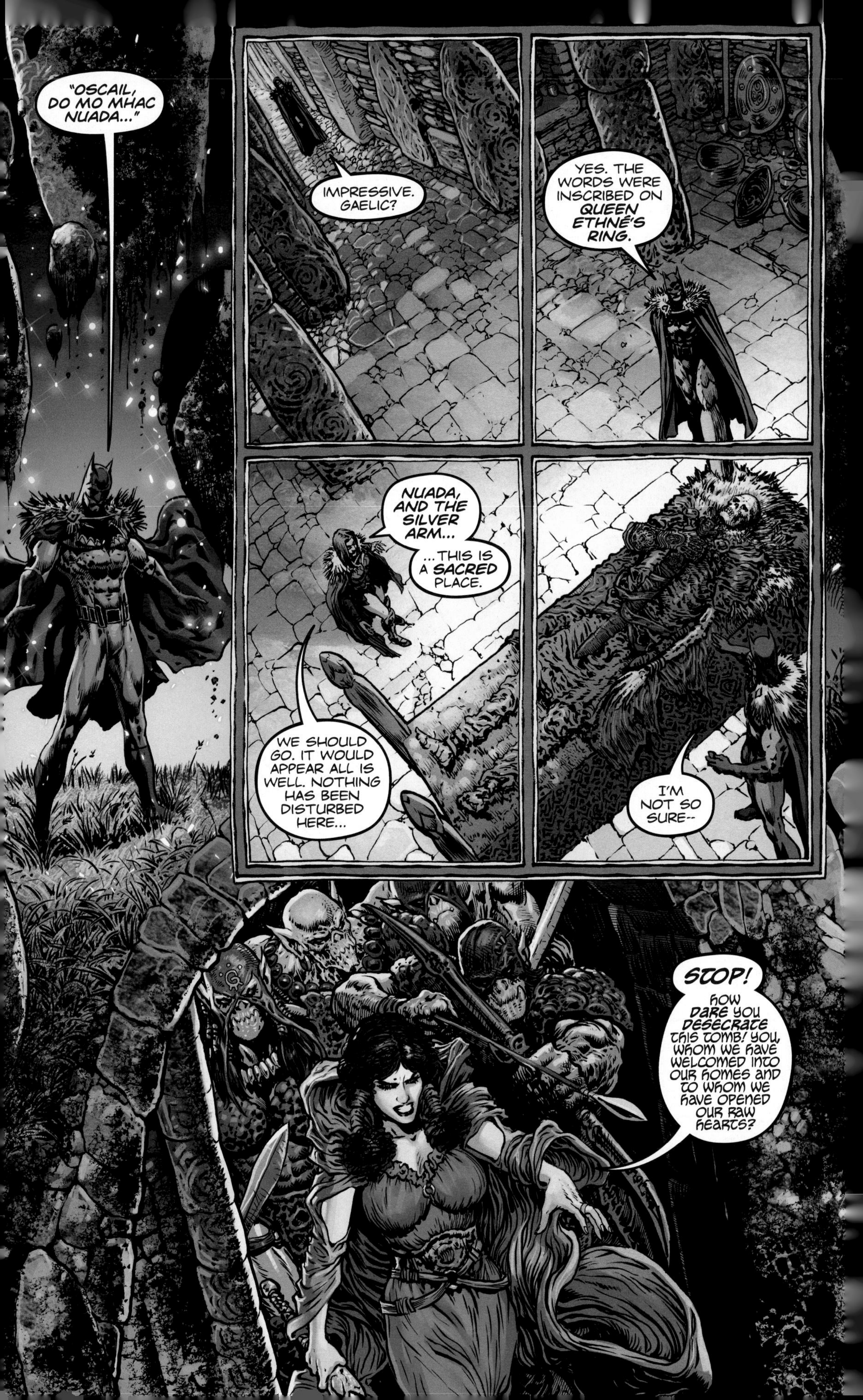
"OSCAIL, DO MO MHAC NUADA..."
IMPRESSIVE. GAELIC?
YES. THE WORDS WERE INSCRIBED ON QUEEN ETHNÉ'S RING.
NUADA, AND THE SILVER ARM...
...THIS IS A SACRED PLACE.
WE SHOULD GO. IT WOULD APPEAR ALL IS WELL. NOTHING HAS BEEN DISTURBED HERE...
I'M NOT SO SURE--
STOP!
HOW DARE YOU DESECRATE THIS TOMB! YOU, WHOM WE HAVE WELCOMED INTO OUR HOMES AND TO WHOM WE HAVE OPENED OUR RAW HEARTS?

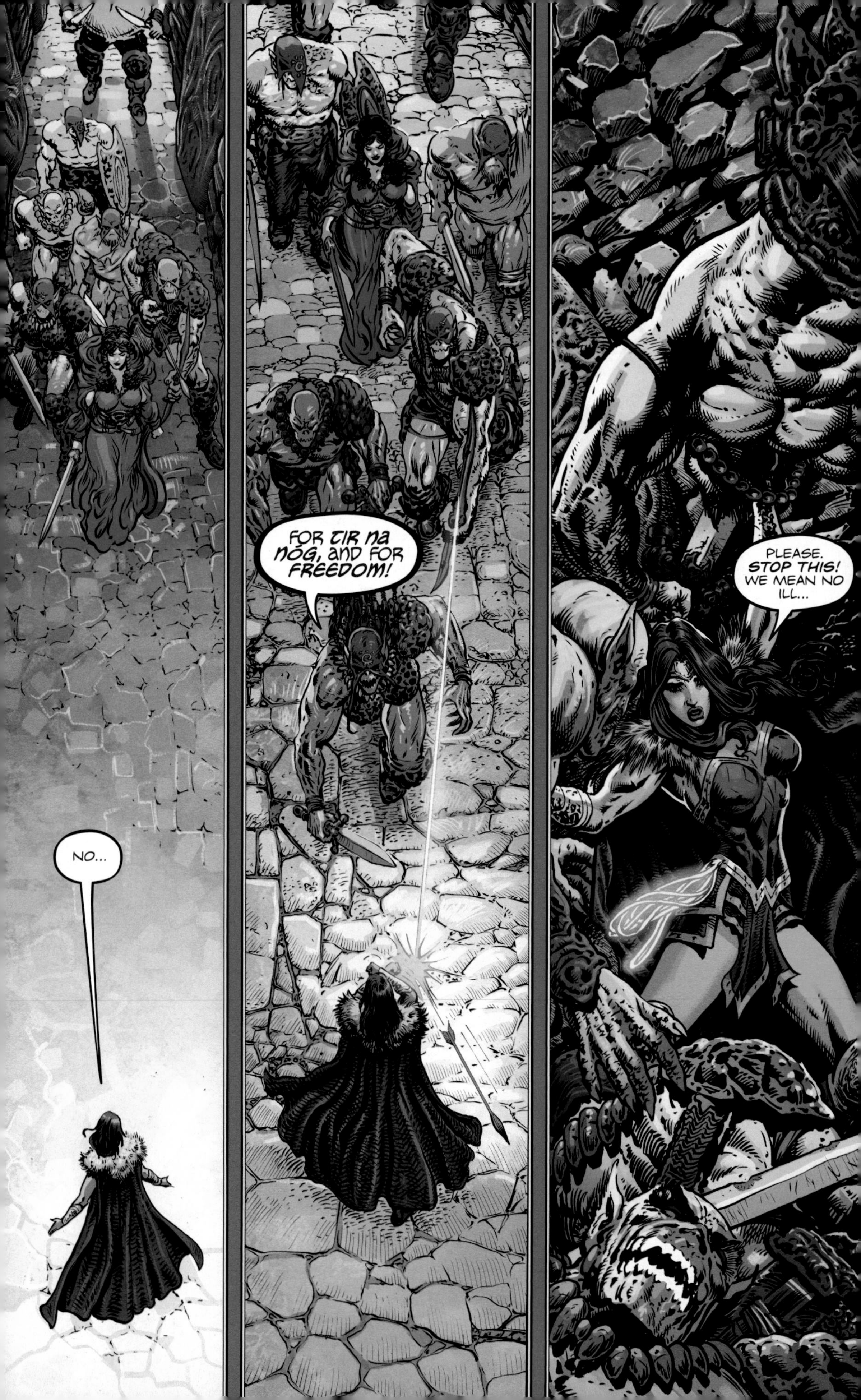
NO...
FOR TIR NA NÓG, AND FOR FREEDOM!
PLEASE. STOP THIS! WE MEAN NO ILL...

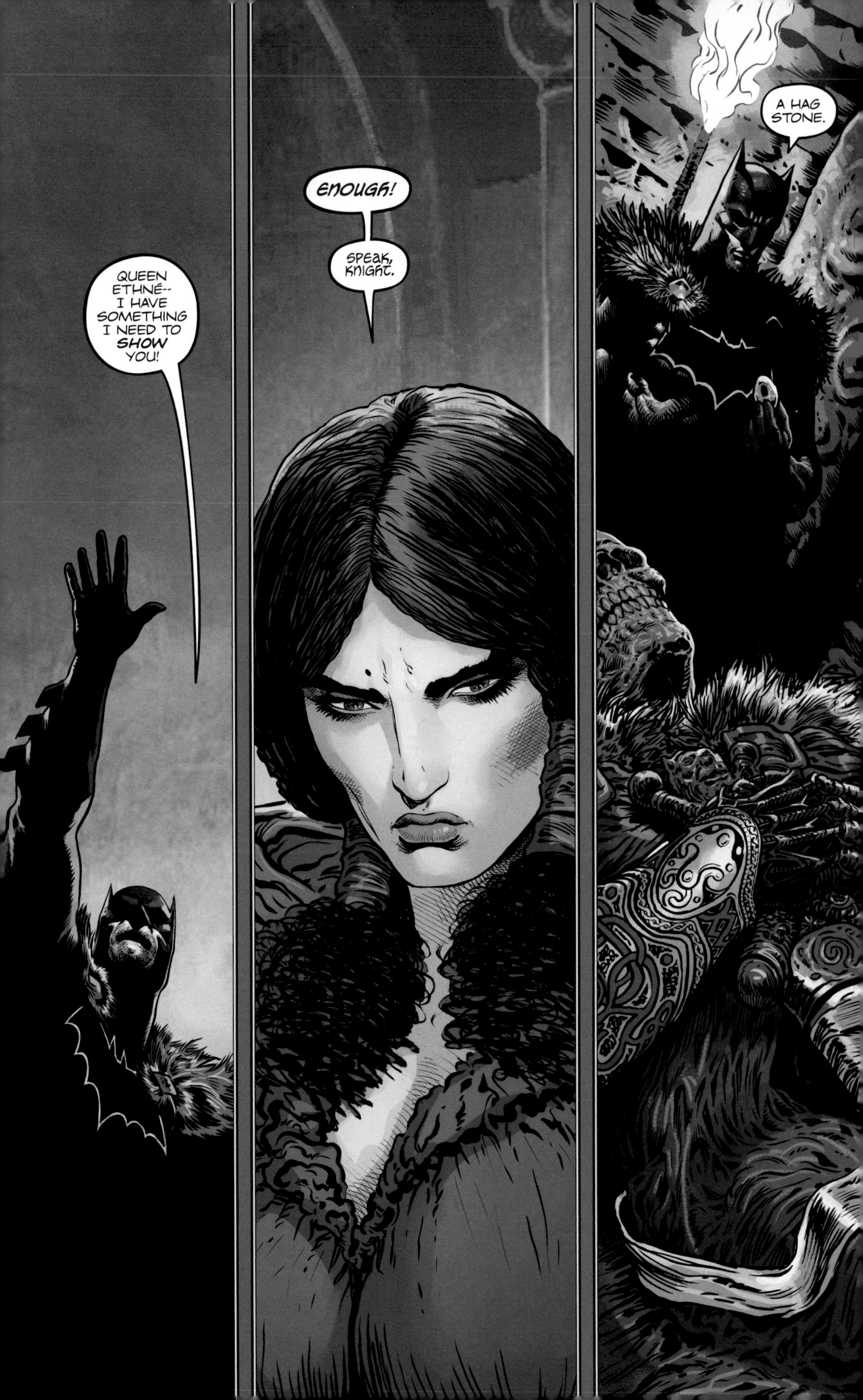
QUEEN ETHNÉ-- I HAVE SOMETHING I NEED TO **SHOW** YOU!
ENOUGH!
SPEAK, KNIGHT.
A HAG STONE.

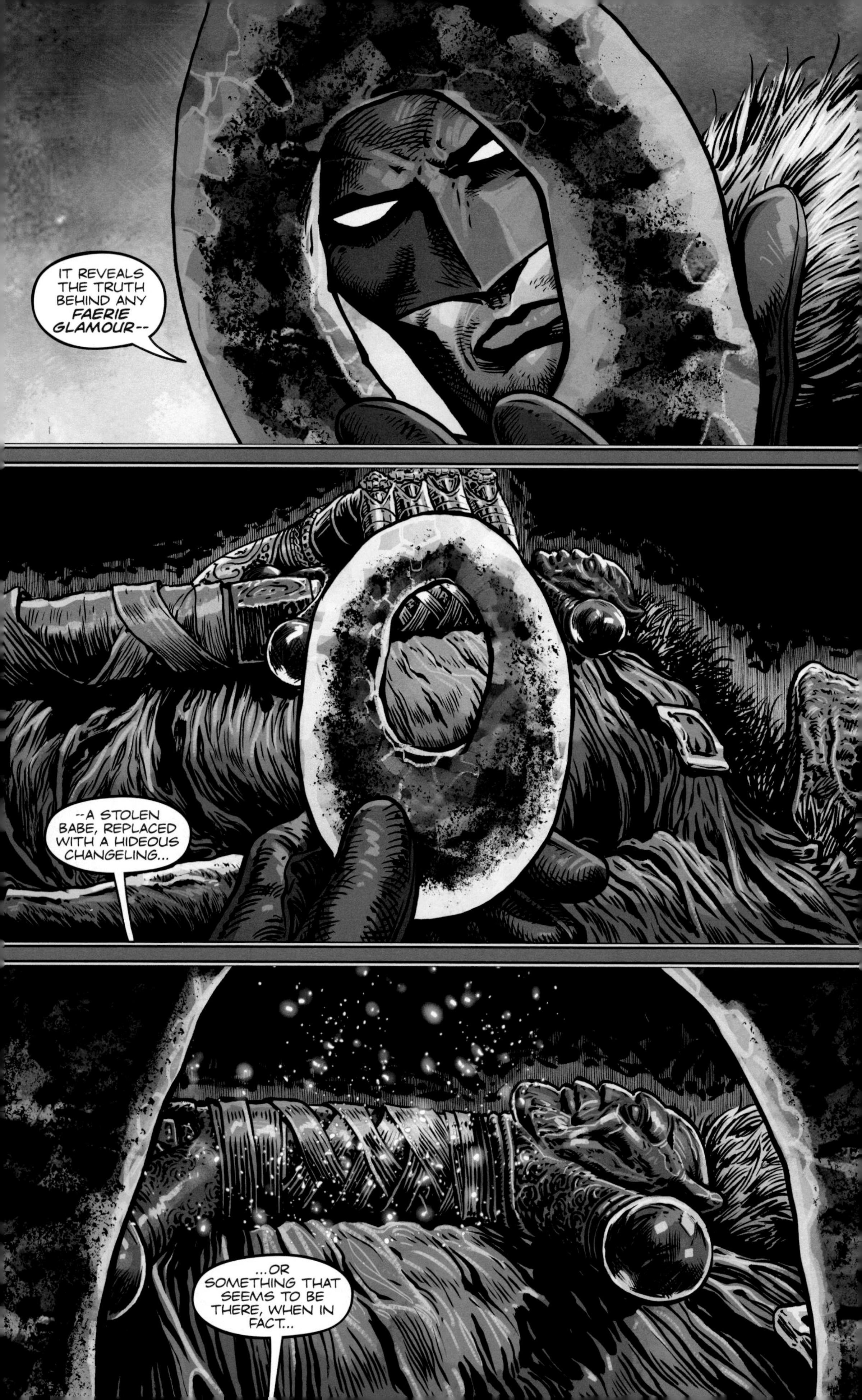
IT REVEALS THE TRUTH BEHIND ANY FAERIE GLAMOUR--
--A STOLEN BABE, REPLACED WITH A HIDEOUS CHANGELING...
...OR SOMETHING THAT SEEMS TO BE THERE, WHEN IN FACT...

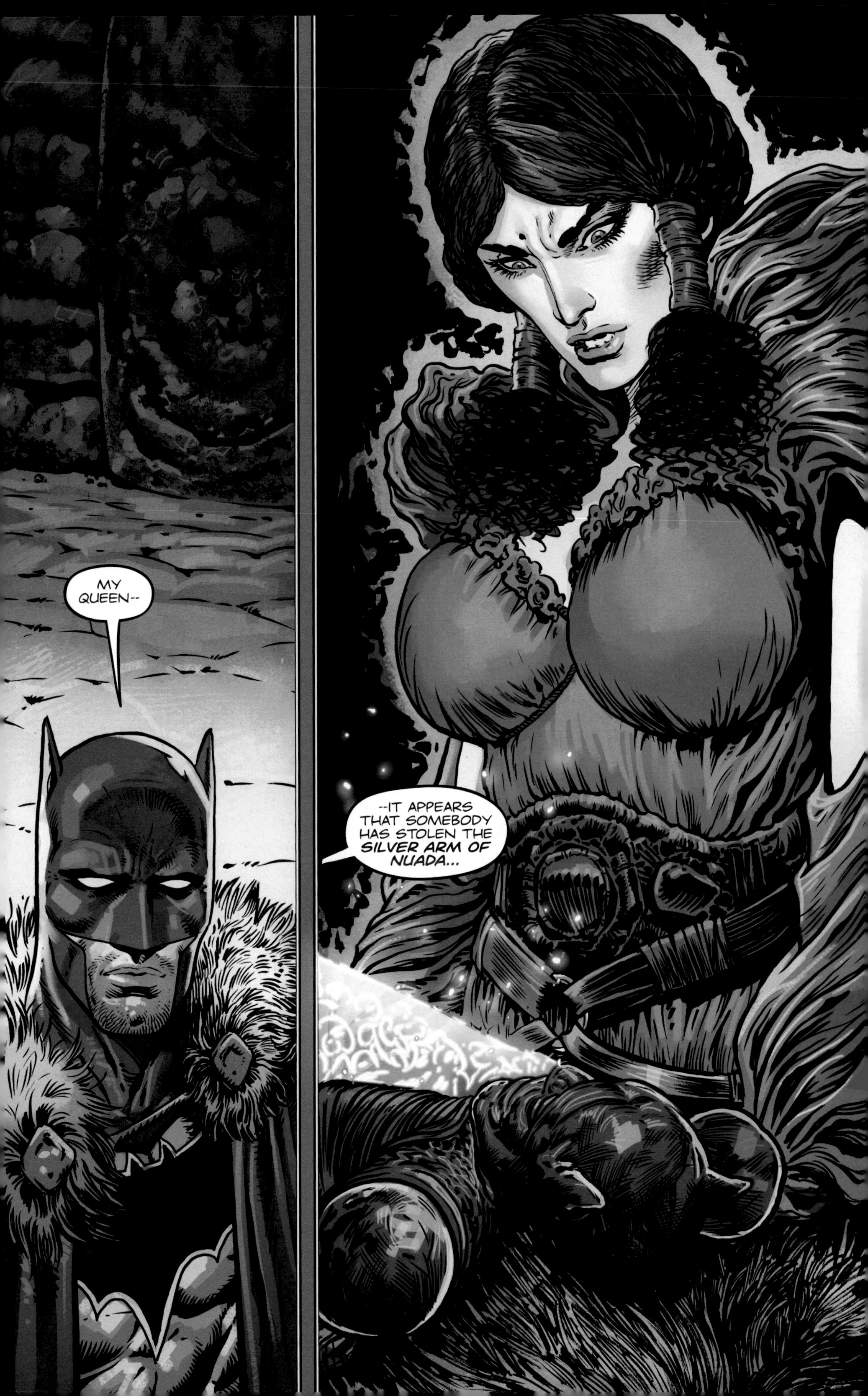
MY QUEEN--
--IT APPEARS THAT SOMEBODY HAS STOLEN THE SILVER ARM OF NUADA...

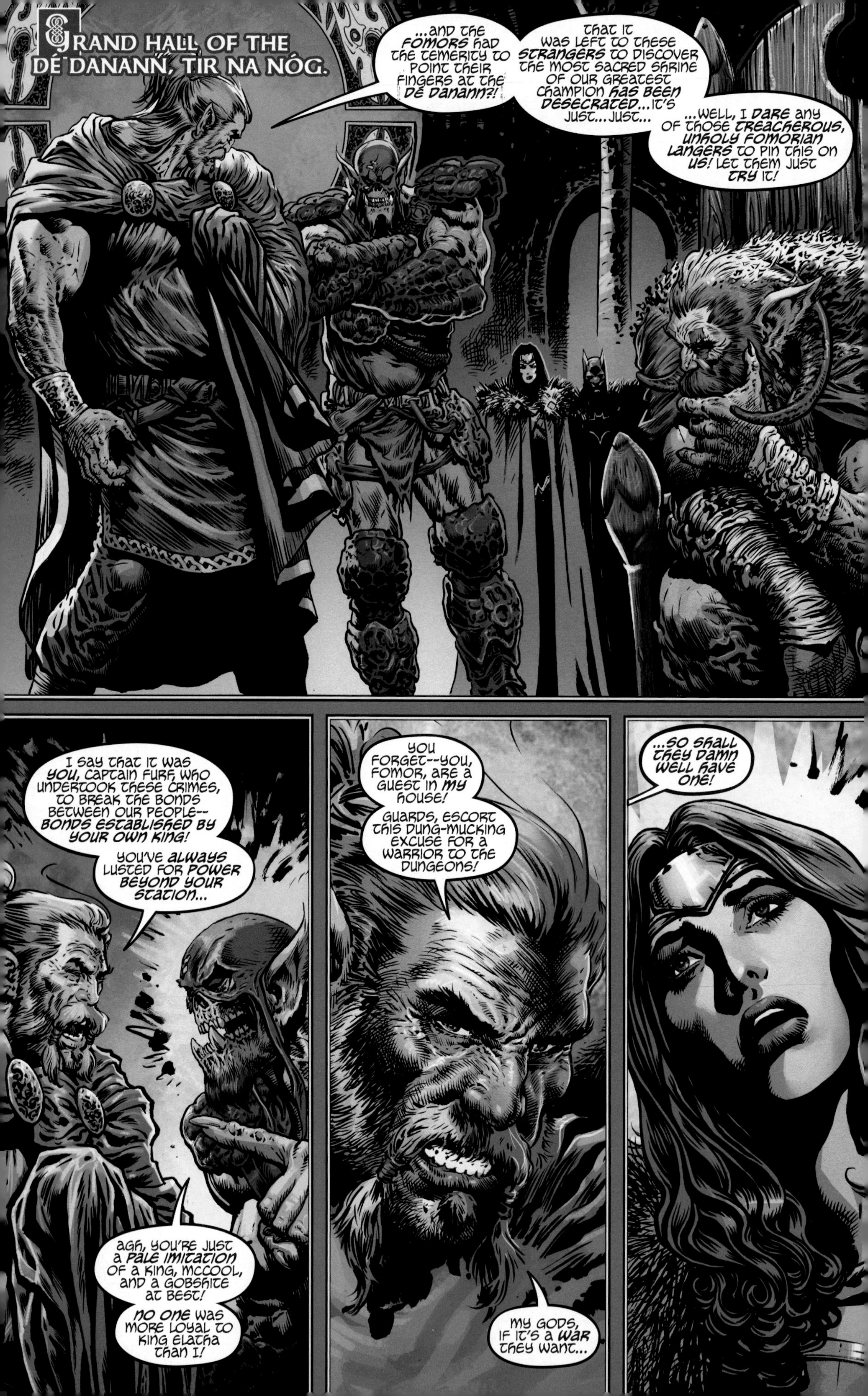
GRAND HALL OF THE DÉ DANANN, TIR NA NÓG.
...AND THE FOMORS HAD THE TEMERITY TO POINT THEIR FINGERS AT THE DÉ DANANN?!
THAT IT WAS LEFT TO THESE STRANGERS TO DISCOVER THE MOST SACRED SHRINE OF OUR GREATEST CHAMPION HAS BEEN DESECRATED... IT'S JUST... JUST...
...WELL, I DARE ANY OF THOSE TREACHEROUS, UNHOLY FOMORIAN LANGERS TO PIN THIS ON US! LET THEM JUST TRY IT!
I SAY THAT IT WAS YOU, CAPTAIN FURF, WHO UNDERTOOK THESE CRIMES, TO BREAK THE BONDS BETWEEN OUR PEOPLE-- BONDS ESTABLISHED BY YOUR OWN KING!
YOU'VE ALWAYS LUSTED FOR POWER BEYOND YOUR STATION...
AGH, YOU'RE JUST A PALE IMITATION OF A KING, MCCOOL, AND A GOBSHITE AT BEST!
NO ONE WAS MORE LOYAL TO KING ELATHA THAN I!
YOU FORGET--YOU, FOMOR, ARE A GUEST IN MY HOUSE!
GUARDS, ESCORT THIS DUNG-MUCKING EXCUSE FOR A WARRIOR TO THE DUNGEONS!
MY GODS, IF IT'S A WAR THEY WANT...
...SO SHALL THEY DAMN WELL HAVE ONE!

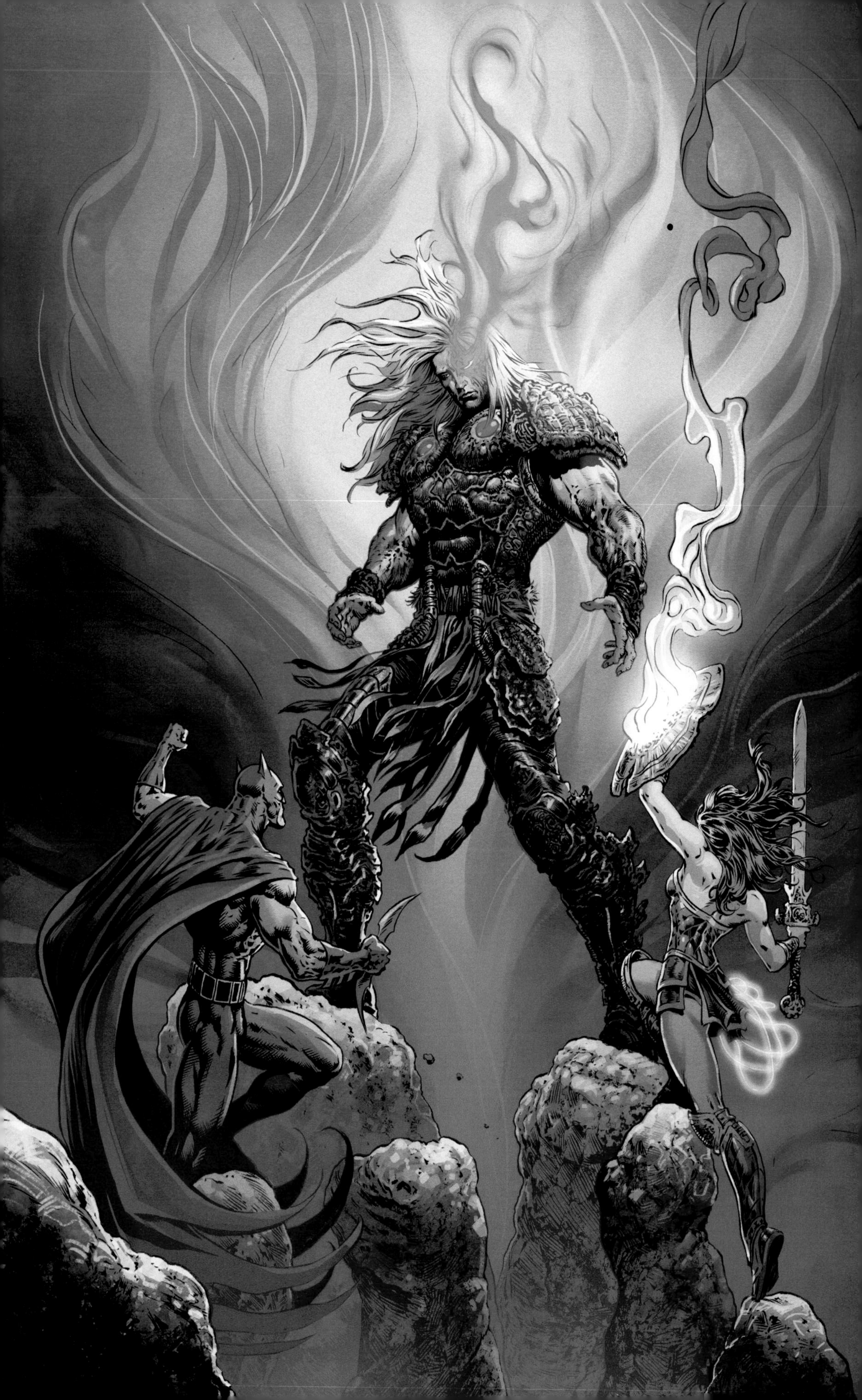

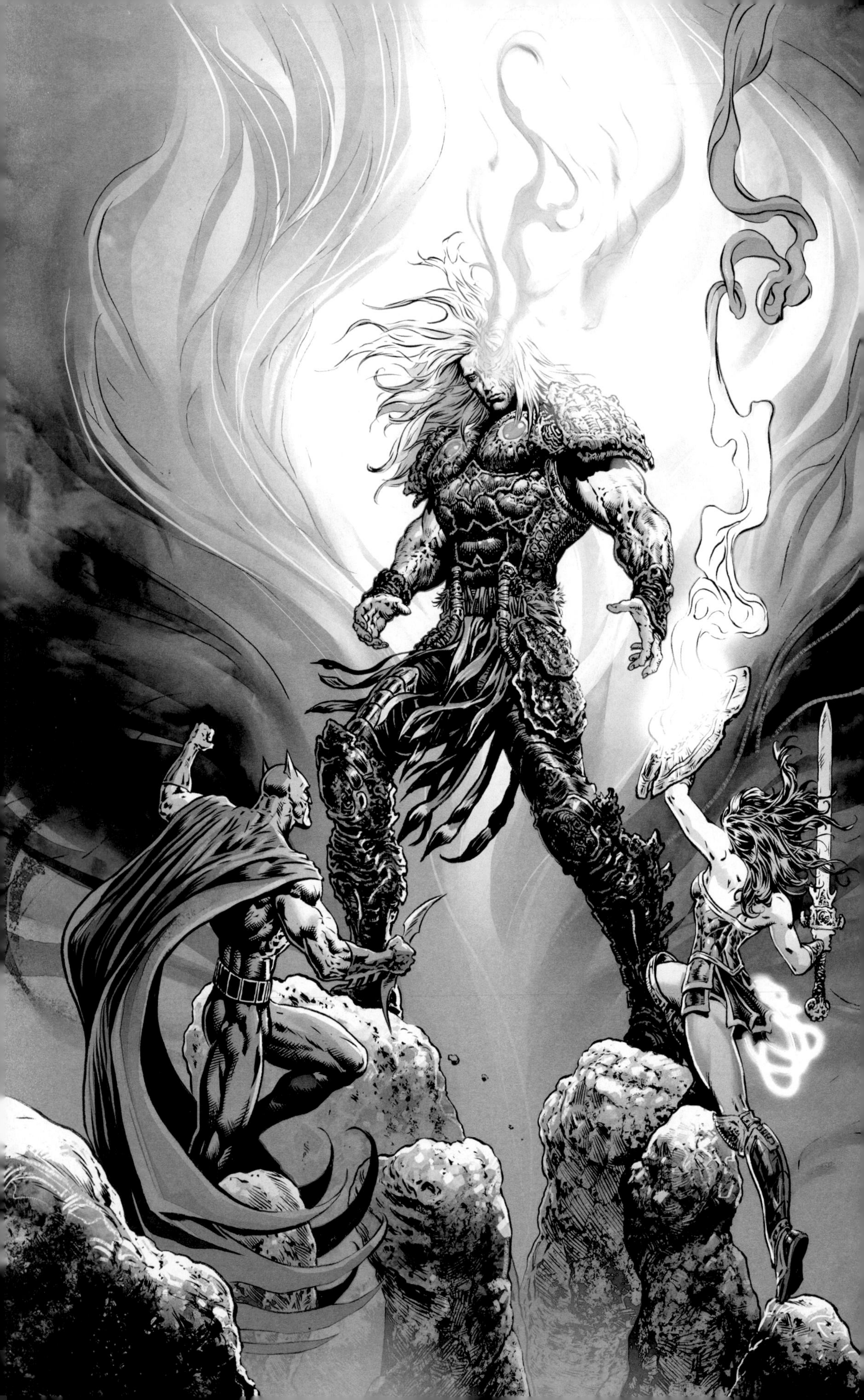

CHAPTER FIVE

THE RETURN OF THE KINGS

LIAM SHARP WRITER/ARTIST
ROMULO FAJARDO JR. COLORS
ALW'S TROY PETERI LETTERER
SHARP & FAJARDO JR. COVER
BRIAN CUNNINGHAM GROUP EDITOR
JESSICA CHEN EDITOR

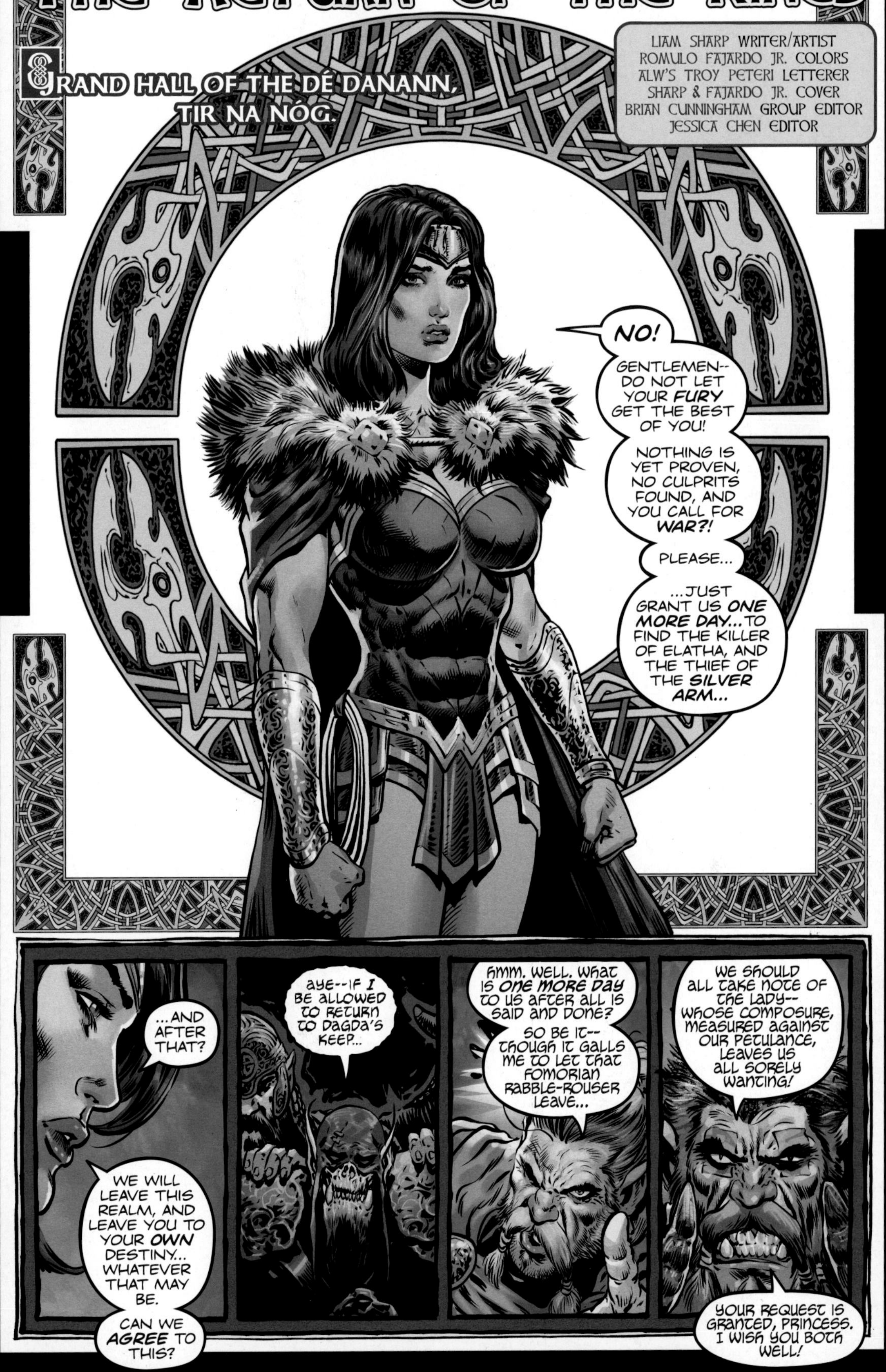
GRAND HALL OF THE DÉ DANANN, TIR NA NÓG.
NO!
GENTLEMEN-- DO NOT LET YOUR FURY GET THE BEST OF YOU!
NOTHING IS YET PROVEN, NO CULPRITS FOUND, AND YOU CALL FOR WAR?!
PLEASE...
...JUST GRANT US ONE MORE DAY... TO FIND THE KILLER OF ELATHA, AND THE THIEF OF THE SILVER ARM...
...AND AFTER THAT?
WE WILL LEAVE THIS REALM, AND LEAVE YOU TO YOUR OWN DESTINY... WHATEVER THAT MAY BE.
CAN WE AGREE TO THIS?
AYE--IF I BE ALLOWED TO RETURN TO DAGDA'S KEEP...
HMM. WELL. WHAT IS ONE MORE DAY TO US AFTER ALL IS SAID AND DONE?
SO BE IT-- THOUGH IT GALLS ME TO LET THAT FOMORIAN RABBLE-ROUSER LEAVE...
WE SHOULD ALL TAKE NOTE OF THE LADY-- WHOSE COMPOSURE, MEASURED AGAINST OUR PETULANCE, LEAVES US ALL SORELY WANTING!
YOUR REQUEST IS GRANTED, PRINCESS. I WISH YOU BOTH WELL!

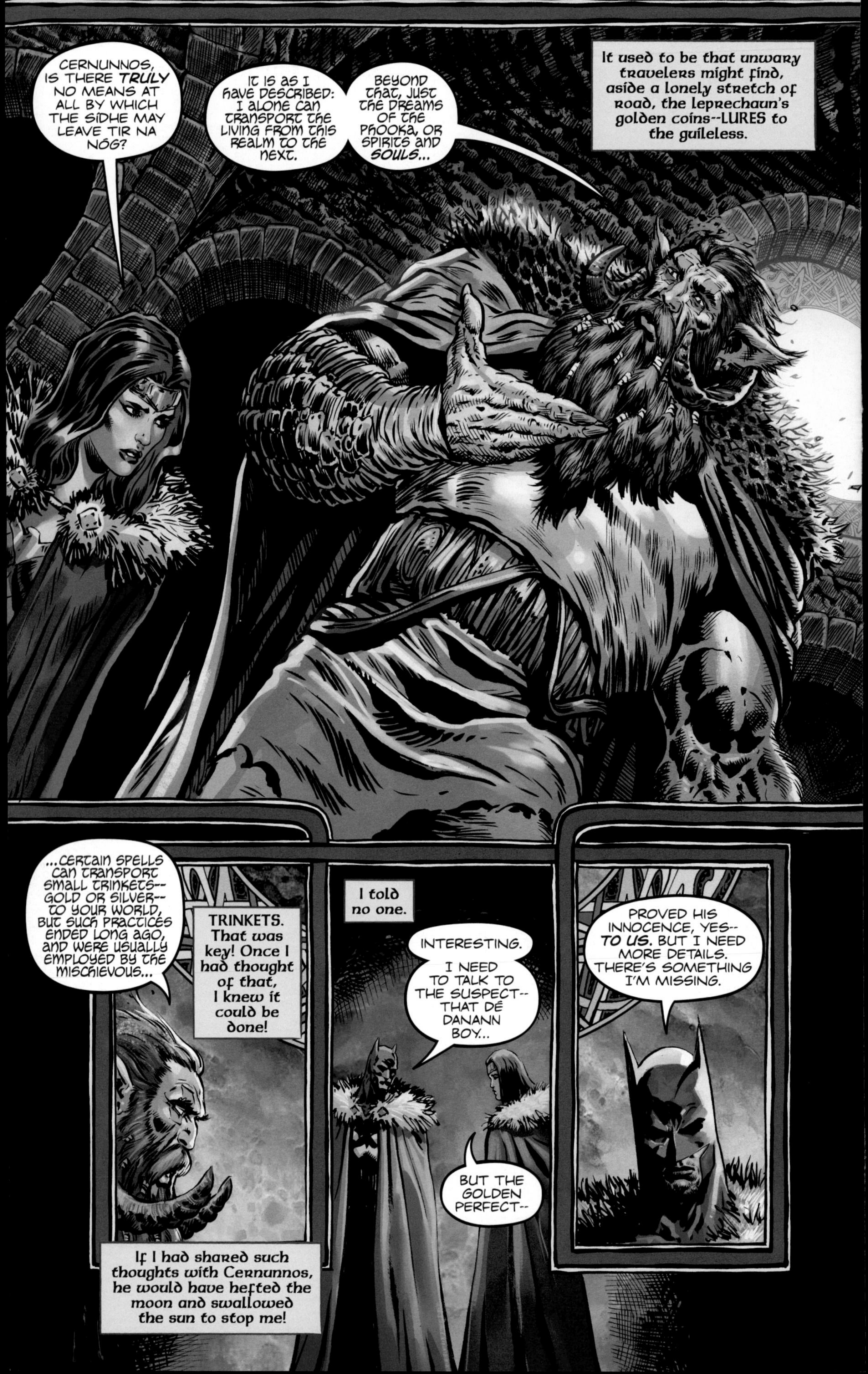
CERNUNNOS, IS THERE TRULY NO MEANS AT ALL BY WHICH THE SIDHE MAY LEAVE TIR NA NÓG?
IT IS AS I HAVE DESCRIBED: I ALONE CAN TRANSPORT THE LIVING FROM THIS REALM TO THE NEXT.
BEYOND THAT, JUST THE DREAMS OF THE PHOOKA, OR SPIRITS AND SOULS...
It used to be that unwary travelers might find, aside a lonely stretch of road, the leprechaun's golden coins--LURES to the guileless.
...CERTAIN SPELLS CAN TRANSPORT SMALL TRINKETS--GOLD OR SILVER--TO YOUR WORLD, BUT SUCH PRACTICES ENDED LONG AGO, AND WERE USUALLY EMPLOYED BY THE MISCHIEVOUS...
TRINKETS. That was key! Once I had thought of that, I knew it could be done!
If I had shared such thoughts with Cernunnos, he would have hefted the moon and swallowed the sun to stop me!
I told no one.
INTERESTING.
I NEED TO TALK TO THE SUSPECT--THAT DÉ DANANN BOY...
BUT THE GOLDEN PERFECT--
PROVED HIS INNOCENCE, YES--TO US. BUT I NEED MORE DETAILS. THERE'S SOMETHING I'M MISSING.

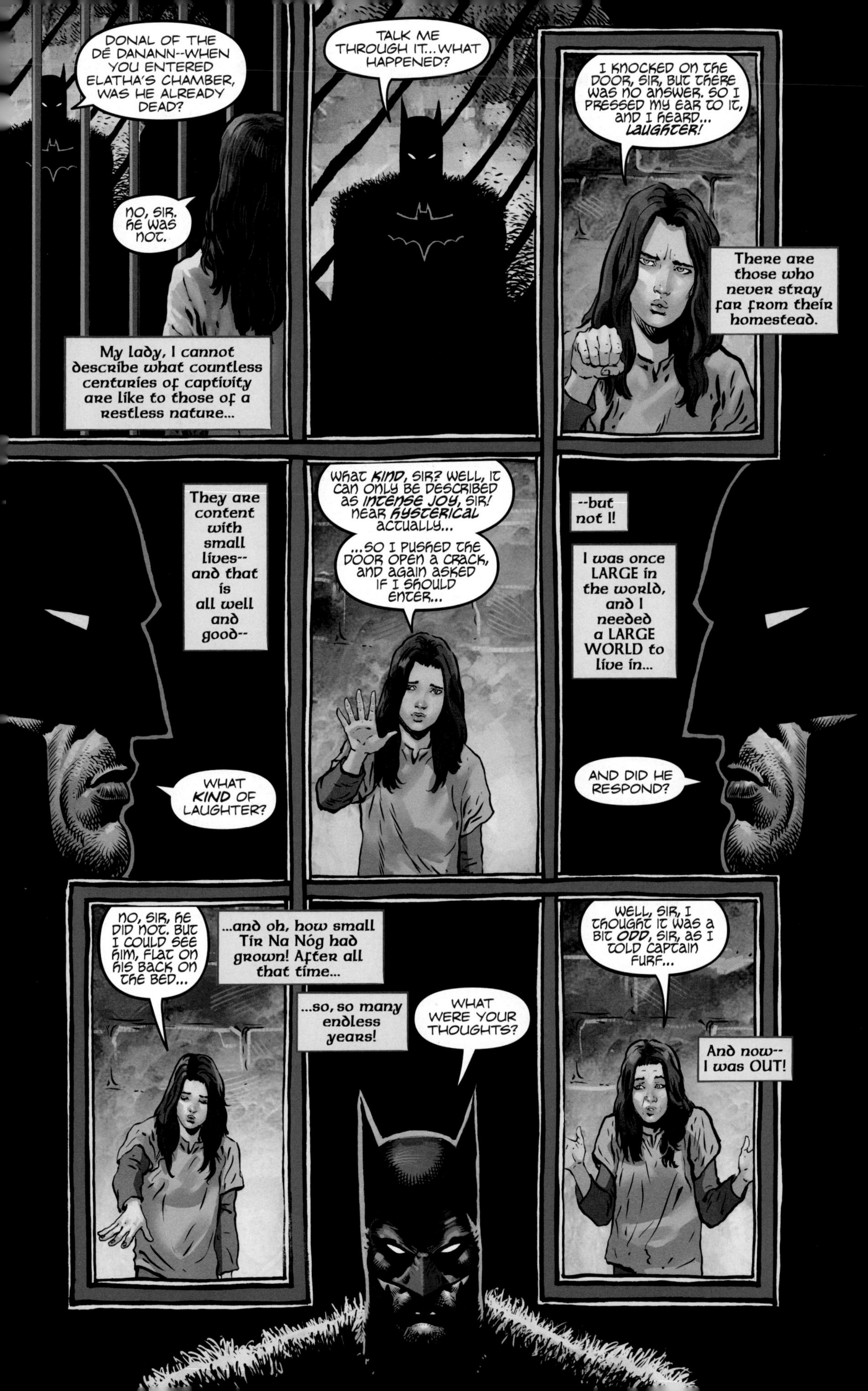
DONAL OF THE DÉ DANANN--WHEN YOU ENTERED ELATHA'S CHAMBER, WAS HE ALREADY DEAD?
NO, SIR. HE WAS NOT.
My lady, I cannot describe what countless centuries of captivity are like to those of a restless nature...
TALK ME THROUGH IT...WHAT HAPPENED?
I KNOCKED ON THE DOOR, SIR, BUT THERE WAS NO ANSWER. SO I PRESSED MY EAR TO IT, AND I HEARD... LAUGHTER!
There are those who never stray far from their homestead.
They are content with small lives--and that is all well and good--
WHAT KIND OF LAUGHTER?
WHAT KIND, SIR? WELL, IT CAN ONLY BE DESCRIBED AS INTENSE JOY, SIR! NEAR HYSTERICAL ACTUALLY...
...SO I PUSHED THE DOOR OPEN A CRACK, AND AGAIN ASKED IF I SHOULD ENTER...
--but not I!
I was once LARGE in the world, and I needed a LARGE WORLD to live in...
AND DID HE RESPOND?
NO, SIR, HE DID NOT. BUT I COULD SEE HIM, FLAT ON HIS BACK ON THE BED...
...and oh, how small Tír Na Nóg had grown! After all that time...
...so, so many endless years!
WHAT WERE YOUR THOUGHTS?
WELL, SIR, I THOUGHT IT WAS A BIT ODD, SIR, AS I TOLD CAPTAIN FURF...
And now--I was OUT!

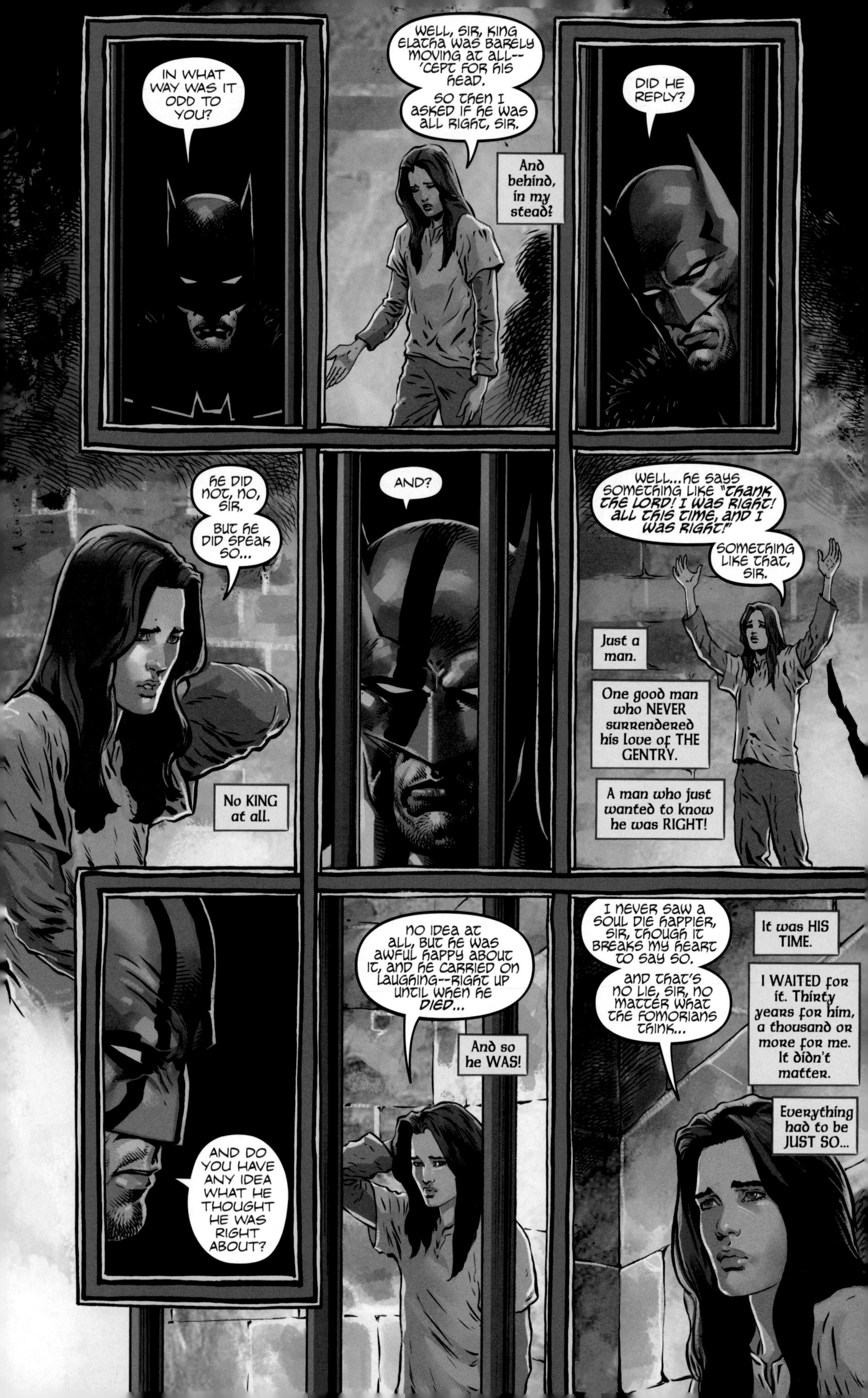
IN WHAT WAY WAS IT ODD TO YOU?
WELL, SIR, KING ELATHA WAS BARELY MOVING AT ALL-- 'CEPT FOR HIS HEAD.
SO THEN I ASKED IF HE WAS ALL RIGHT, SIR.
And behind, in my stead?
DID HE REPLY?
HE DID NOT, NO, SIR.
BUT HE DID SPEAK SO...
No KING at all.
AND?
WELL...HE SAYS SOMETHING LIKE "THANK THE LORD! I WAS RIGHT! ALL THIS TIME, AND I WAS RIGHT!"
SOMETHING LIKE THAT, SIR.
Just a man.
One good man who NEVER surrendered his love of THE GENTRY.
A man who just wanted to know he was RIGHT!
AND DO YOU HAVE ANY IDEA WHAT HE THOUGHT HE WAS RIGHT ABOUT?
NO IDEA AT ALL, BUT HE WAS AWFUL HAPPY ABOUT IT, AND HE CARRIED ON LAUGHING--RIGHT UP UNTIL WHEN HE DIED...
And so he WAS!
I NEVER SAW A SOUL DIE HAPPIER, SIR, THOUGH IT BREAKS MY HEART TO SAY SO.
AND THAT'S NO LIE, SIR, NO MATTER WHAT THE FOMORIANS THINK...
It was HIS TIME.
I WAITED for it. Thirty years for him, a thousand or more for me. It didn't matter.
Everything had to be JUST SO...

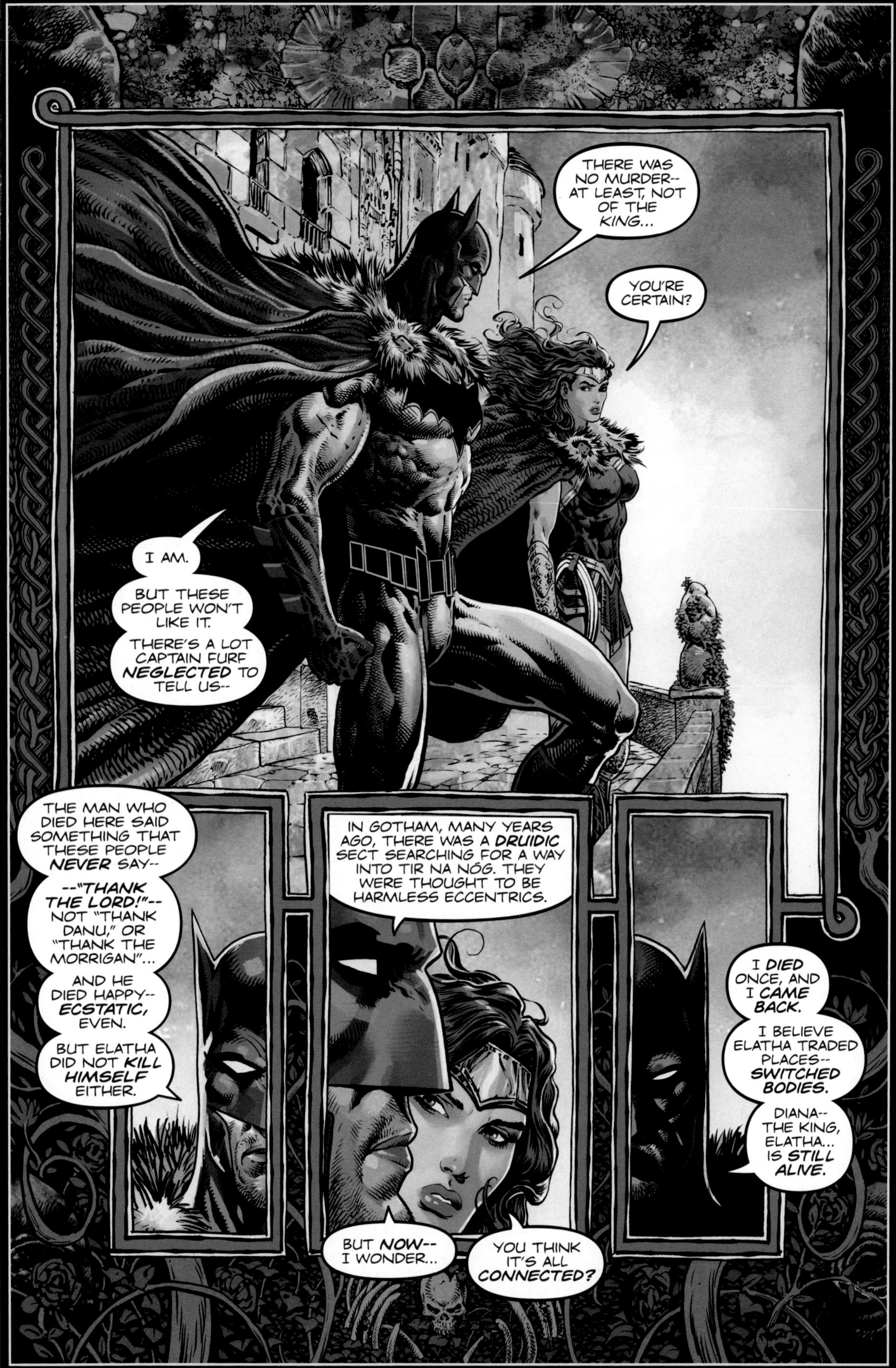
THERE WAS NO MURDER-- AT LEAST, NOT OF THE KING...
YOU'RE CERTAIN?
I AM.
BUT THESE PEOPLE WON'T LIKE IT.
THERE'S A LOT CAPTAIN FURF NEGLECTED TO TELL US--
THE MAN WHO DIED HERE SAID SOMETHING THAT THESE PEOPLE NEVER SAY--
--"THANK THE LORD!"-- NOT "THANK DANU," OR "THANK THE MORRIGAN"...
AND HE DIED HAPPY-- ECSTATIC, EVEN.
BUT ELATHA DID NOT KILL HIMSELF EITHER.
IN GOTHAM, MANY YEARS AGO, THERE WAS A DRUIDIC SECT SEARCHING FOR A WAY INTO TIR NA NÓG. THEY WERE THOUGHT TO BE HARMLESS ECCENTRICS.
BUT NOW-- I WONDER...
YOU THINK IT'S ALL CONNECTED?
I DIED ONCE, AND I CAME BACK.
I BELIEVE ELATHA TRADED PLACES-- SWITCHED BODIES.
DIANA-- THE KING, ELATHA... IS STILL ALIVE.

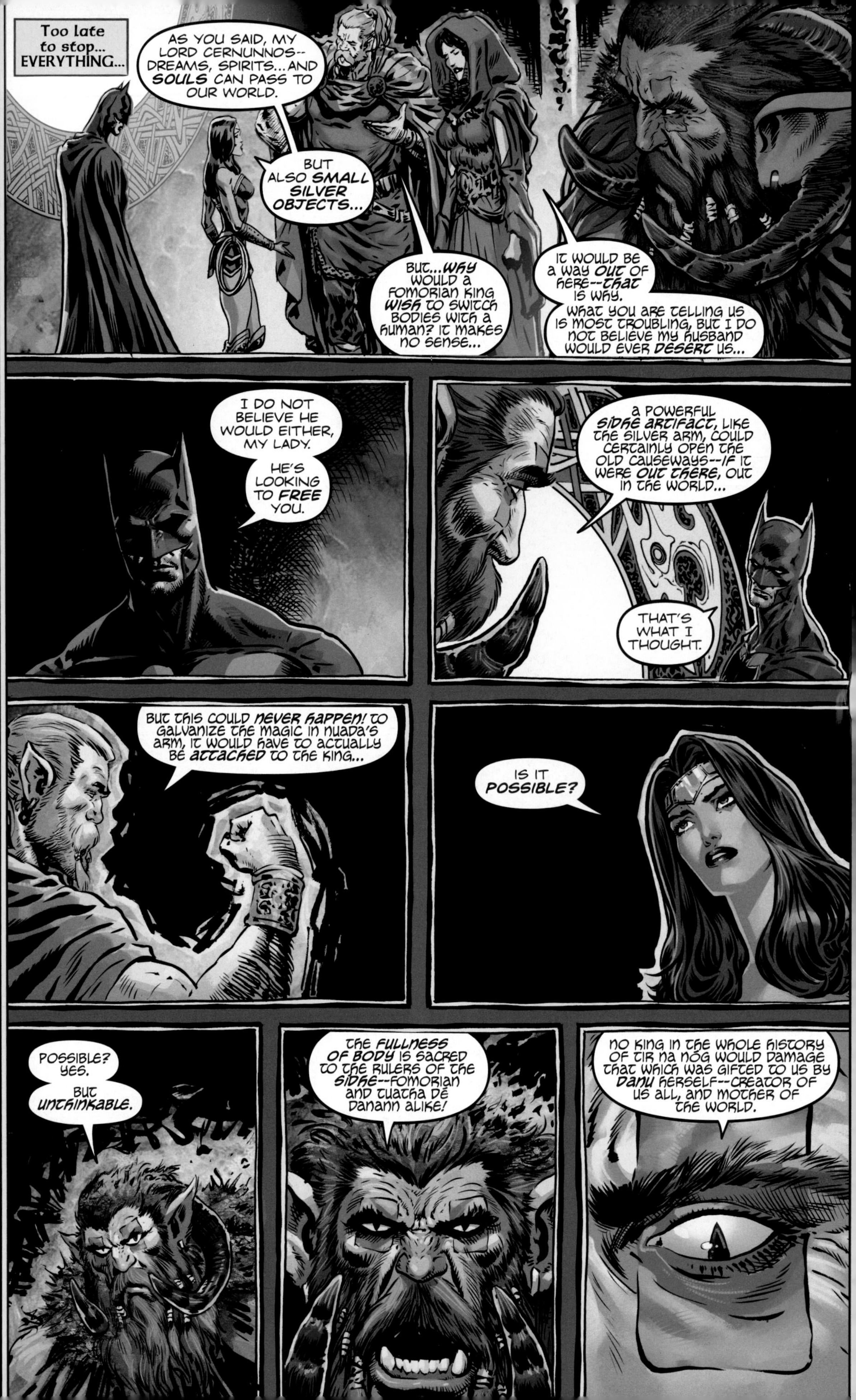
Too late to stop... EVERYTHING...
AS YOU SAID, MY LORD CERNUNNOS--DREAMS, SPIRITS...AND SOULS CAN PASS TO OUR WORLD.
BUT ALSO SMALL SILVER OBJECTS...
BUT...WHY WOULD A FOMORIAN KING WISH TO SWITCH BODIES WITH A HUMAN? IT MAKES NO SENSE...
IT WOULD BE A WAY OUT OF HERE--THAT IS WHY.
WHAT YOU ARE TELLING US IS MOST TROUBLING, BUT I DO NOT BELIEVE MY HUSBAND WOULD EVER DESERT US...
I DO NOT BELIEVE HE WOULD EITHER, MY LADY.
HE'S LOOKING TO FREE YOU.
A POWERFUL SIDHE ARTIFACT, LIKE THE SILVER ARM, COULD CERTAINLY OPEN THE OLD CAUSEWAYS--IF IT WERE OUT THERE, OUT IN THE WORLD...
THAT'S WHAT I THOUGHT.
BUT THIS COULD NEVER HAPPEN! TO GALVANIZE THE MAGIC IN NUADA'S ARM, IT WOULD HAVE TO ACTUALLY BE ATTACHED TO THE KING...
IS IT POSSIBLE?
POSSIBLE? YES.
BUT UNTHINKABLE.
THE FULLNESS OF BODY IS SACRED TO THE RULERS OF THE SIDHE--FOMORIAN AND TUATHA DÉ DANANN ALIKE!
NO KING IN THE WHOLE HISTORY OF TIR NA NÓG WOULD DAMAGE THAT WHICH WAS GIFTED TO US BY DANU HERSELF--CREATOR OF US ALL, AND MOTHER OF THE WORLD.

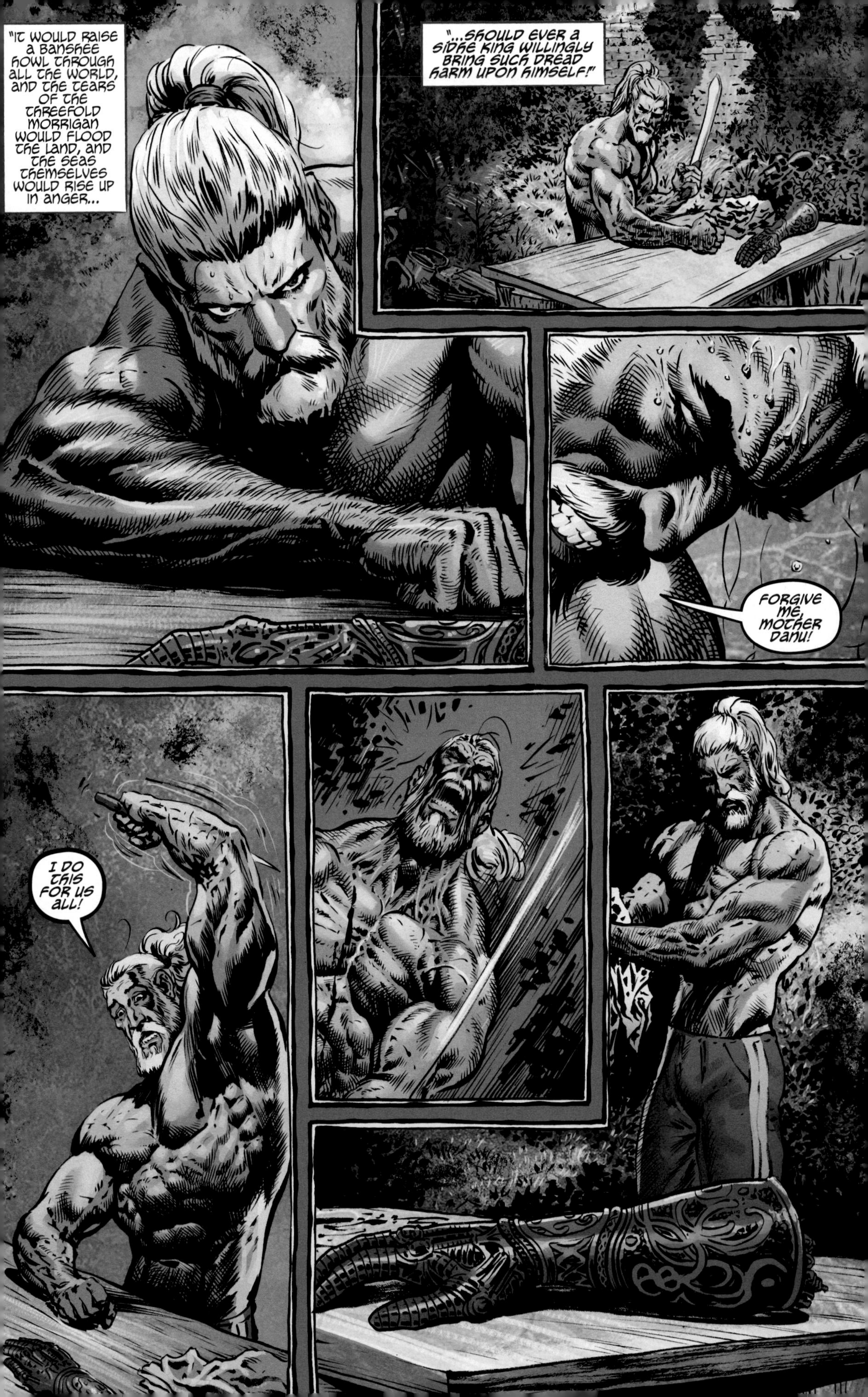
"IT WOULD RAISE A BANSHEE HOWL THROUGH ALL THE WORLD, AND THE TEARS OF THE THREEFOLD MORRIGAN WOULD FLOOD THE LAND, AND THE SEAS THEMSELVES WOULD RISE UP IN ANGER...
"...SHOULD EVER A SIDHE KING WILLINGLY BRING SUCH DREAD HARM UPON HIMSELF!"
FORGIVE ME, MOTHER DANU!
I DO THIS FOR US ALL!

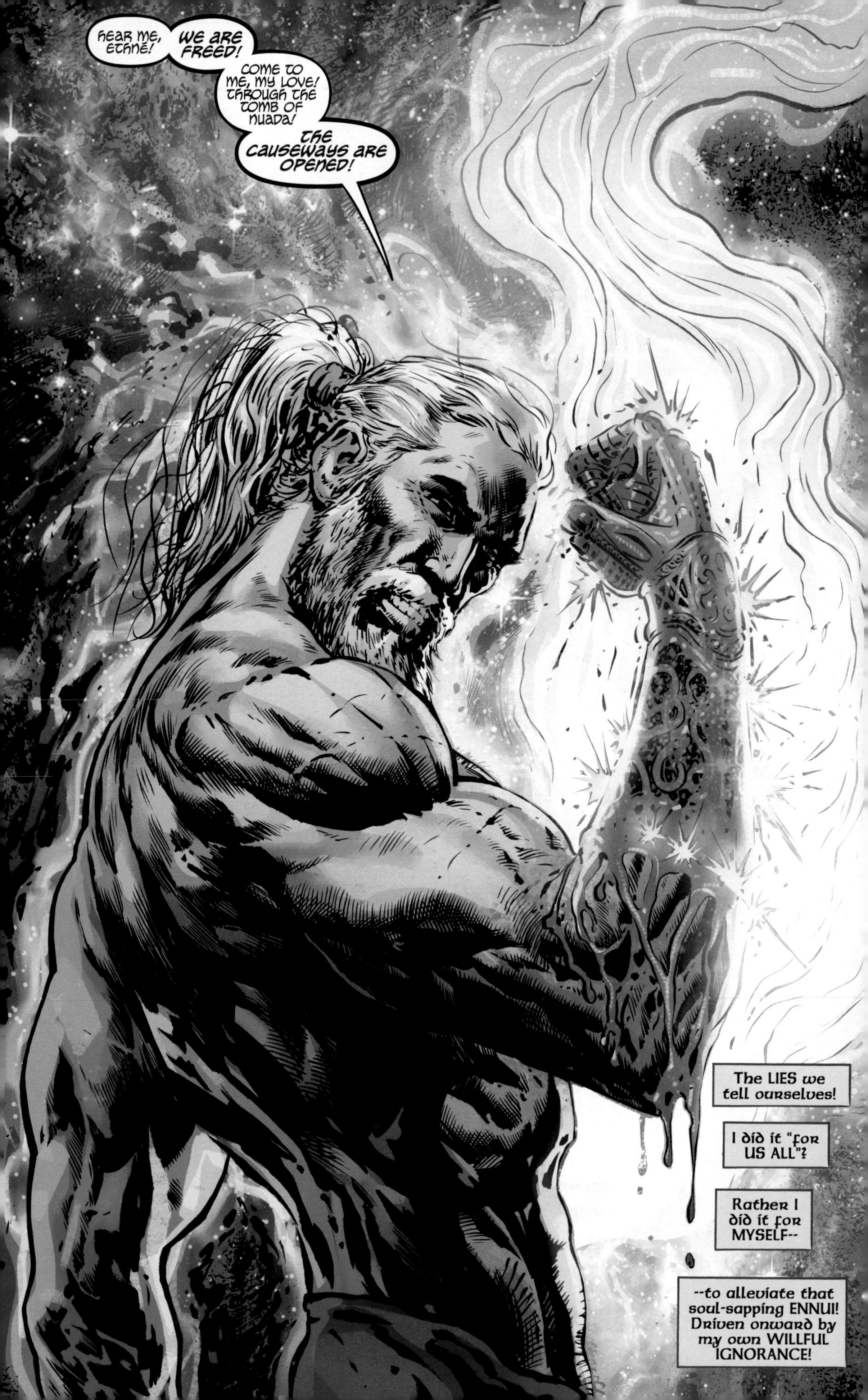
Hear me, Ethne!
We are freed!
Come to me, my love! Through the tomb of Nuada!
The causeways are opened!
The LIES we tell ourselves!
I did it "for US ALL"?
Rather I did it for MYSELF--
--to alleviate that soul-sapping ENNUI! Driven onward by my own WILLFUL IGNORANCE!

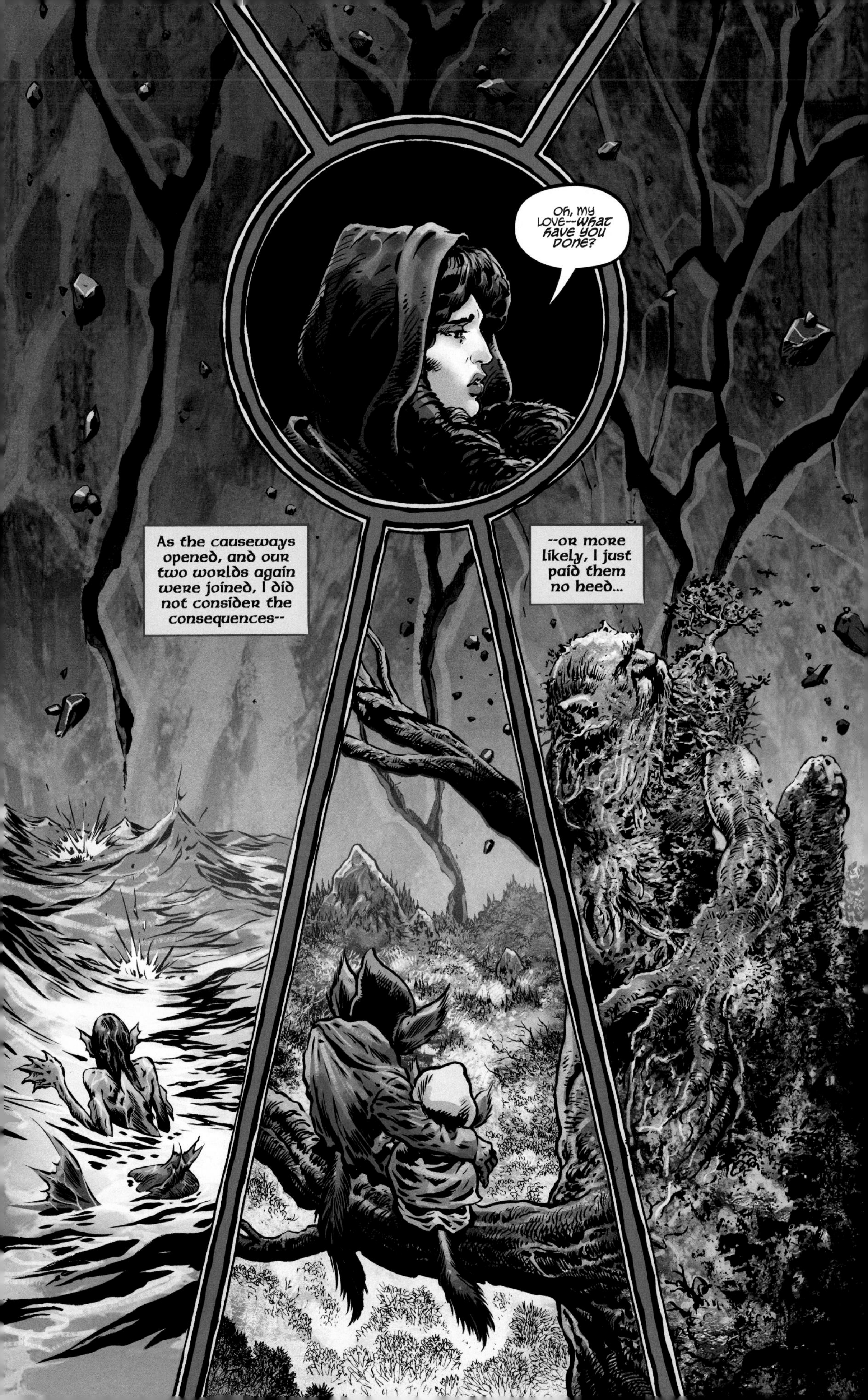
OH, MY LOVE--WHAT HAVE YOU DONE?
As the causeways opened, and our two worlds again were joined, I did not consider the consequences--
--or more likely, I just paid them no heed...

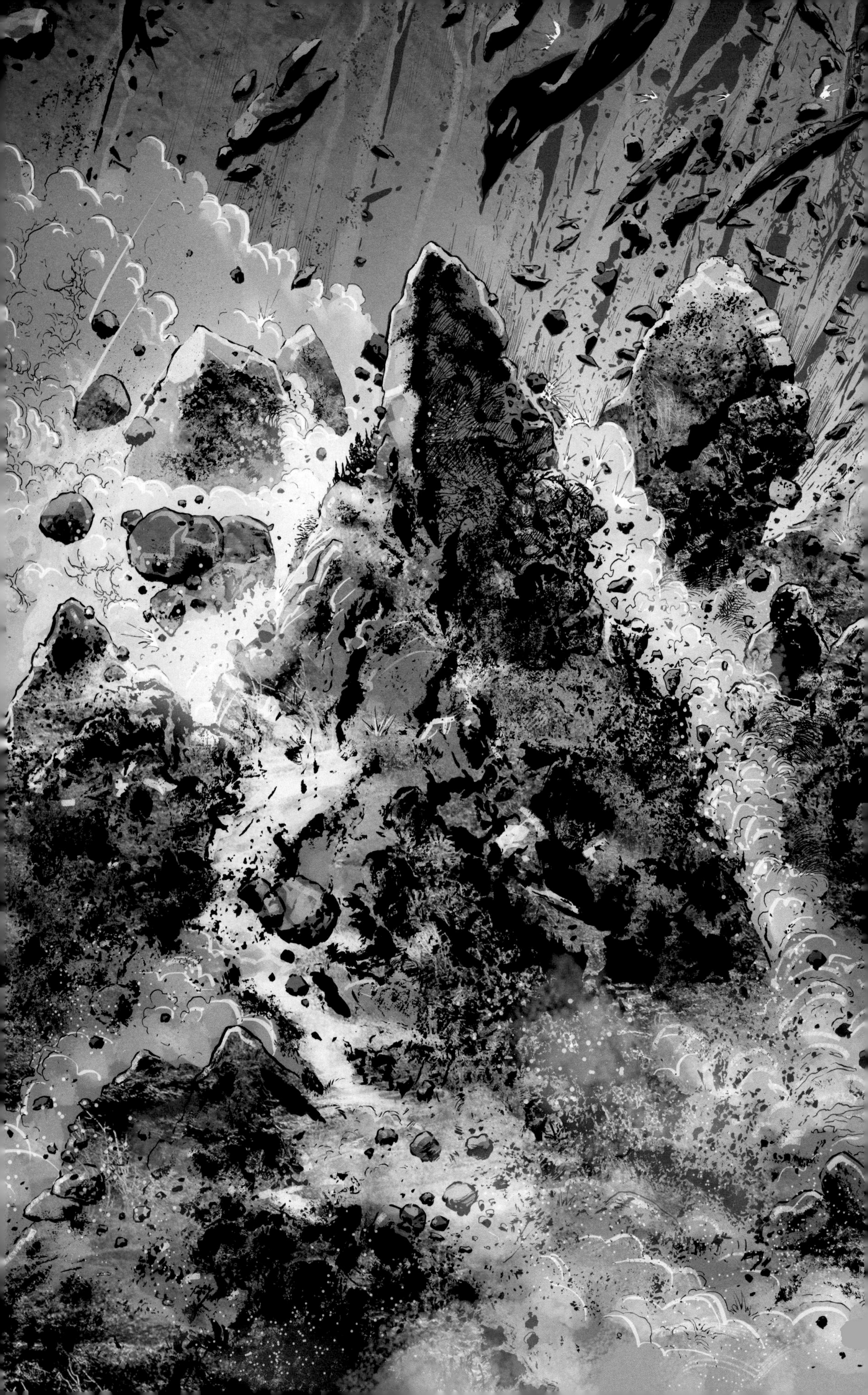

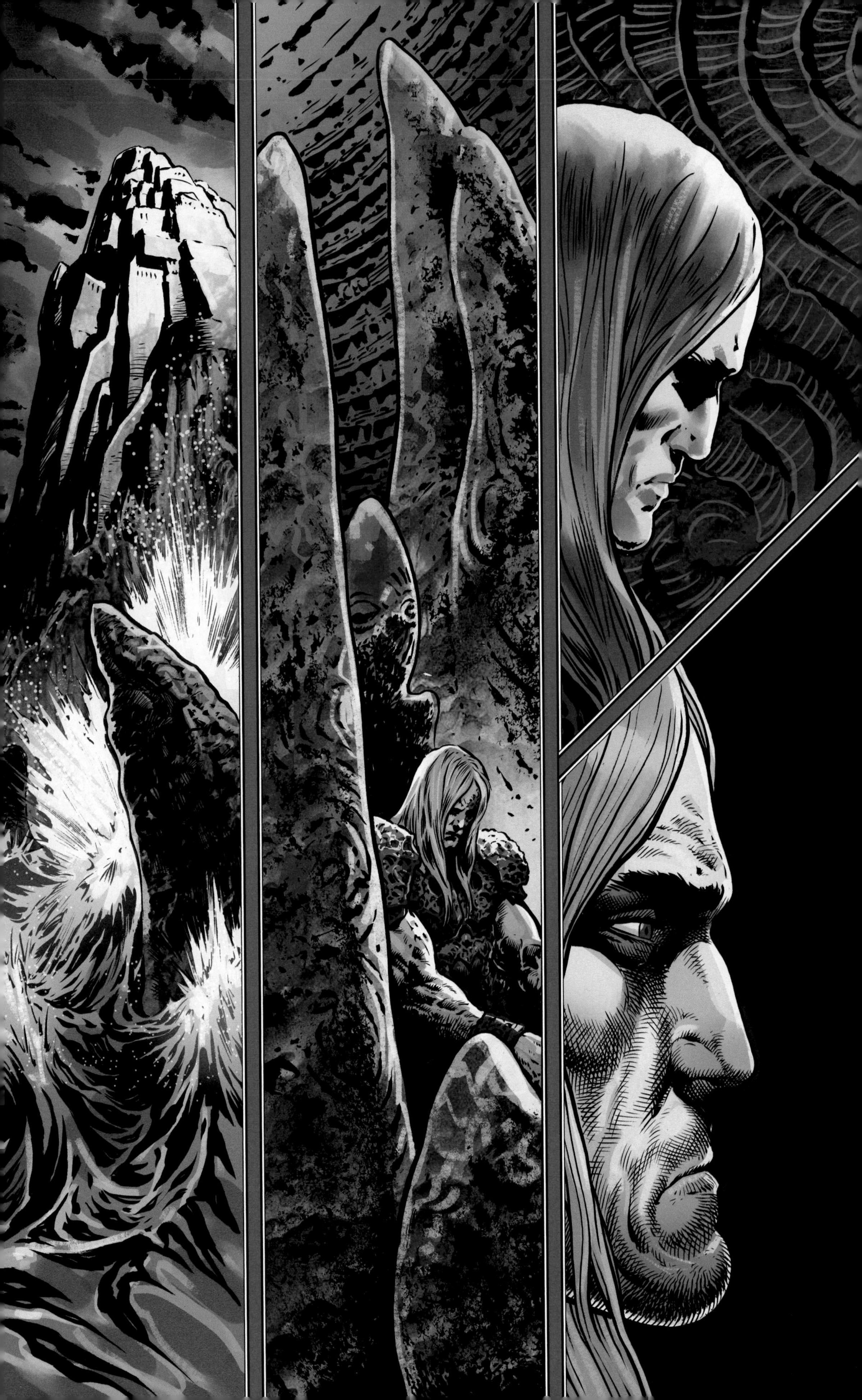

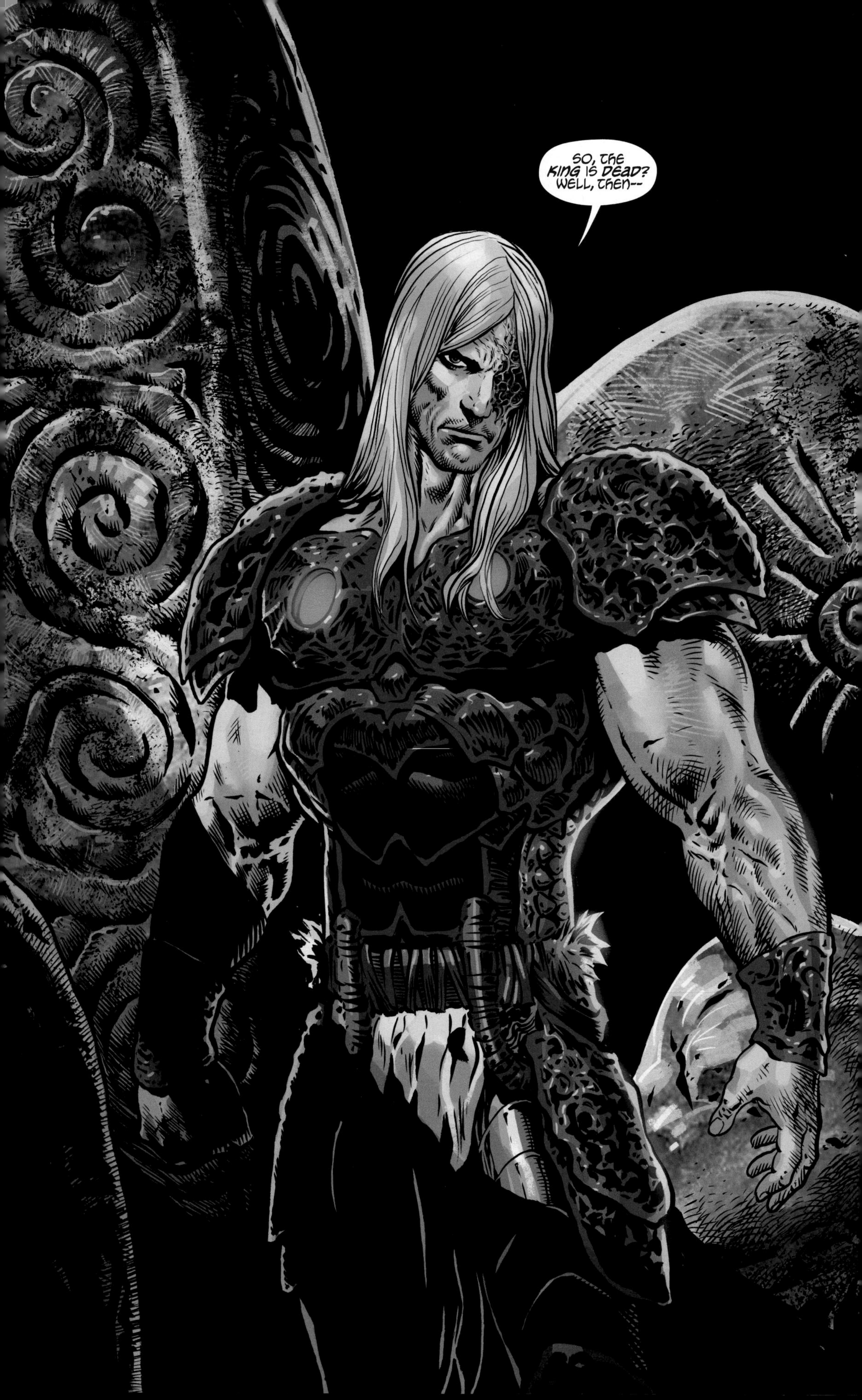
SO, THE KING IS DEAD? WELL, THEN--

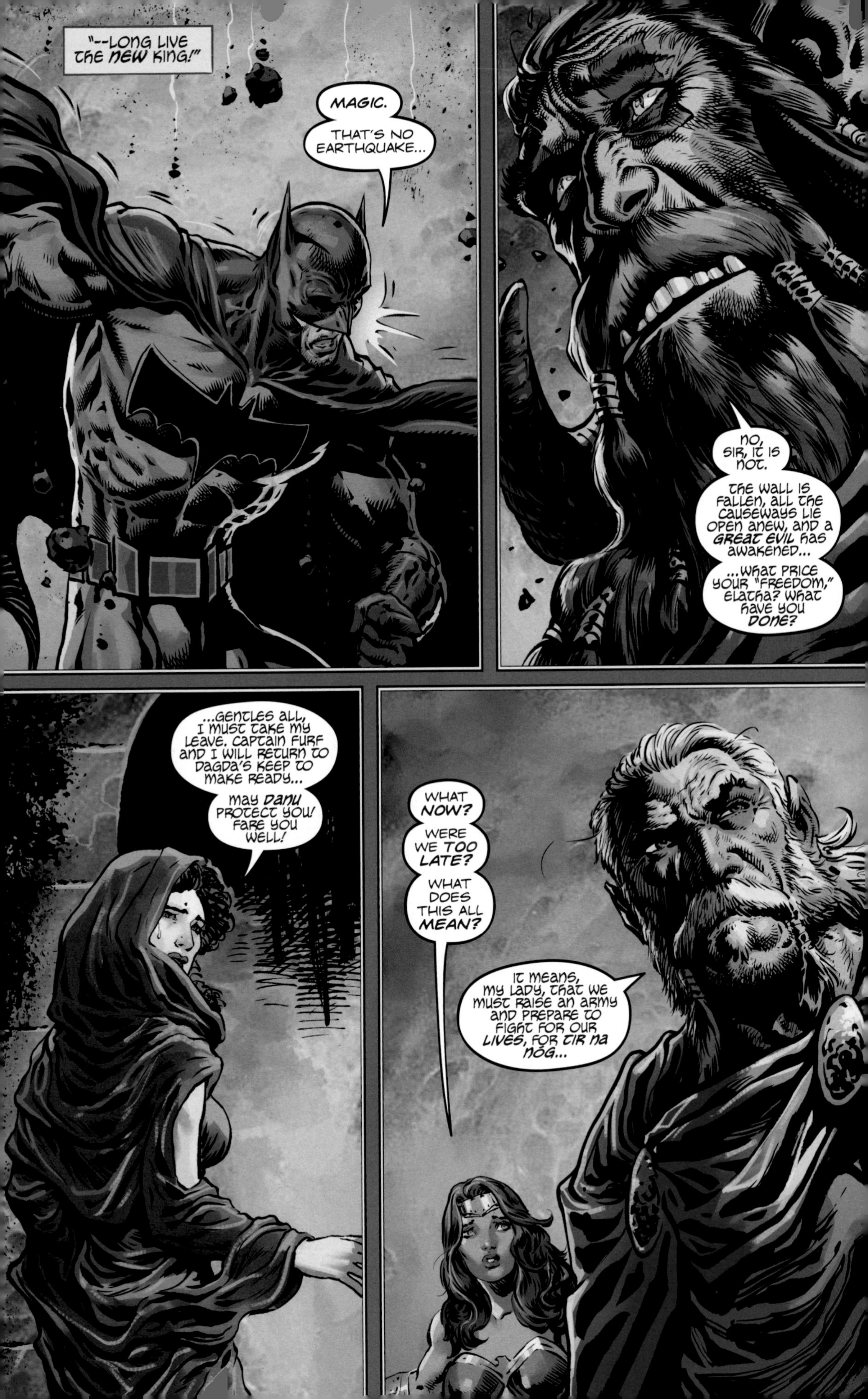
"--LONG LIVE THE NEW KING!"
MAGIC.
THAT'S NO EARTHQUAKE...
NO, SIR, IT IS NOT.
THE WALL IS FALLEN, ALL THE CAUSEWAYS LIE OPEN ANEW, AND A GREAT EVIL HAS AWAKENED...
...WHAT PRICE YOUR "FREEDOM," ELATHA? WHAT HAVE YOU DONE?
...GENTLES ALL, I MUST TAKE MY LEAVE. CAPTAIN FURF AND I WILL RETURN TO DAGDA'S KEEP TO MAKE READY...
MAY DANU PROTECT YOU! FARE YOU WELL!
WHAT NOW?
WERE WE TOO LATE?
WHAT DOES THIS ALL MEAN?
IT MEANS, MY LADY, THAT WE MUST RAISE AN ARMY AND PREPARE TO FIGHT FOR OUR LIVES, FOR TIR NA NÓG...

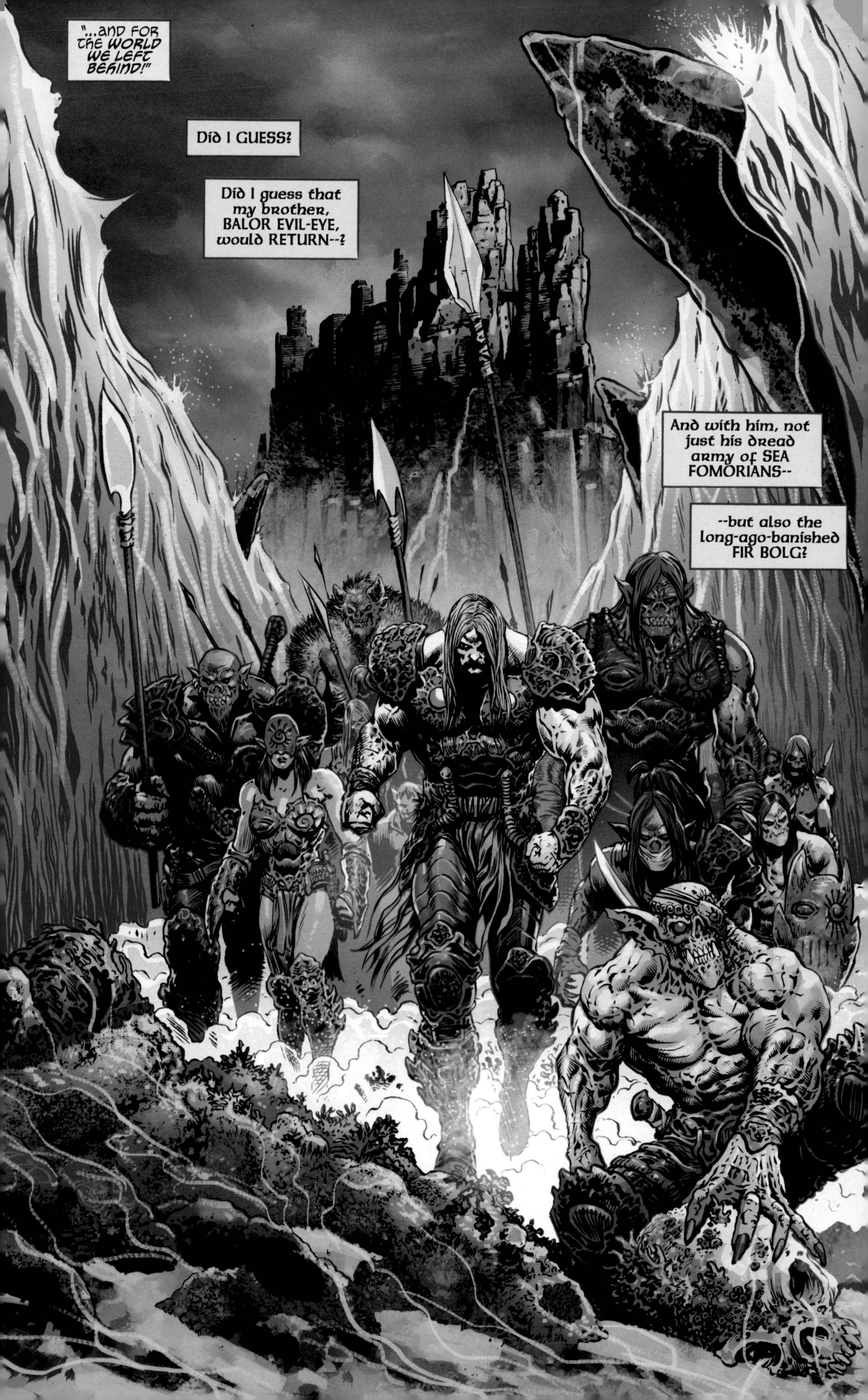
"...AND FOR THE WORLD WE LEFT BEHIND!"
Did I GUESS?
Did I guess that my brother, BALOR EVIL-EYE, would RETURN--?
And with him, not just his dread army of SEA FOMORIANS--
--but also the long-ago-banished FIR BOLG?

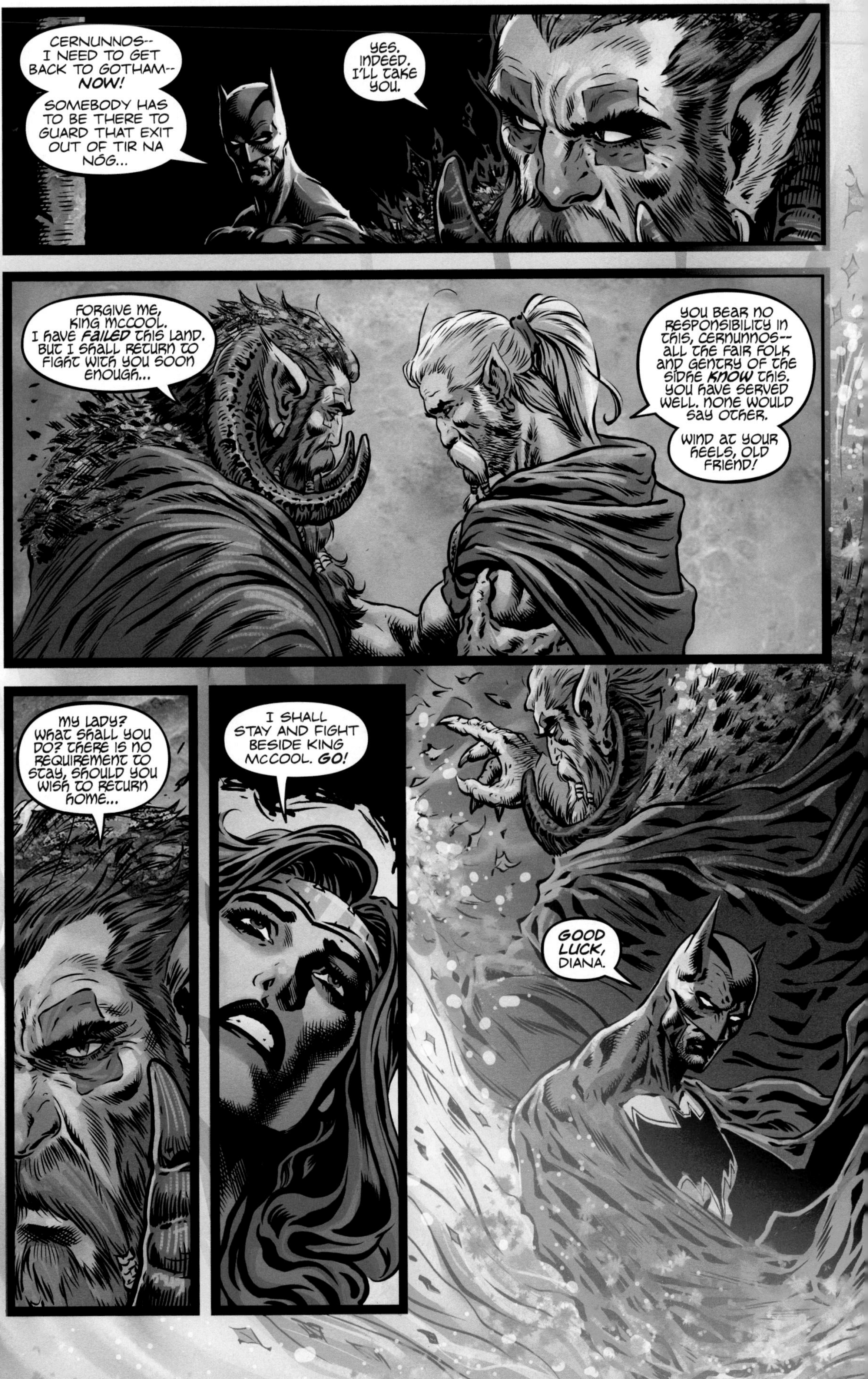
CERNUNNOS-- I NEED TO GET BACK TO GOTHAM-- NOW!
SOMEBODY HAS TO BE THERE TO GUARD THAT EXIT OUT OF TIR NA NÓG...
YES. INDEED. I'LL TAKE YOU.
FORGIVE ME, KING McCOOL. I HAVE FAILED THIS LAND. BUT I SHALL RETURN TO FIGHT WITH YOU SOON ENOUGH...
YOU BEAR NO RESPONSIBILITY IN THIS, CERNUNNOS-- ALL THE FAIR FOLK AND GENTRY OF THE SIDHE KNOW THIS. YOU HAVE SERVED WELL. NONE WOULD SAY OTHER.
WIND AT YOUR HEELS, OLD FRIEND!
MY LADY? WHAT SHALL YOU DO? THERE IS NO REQUIREMENT TO STAY, SHOULD YOU WISH TO RETURN HOME...
I SHALL STAY AND FIGHT BESIDE KING McCOOL. GO!
GOOD LUCK, DIANA.

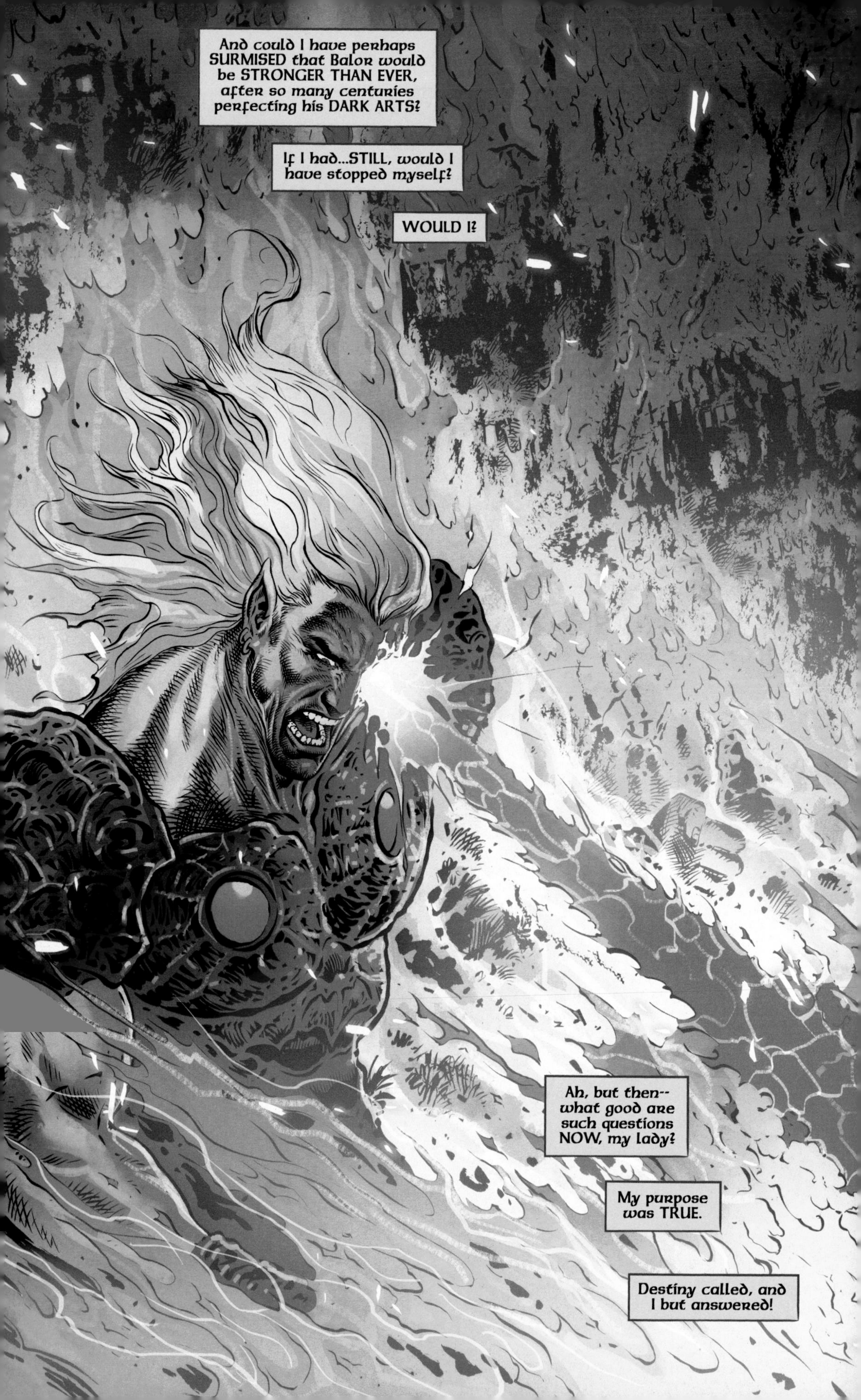
And could I have perhaps SURMISED that Balor would be STRONGER THAN EVER, after so many centuries perfecting his DARK ARTS?
If I had...STILL, would I have stopped myself?
WOULD I?
Ah, but then-- what good are such questions NOW, my lady?
My purpose was TRUE.
Destiny called, and I but answered!

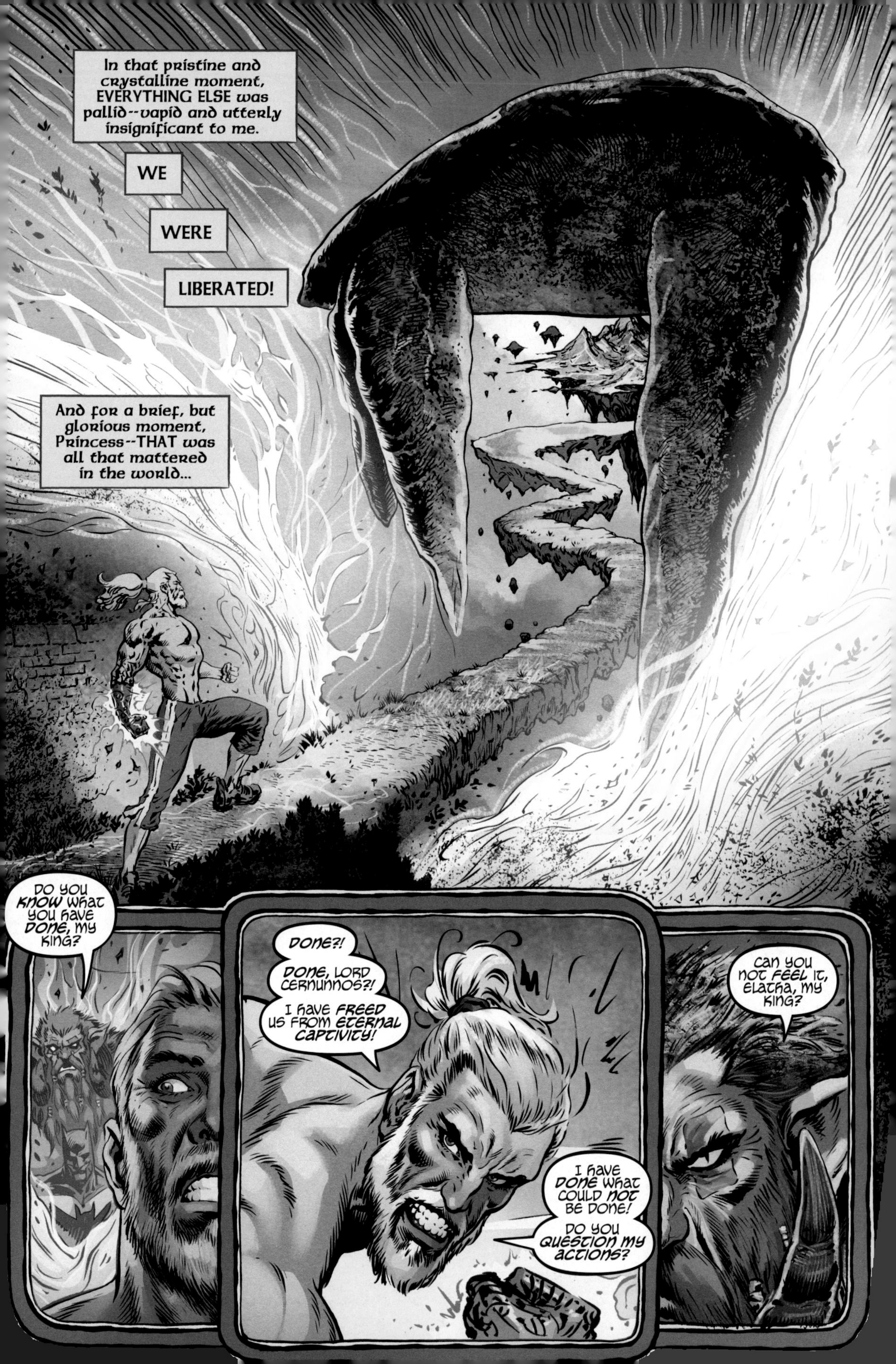
In that pristine and crystalline moment, EVERYTHING ELSE was pallid--vapid and utterly insignificant to me.
WE
WERE
LIBERATED!
And for a brief, but glorious moment, Princess--THAT was all that mattered in the world...
DO YOU KNOW WHAT YOU HAVE DONE, MY KING?
DONE?!
DONE, LORD CERNUNNOS?!
I HAVE FREED US FROM ETERNAL CAPTIVITY!
I HAVE DONE WHAT COULD NOT BE DONE!
DO YOU QUESTION MY ACTIONS?
CAN YOU NOT FEEL IT, ELATHA, MY KING?

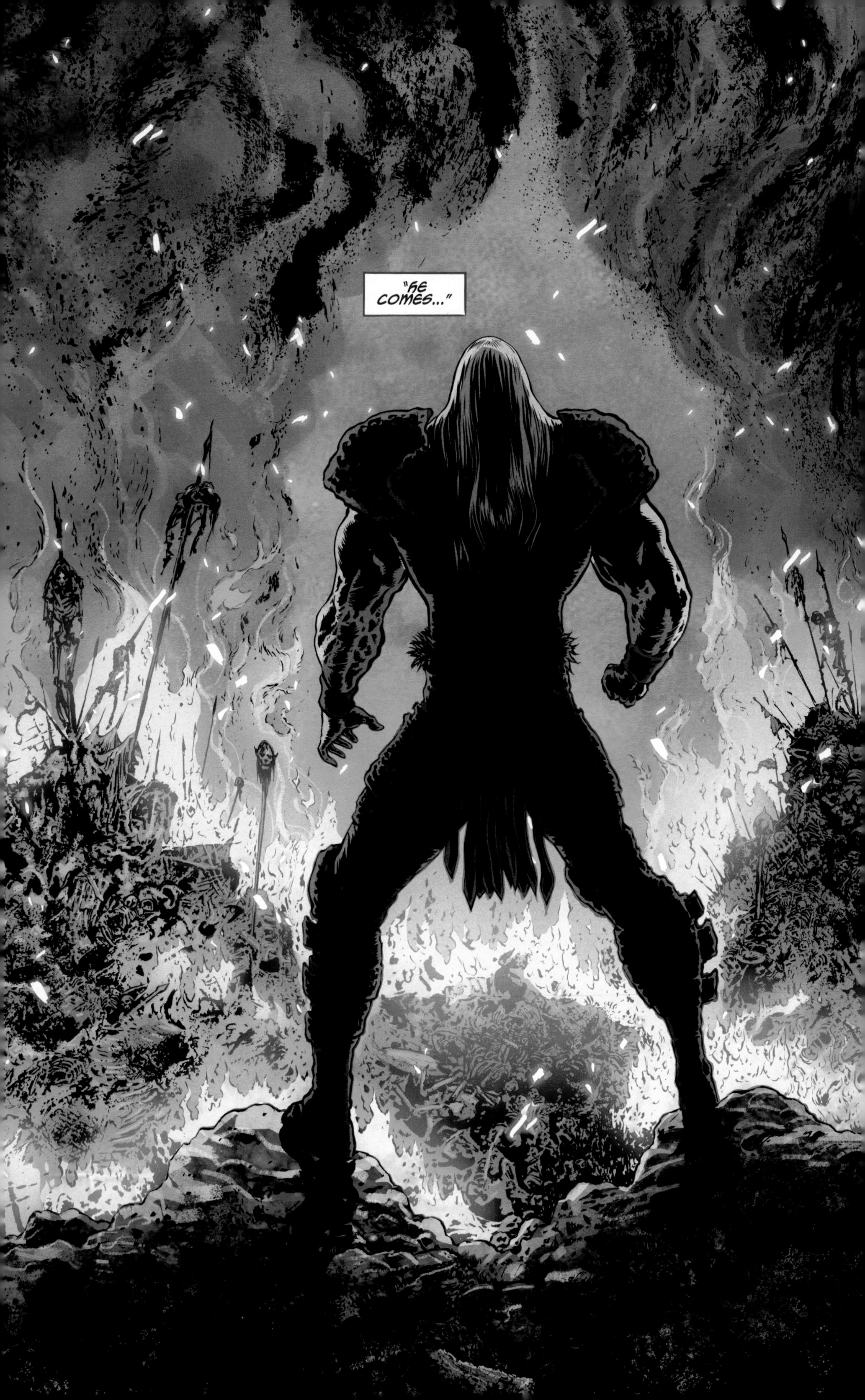
"HE COMES..."

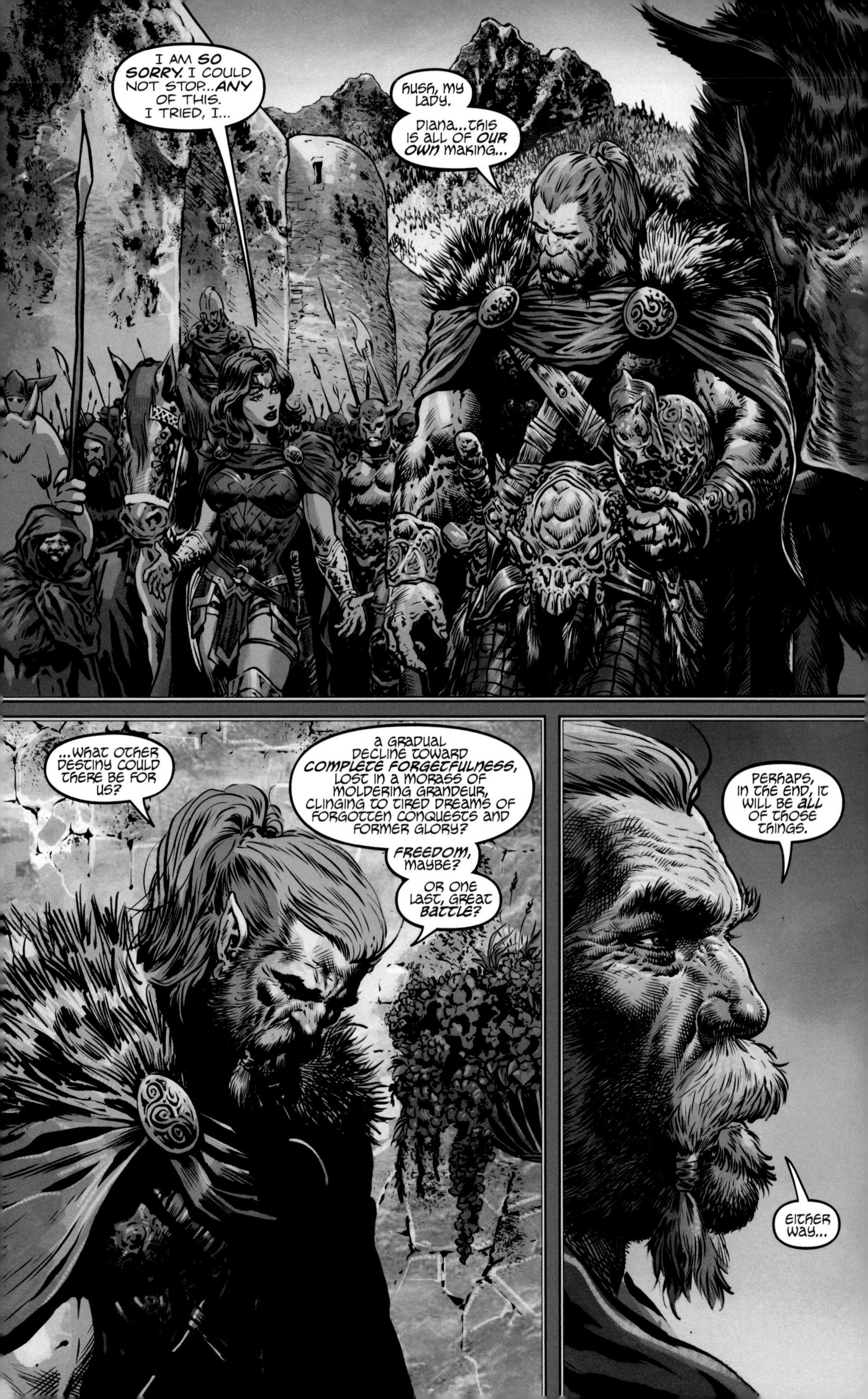
I AM SO SORRY. I COULD NOT STOP...ANY OF THIS. I TRIED, I...
HUSH, MY LADY.
DIANA...THIS IS ALL OF OUR OWN MAKING...
...WHAT OTHER DESTINY COULD THERE BE FOR US?
A GRADUAL DECLINE TOWARD COMPLETE FORGETFULNESS, LOST IN A MORASS OF MOLDERING GRANDEUR, CLINGING TO TIRED DREAMS OF FORGOTTEN CONQUESTS AND FORMER GLORY?
FREEDOM, MAYBE?
OR ONE LAST, GREAT BATTLE?
PERHAPS, IN THE END, IT WILL BE ALL OF THOSE THINGS.
EITHER WAY...

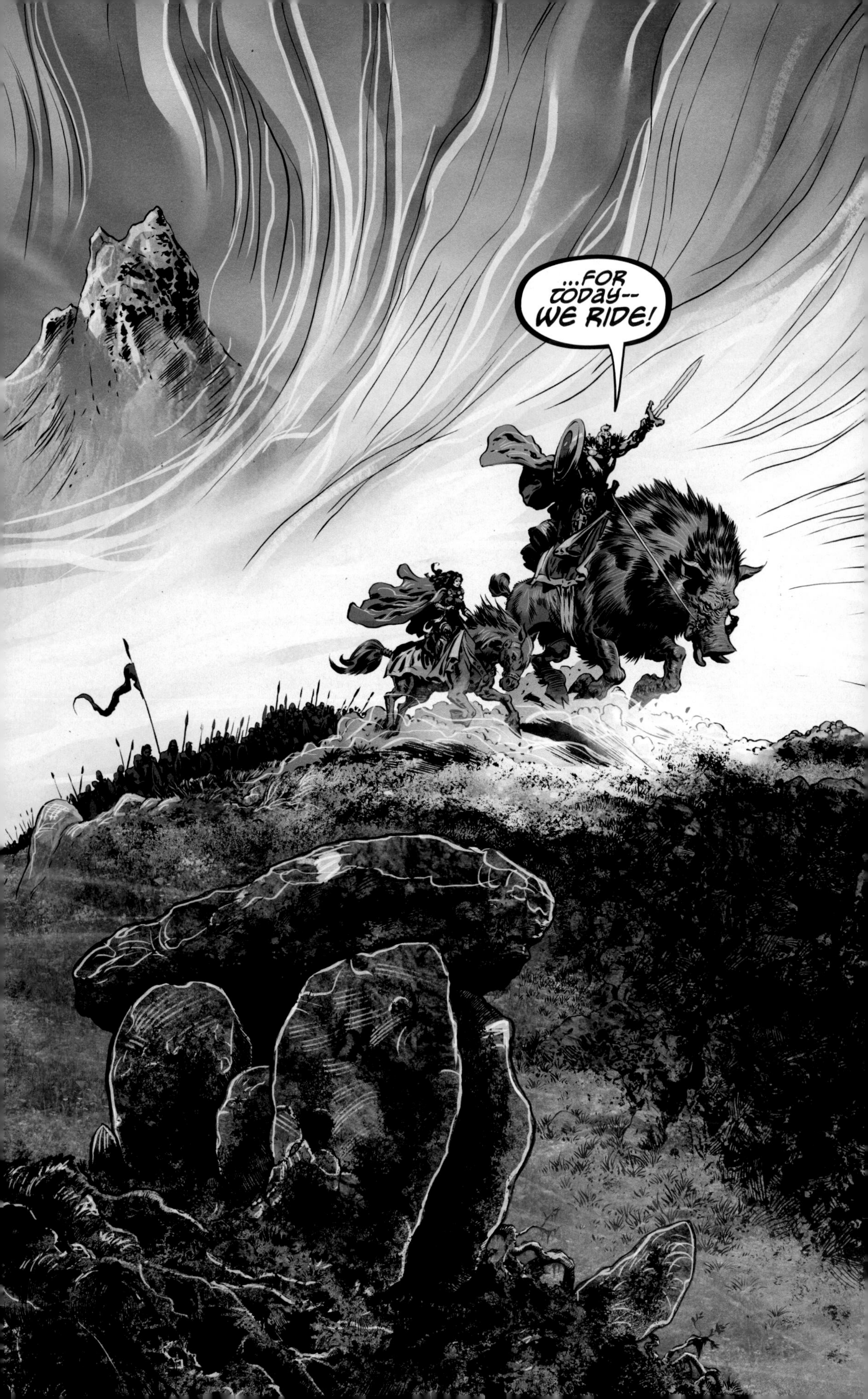
...FOR TODAY-- WE RIDE!

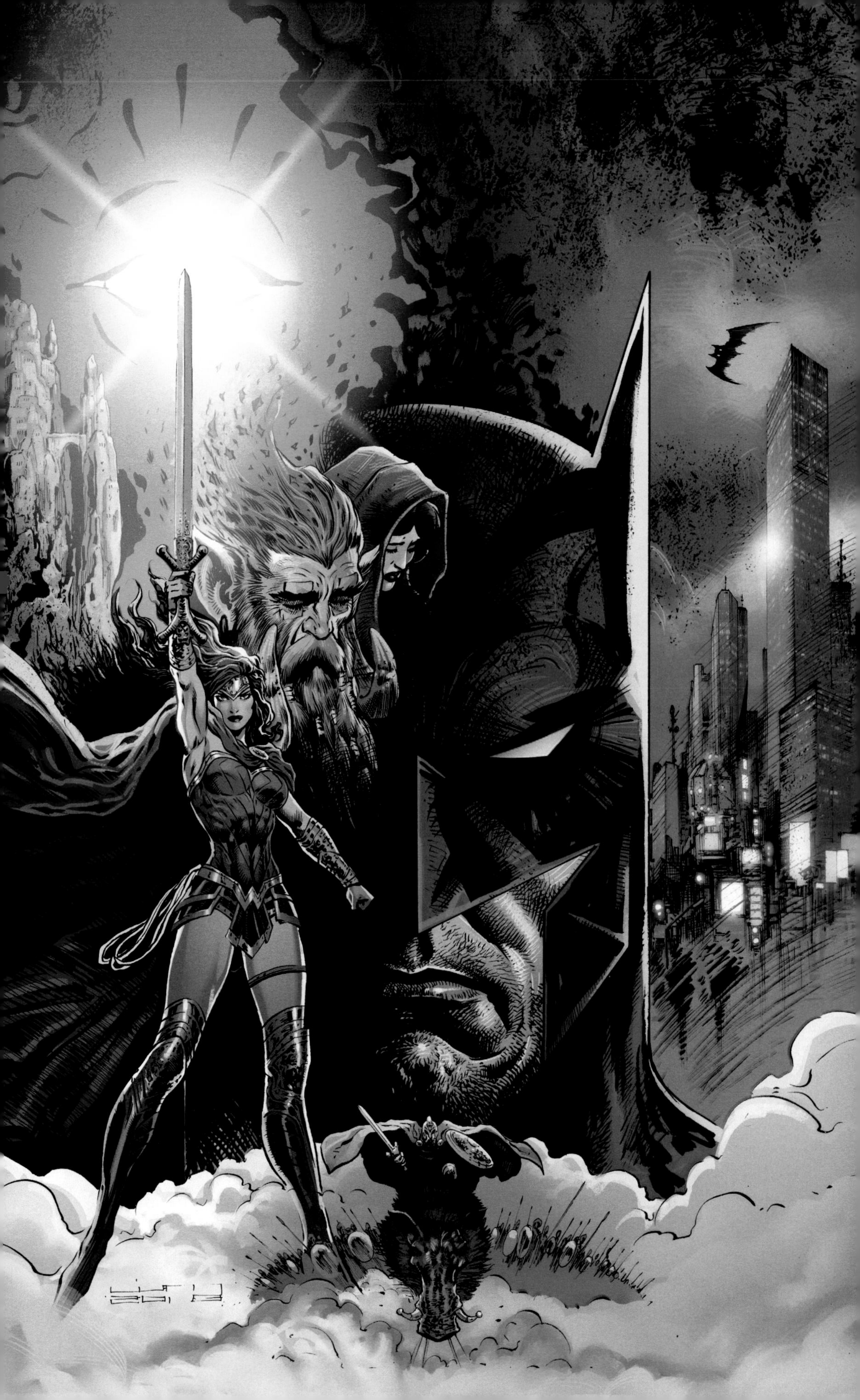

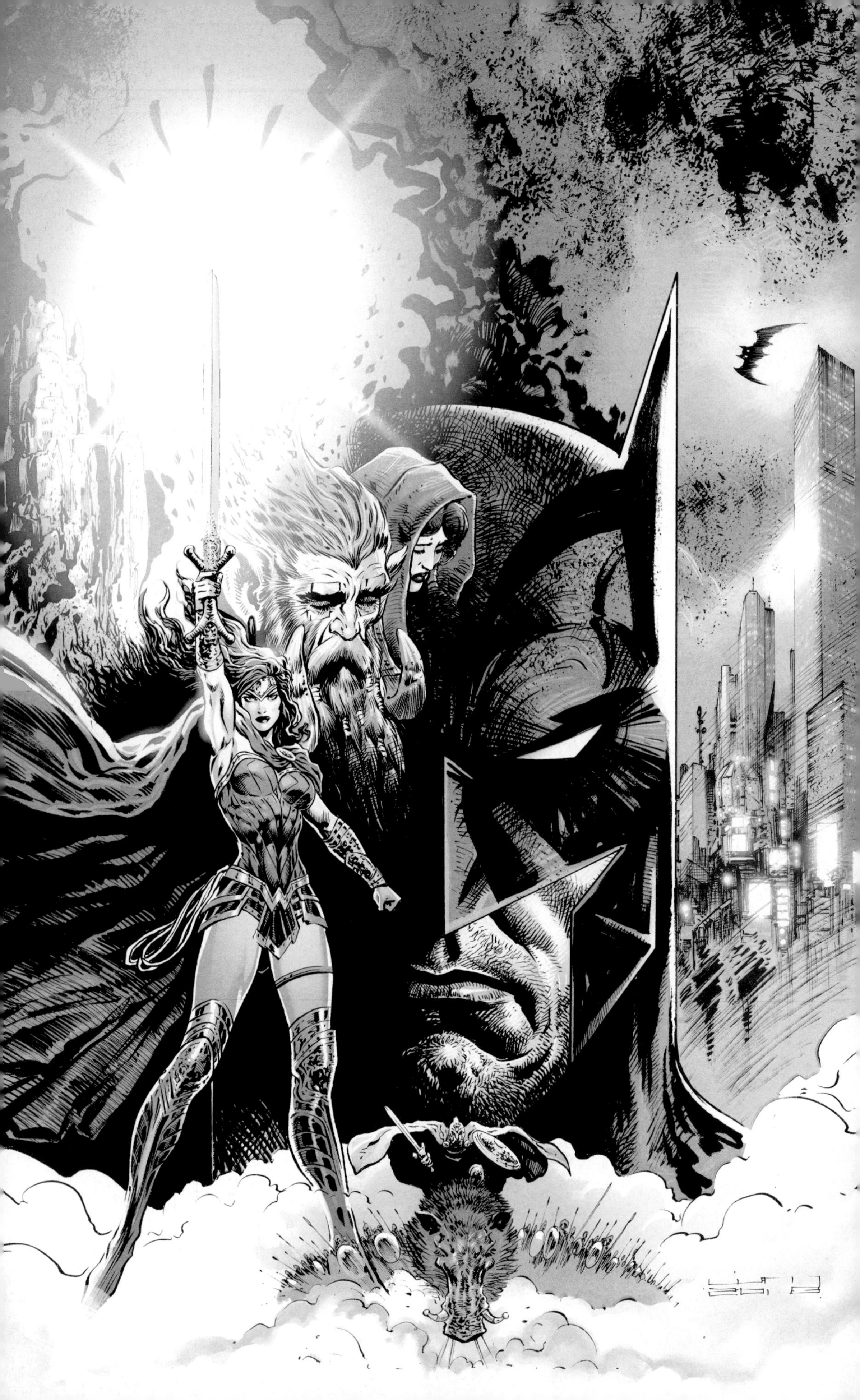

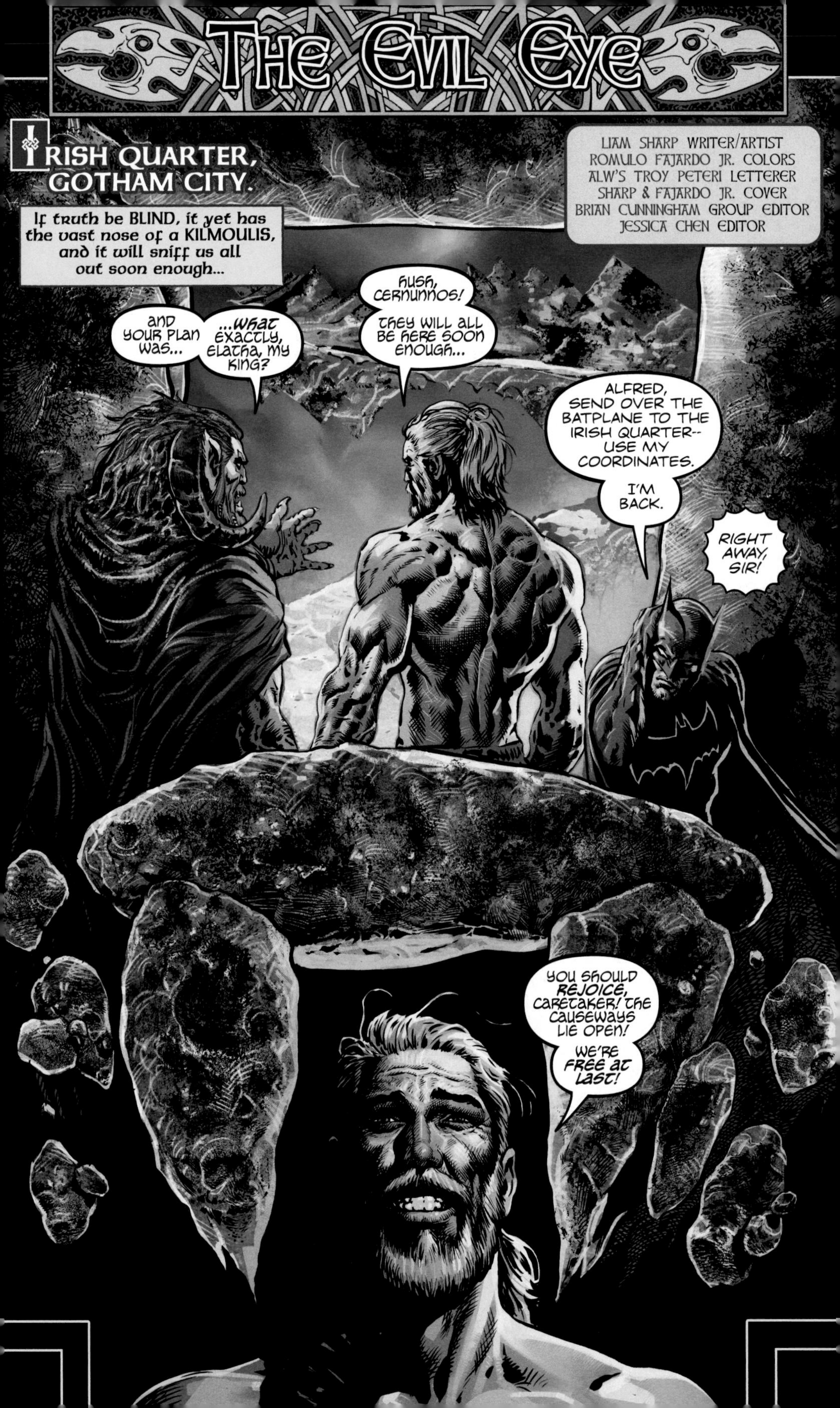
THE EVIL EYE
IRISH QUARTER, GOTHAM CITY.
LIAM SHARP WRITER/ARTIST
ROMULO FAJARDO JR. COLORS
ALW'S TROY PETERI LETTERER
SHARP & FAJARDO JR. COVER
BRIAN CUNNINGHAM GROUP EDITOR
JESSICA CHEN EDITOR
If truth be BLIND, it yet has the vast nose of a KILMOULIS, and it will sniff us all out soon enough...
AND YOUR PLAN WAS...
...WHAT EXACTLY, ELATHA, MY KING?
HUSH, CERNUNNOS!
THEY WILL ALL BE HERE SOON ENOUGH...
ALFRED, SEND OVER THE BATPLANE TO THE IRISH QUARTER-- USE MY COORDINATES.
I'M BACK.
RIGHT AWAY, SIR!
YOU SHOULD REJOICE, CARETAKER! THE CAUSEWAYS LIE OPEN!
WE'RE FREE AT LAST!

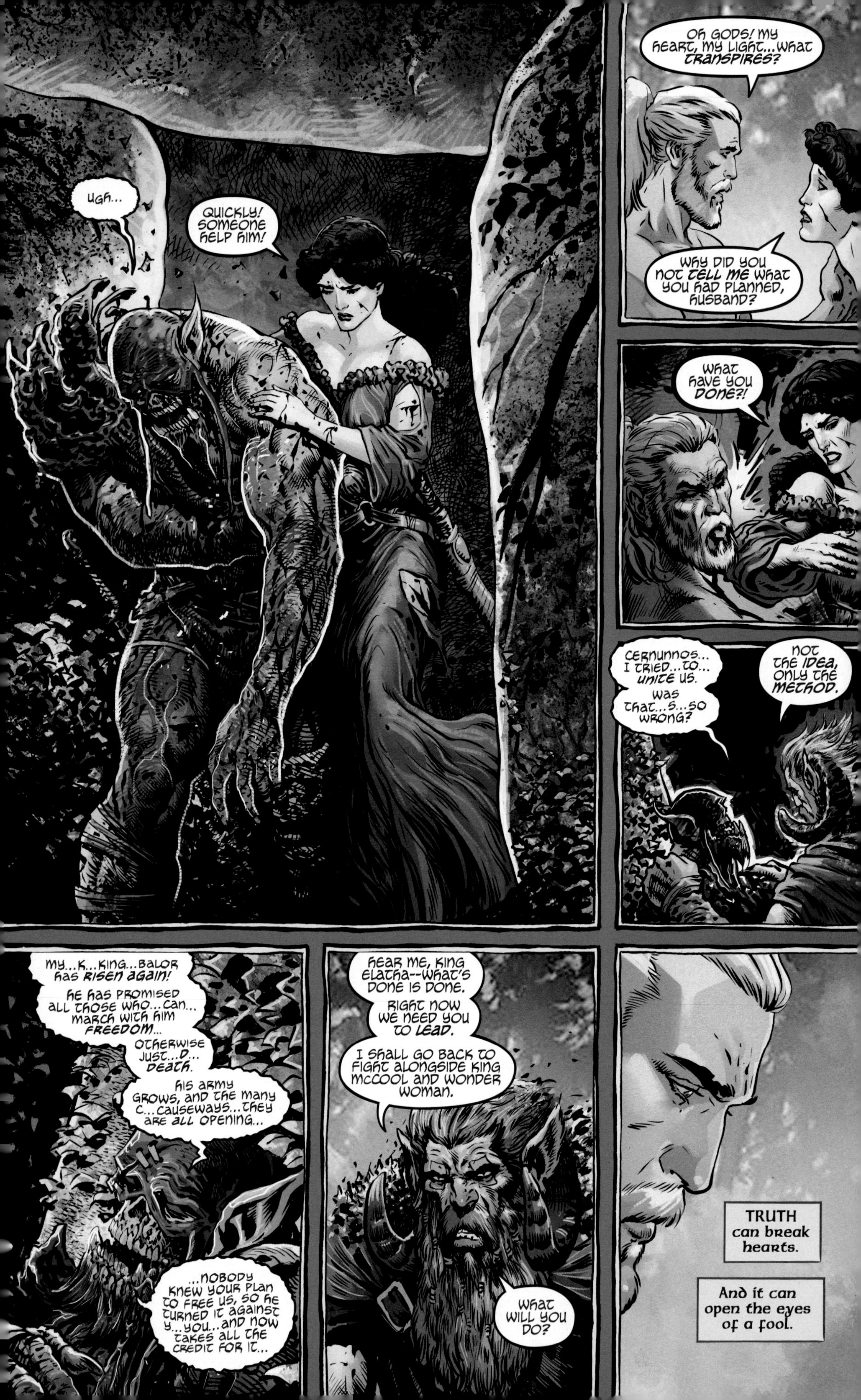

UGH...
QUICKLY! SOMEONE HELP HIM!
OH GODS! MY HEART, MY LIGHT...WHAT TRANSPIRES?
WHY DID YOU NOT TELL ME WHAT YOU HAD PLANNED, HUSBAND?
WHAT HAVE YOU DONE?!
CERNUNNOS... I TRIED...TO... UNITE US.
WAS THAT...S...SO WRONG?
NOT THE IDEA, ONLY THE METHOD.
MY...K...KING...BALOR HAS RISEN AGAIN!
HE HAS PROMISED ALL THOSE WHO...CAN... MARCH WITH HIM FREEDOM...
OTHERWISE JUST...D... DEATH.
HIS ARMY GROWS, AND THE MANY C...CAUSEWAYS...THEY ARE ALL OPENING...
...NOBODY KNEW YOUR PLAN TO FREE US, SO HE TURNED IT AGAINST Y...YOU...AND NOW TAKES ALL THE CREDIT FOR IT...
HEAR ME, KING ELATHA--WHAT'S DONE IS DONE.
RIGHT NOW WE NEED YOU TO LEAD.
I SHALL GO BACK TO FIGHT ALONGSIDE KING McCOOL AND WONDER WOMAN.
WHAT WILL YOU DO?
TRUTH can break hearts.
And it can open the eyes of a fool.

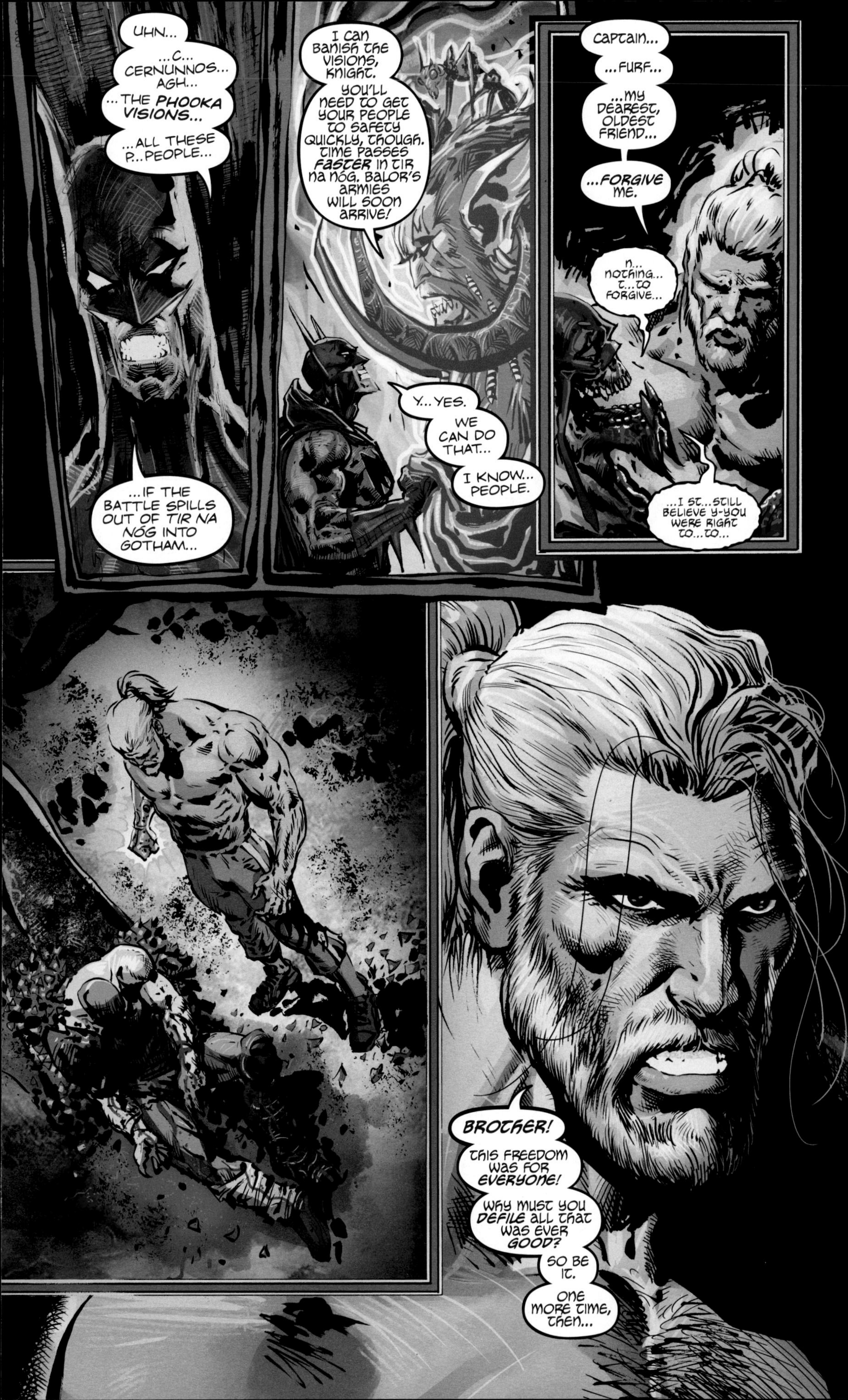
UHN...
...C... CERNUNNOS... AGH...
...THE PHOOKA VISIONS...
...ALL THESE P...PEOPLE...
...IF THE BATTLE SPILLS OUT OF TIR NA NÓG INTO GOTHAM...
I CAN BANISH THE VISIONS, KNIGHT.
YOU'LL NEED TO GET YOUR PEOPLE TO SAFETY QUICKLY, THOUGH. TIME PASSES FASTER IN TIR NA NÓG. BALOR'S ARMIES WILL SOON ARRIVE!
Y...YES.
WE CAN DO THAT...
I KNOW... PEOPLE.
CAPTAIN...
...FURF...
...MY DEAREST, OLDEST FRIEND...
...FORGIVE ME.
N... NOTHING... T...TO FORGIVE...
...I ST...STILL BELIEVE Y-YOU WERE RIGHT TO...TO...
BROTHER!
THIS FREEDOM WAS FOR EVERYONE!
WHY MUST YOU DEFILE ALL THAT WAS EVER GOOD?
SO BE IT.
ONE MORE TIME, THEN...

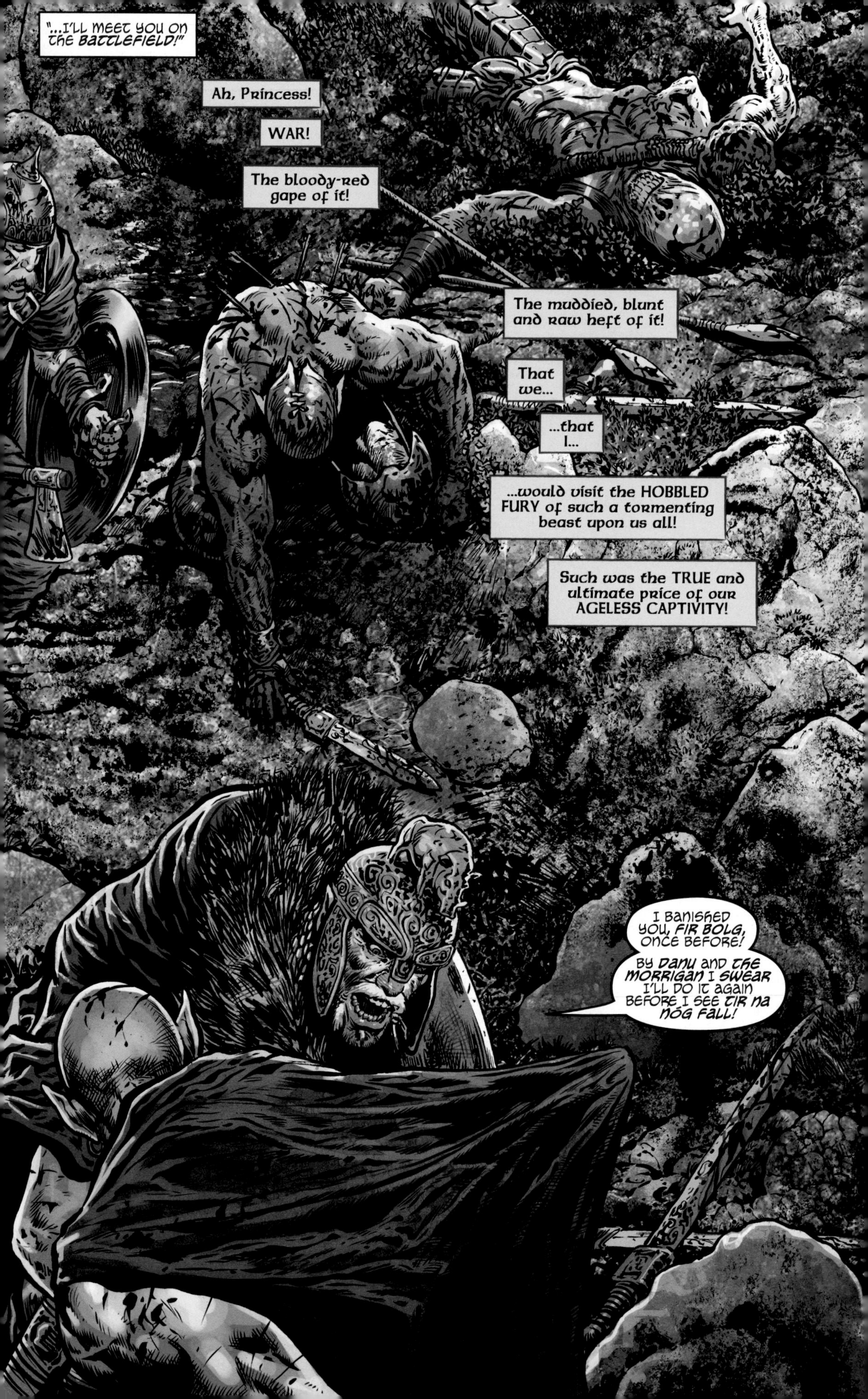
"...I'LL MEET YOU ON THE BATTLEFIELD!"
Ah, Princess!
WAR!
The bloody-red gape of it!
The muddied, blunt and raw heft of it!
That we...
...that I...
...would visit the HOBBLED FURY of such a tormenting beast upon us all!
Such was the TRUE and ultimate price of our AGELESS CAPTIVITY!
I BANISHED YOU, FIR BOLG, ONCE BEFORE!
BY DANU AND THE MORRIGAN I SWEAR I'LL DO IT AGAIN BEFORE I SEE TIR NA NÓG FALL!

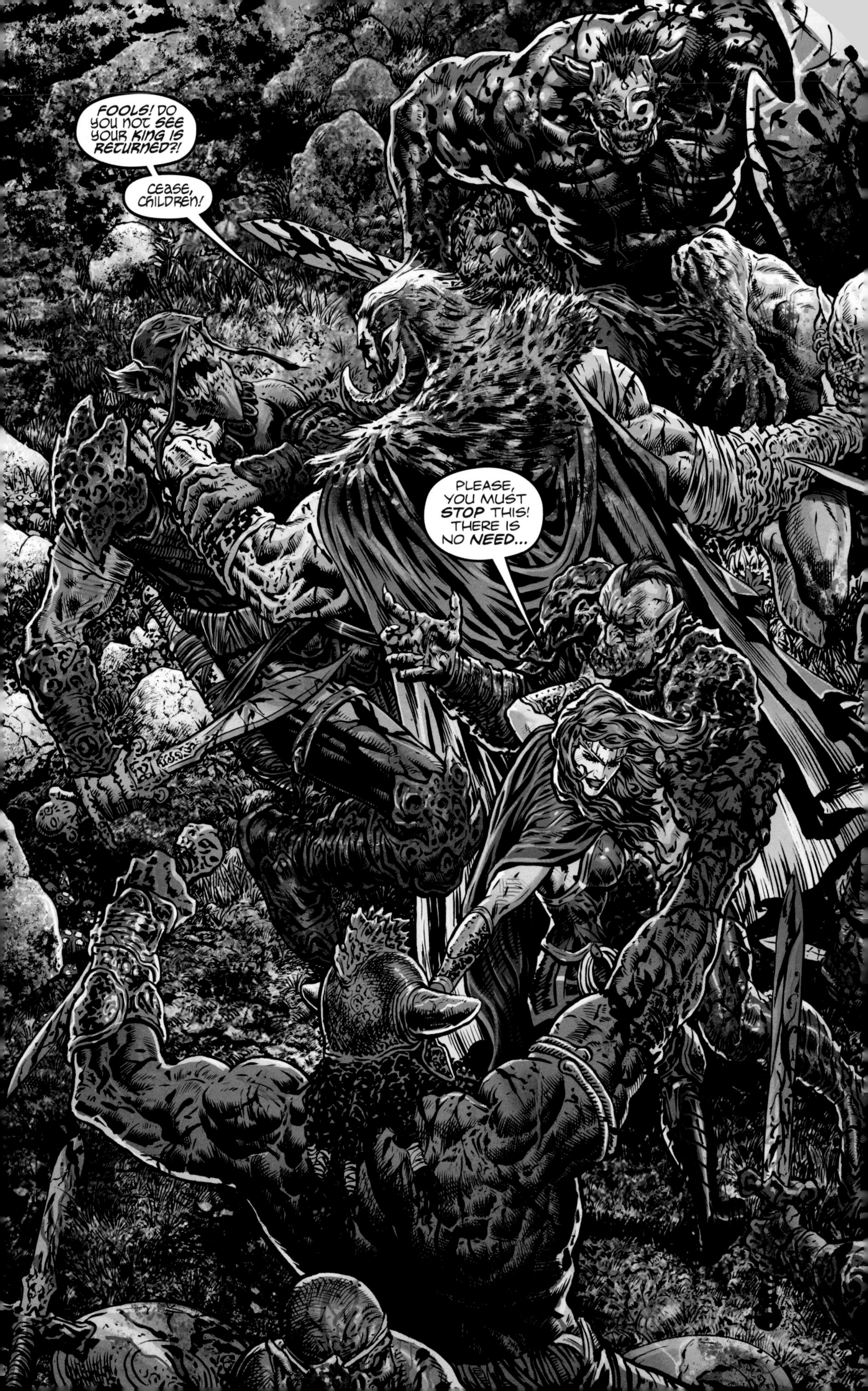
FOOLS! DO YOU NOT SEE YOUR KING IS RETURNED?!
CEASE, CHILDREN!
PLEASE, YOU MUST STOP THIS! THERE IS NO NEED...

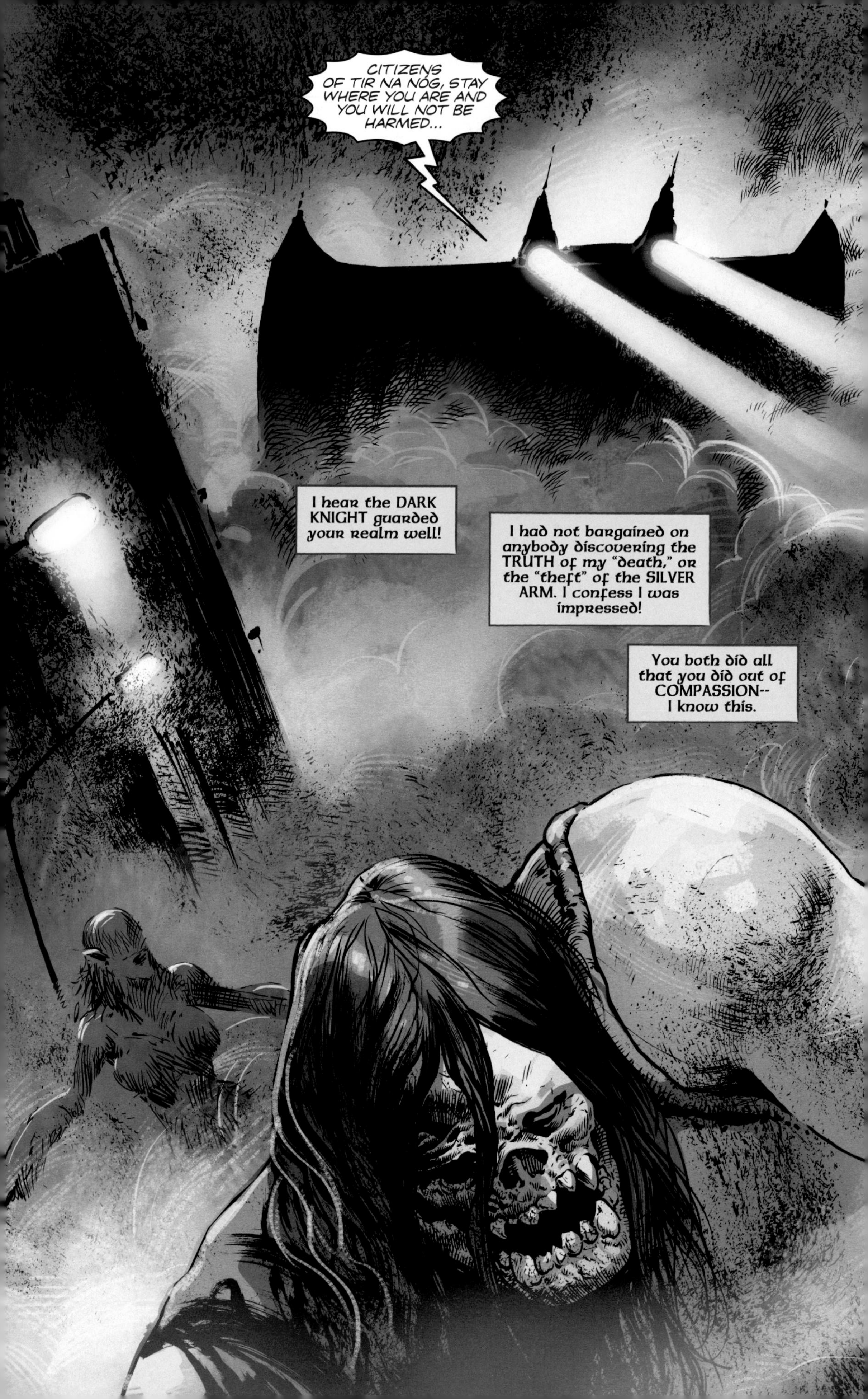
CITIZENS OF TIR NA NÓG, STAY WHERE YOU ARE AND YOU WILL NOT BE HARMED...
I hear the DARK KNIGHT guarded your realm well!
I had not bargained on anybody discovering the TRUTH of my "death," or the "theft" of the SILVER ARM. I confess I was impressed!
You both did all that you did out of COMPASSION-- I know this.

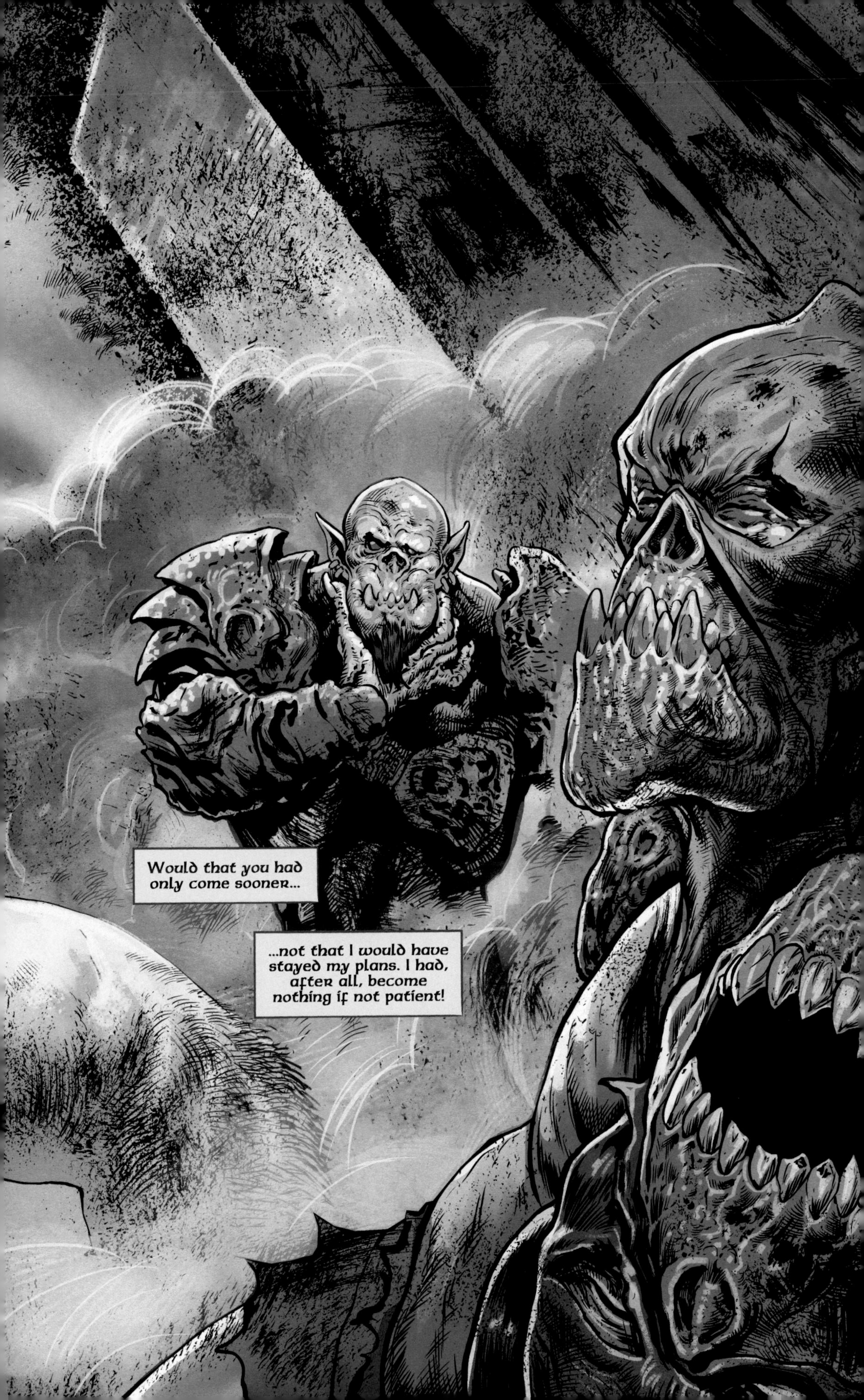
Would that you had only come sooner...
...not that I would have stayed my plans. I had, after all, become nothing if not patient!

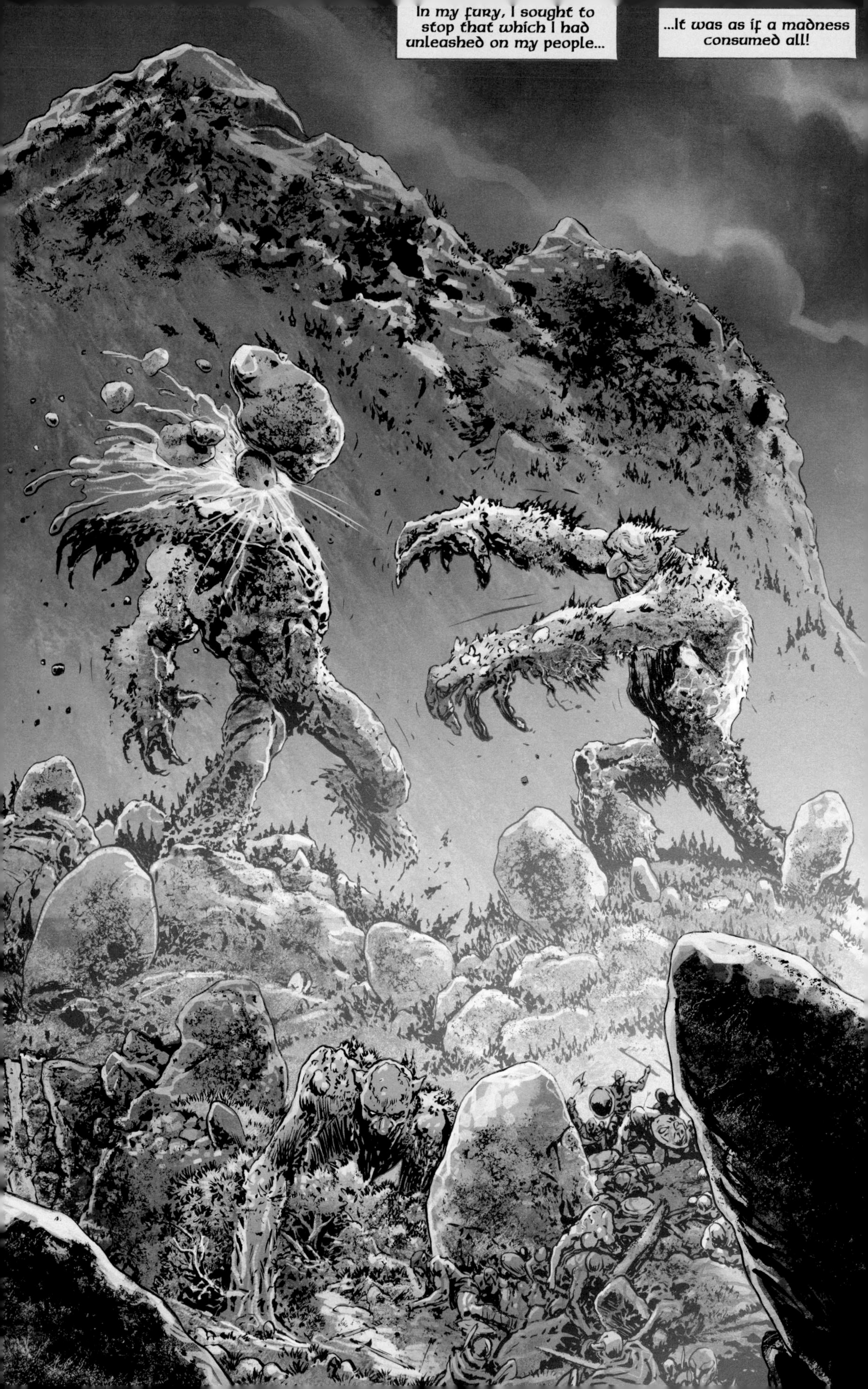
In my fury, I sought to stop that which I had unleashed on my people...
...It was as if a madness consumed all!

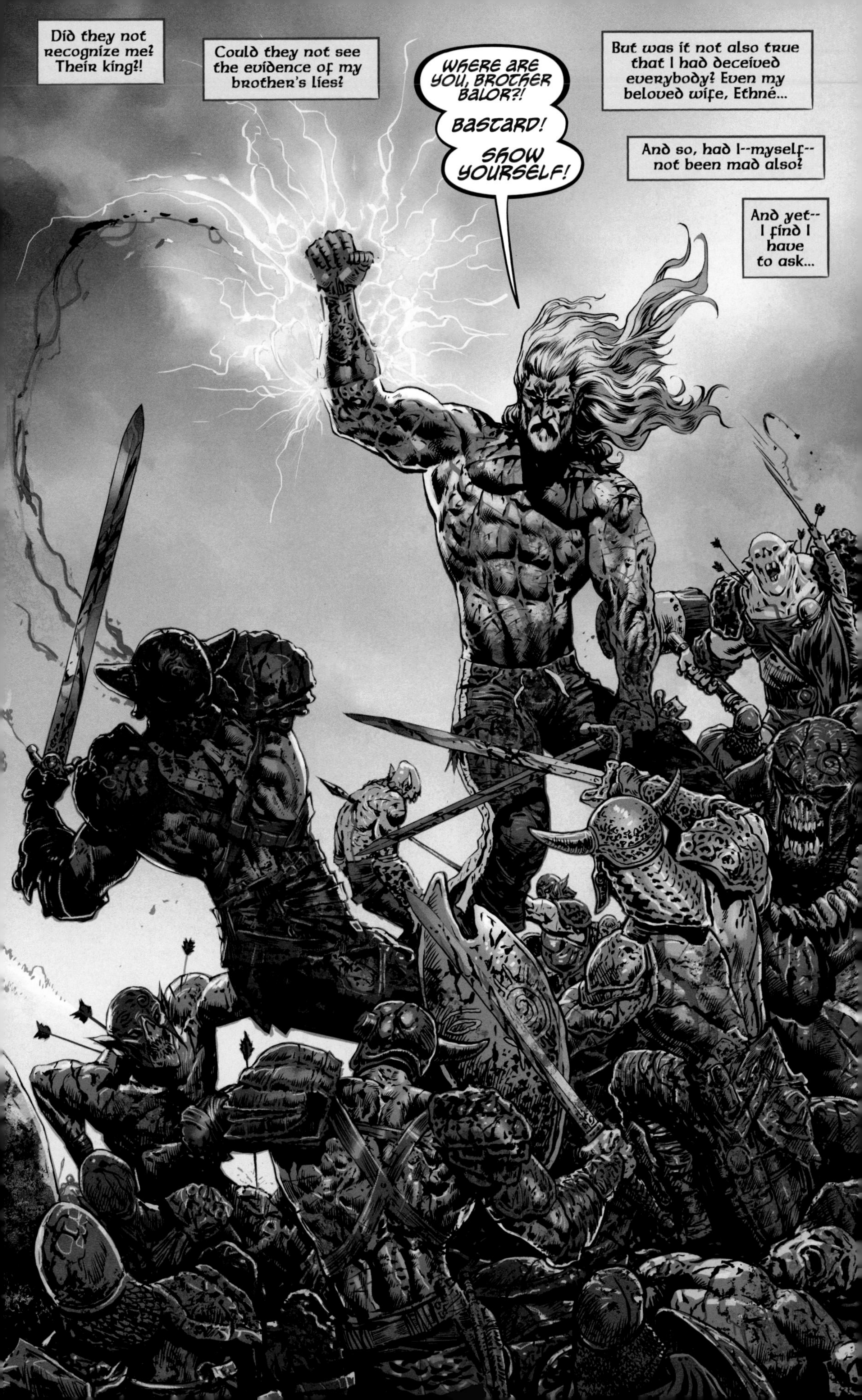

Did they not recognize me? Their king?!
Could they not see the evidence of my brother's lies?
WHERE ARE YOU, BROTHER BALOR?!
BASTARD!
SHOW YOURSELF!
But was it not also true that I had deceived everybody? Even my beloved wife, Ethné...
And so, had I--myself--not been mad also?
And yet--I find I have to ask...

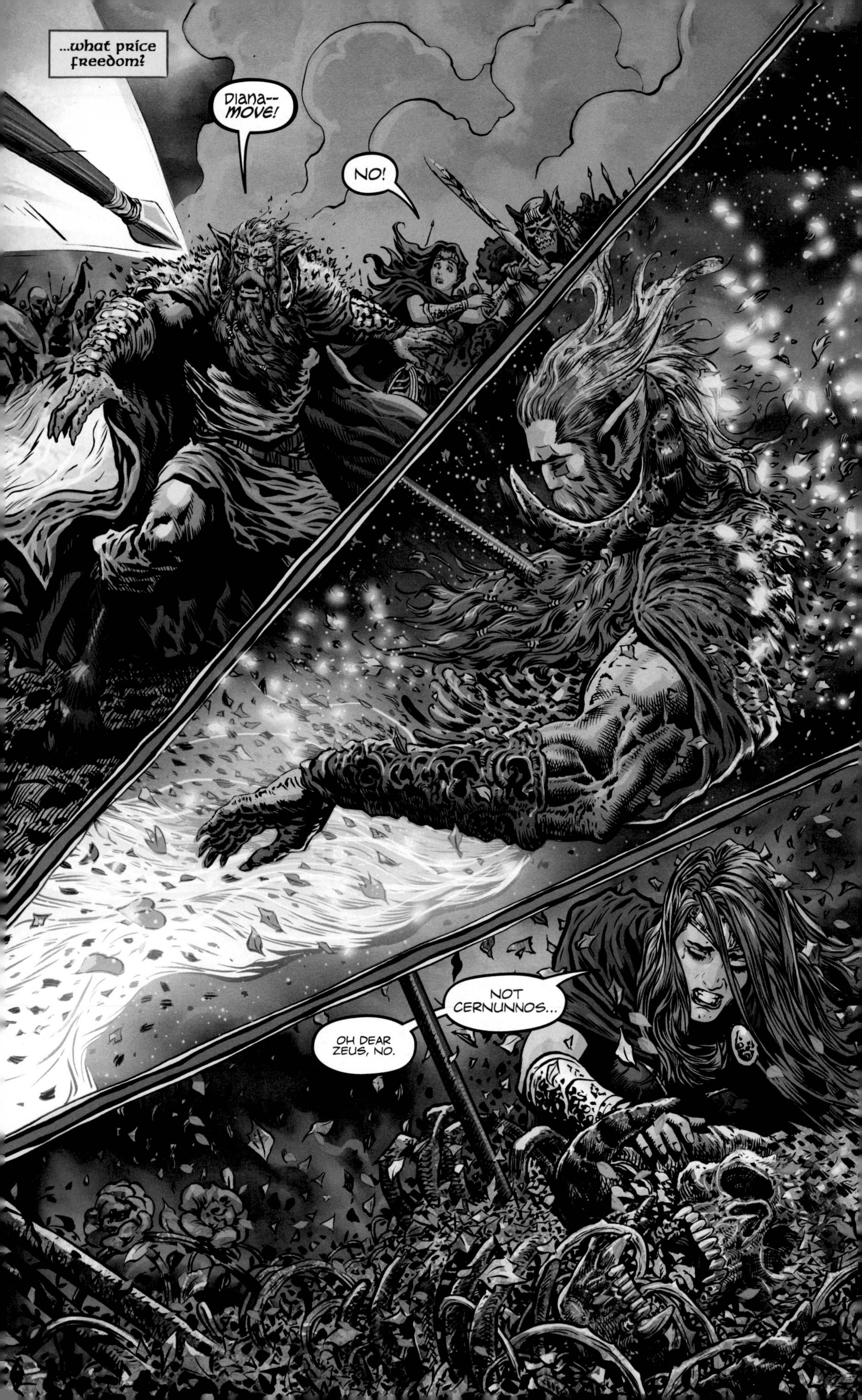
...what price freedom?
DIANA--
MOVE!
NO!
NOT CERNUNNOS...
OH DEAR ZEUS, NO.

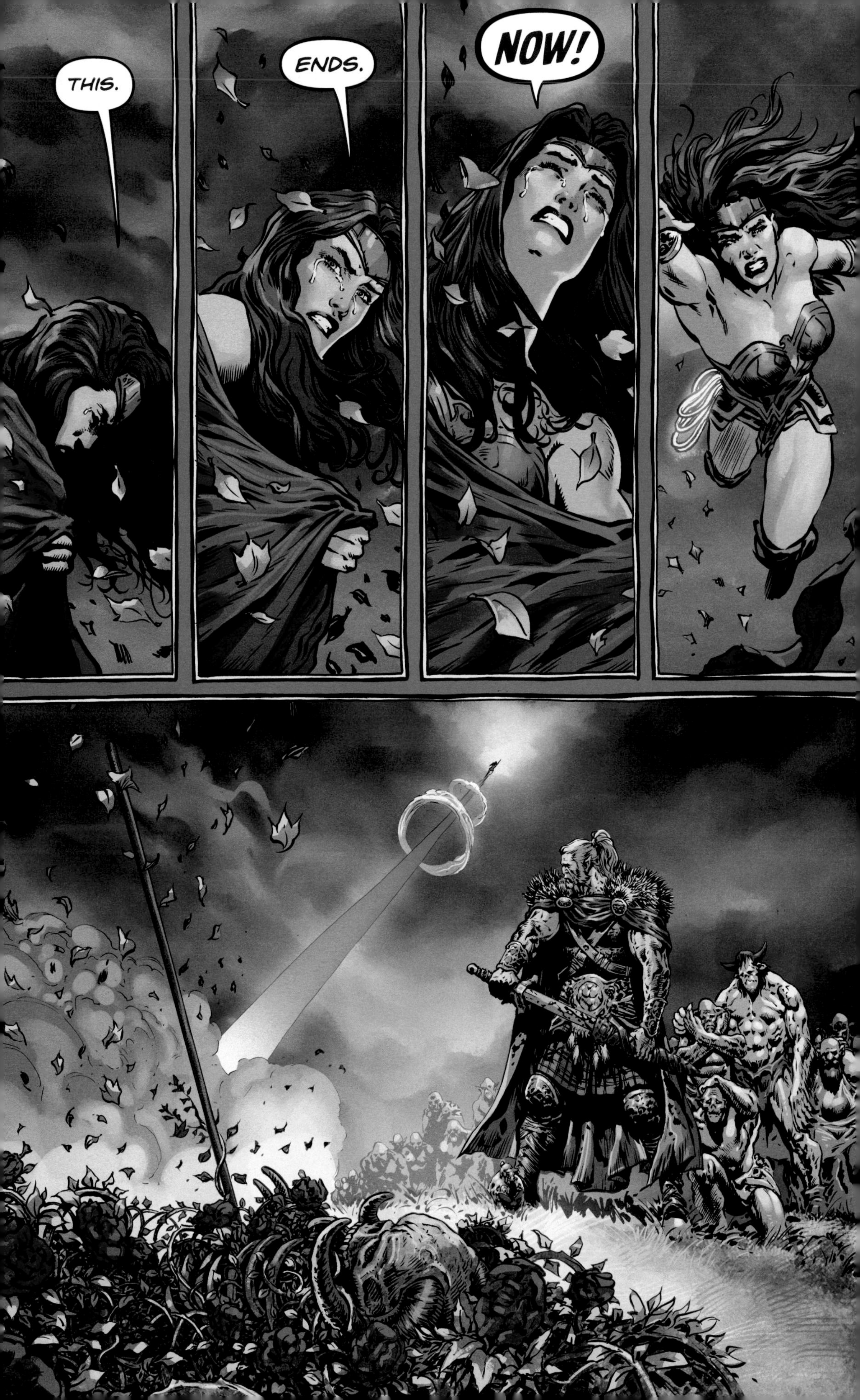
THIS.
ENDS.
NOW!

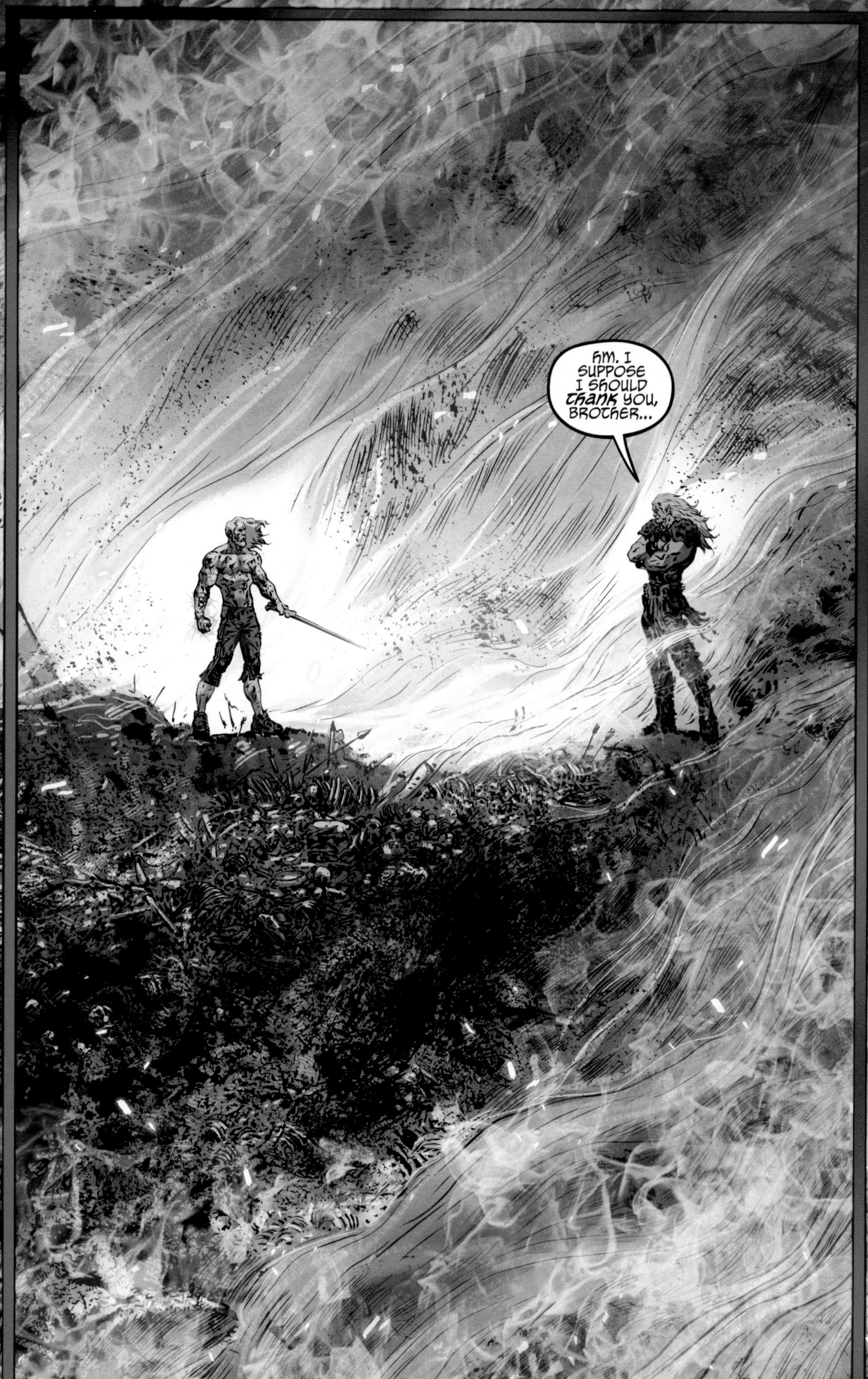
HM. I SUPPOSE I SHOULD *THANK* YOU, BROTHER...

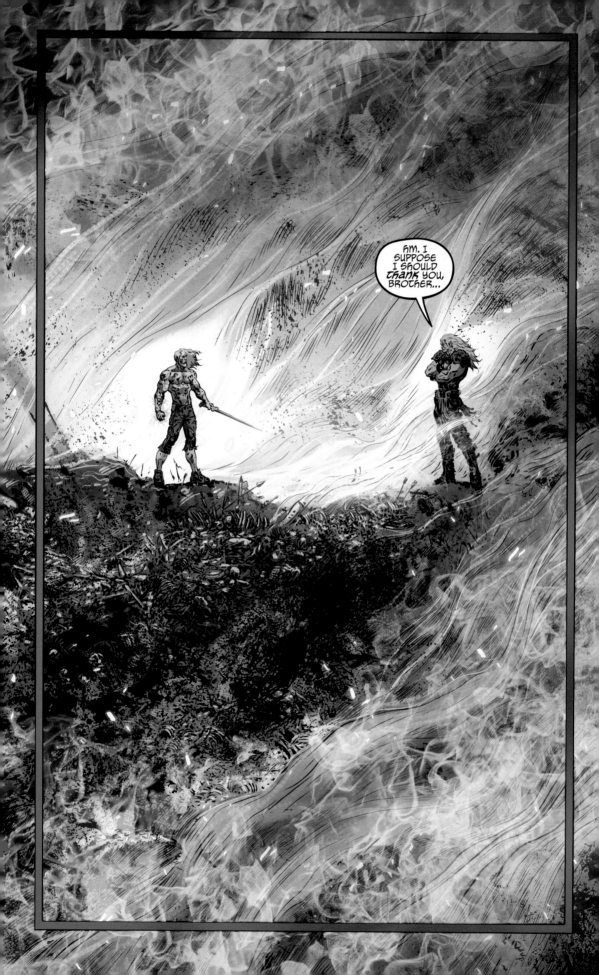

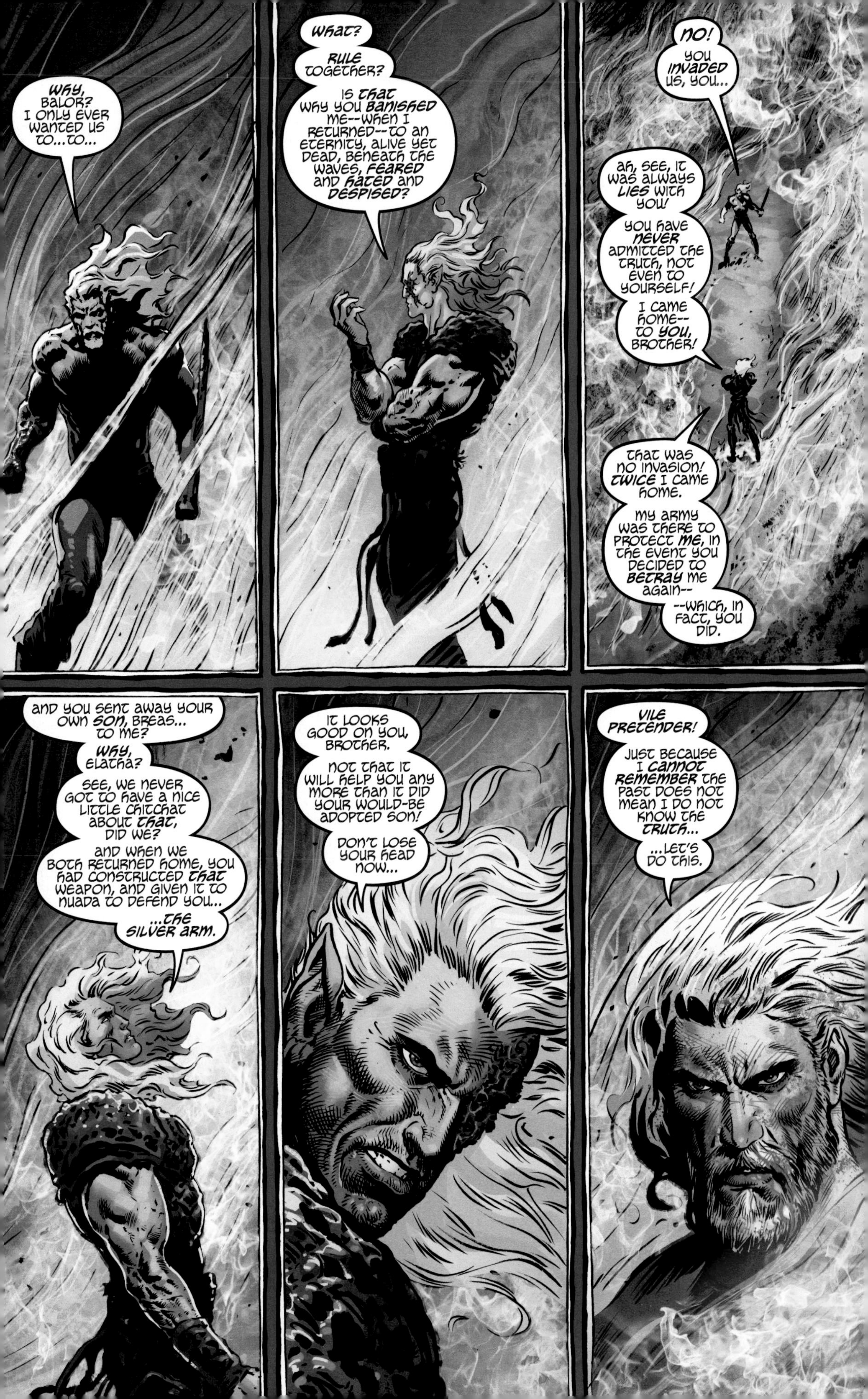
WHY, BALOR? I ONLY EVER WANTED US TO...TO...
WHAT?
RULE TOGETHER?
IS THAT WHY YOU BANISHED ME--WHEN I RETURNED--TO AN ETERNITY, ALIVE YET DEAD, BENEATH THE WAVES, FEARED AND HATED AND DESPISED?
NO!
YOU INVADED US, YOU...
AH, SEE, IT WAS ALWAYS LIES WITH YOU!
YOU HAVE NEVER ADMITTED THE TRUTH, NOT EVEN TO YOURSELF!
I CAME HOME--TO YOU, BROTHER!
THAT WAS NO INVASION! TWICE I CAME HOME.
MY ARMY WAS THERE TO PROTECT ME, IN THE EVENT YOU DECIDED TO BETRAY ME AGAIN--
--WHICH, IN FACT, YOU DID.
AND YOU SENT AWAY YOUR OWN SON, BREAS... TO ME?
WHY, ELATHA?
SEE, WE NEVER GOT TO HAVE A NICE LITTLE CHITCHAT ABOUT THAT, DID WE?
AND WHEN WE BOTH RETURNED HOME, YOU HAD CONSTRUCTED THAT WEAPON, AND GIVEN IT TO NUADA TO DEFEND YOU...
...THE SILVER ARM.
IT LOOKS GOOD ON YOU, BROTHER.
NOT THAT IT WILL HELP YOU ANY MORE THAN IT DID YOUR WOULD-BE ADOPTED SON!
DON'T LOSE YOUR HEAD NOW...
VILE PRETENDER!
JUST BECAUSE I CANNOT REMEMBER THE PAST DOES NOT MEAN I DO NOT KNOW THE TRUTH...
...LET'S DO THIS.

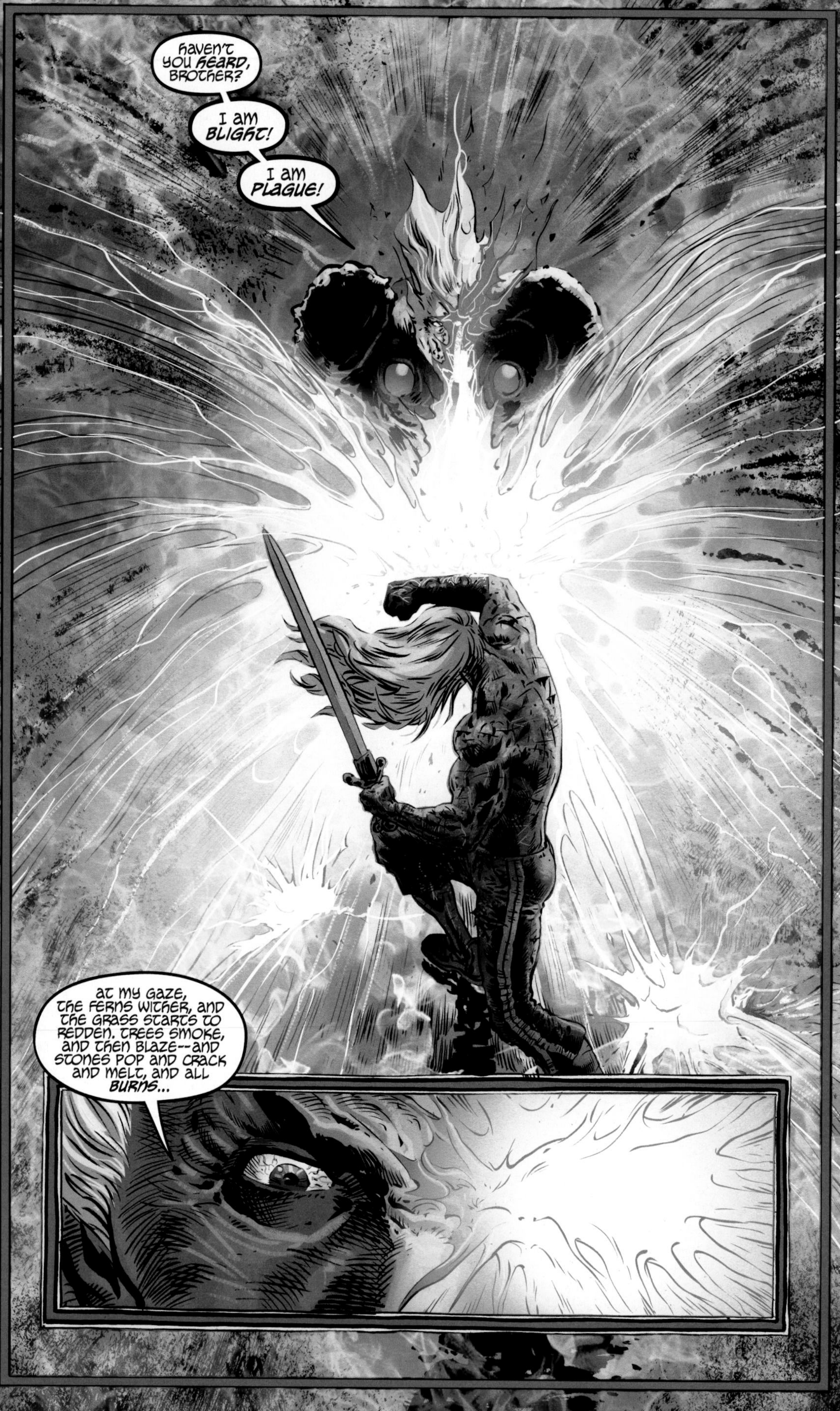
HAVEN'T YOU HEARD, BROTHER?
I AM BLIGHT!
I AM PLAGUE!
AT MY GAZE, THE FERNS WITHER, AND THE GRASS STARTS TO REDDEN. TREES SMOKE, AND THEN BLAZE--AND STONES POP AND CRACK AND MELT, AND ALL BURNS...

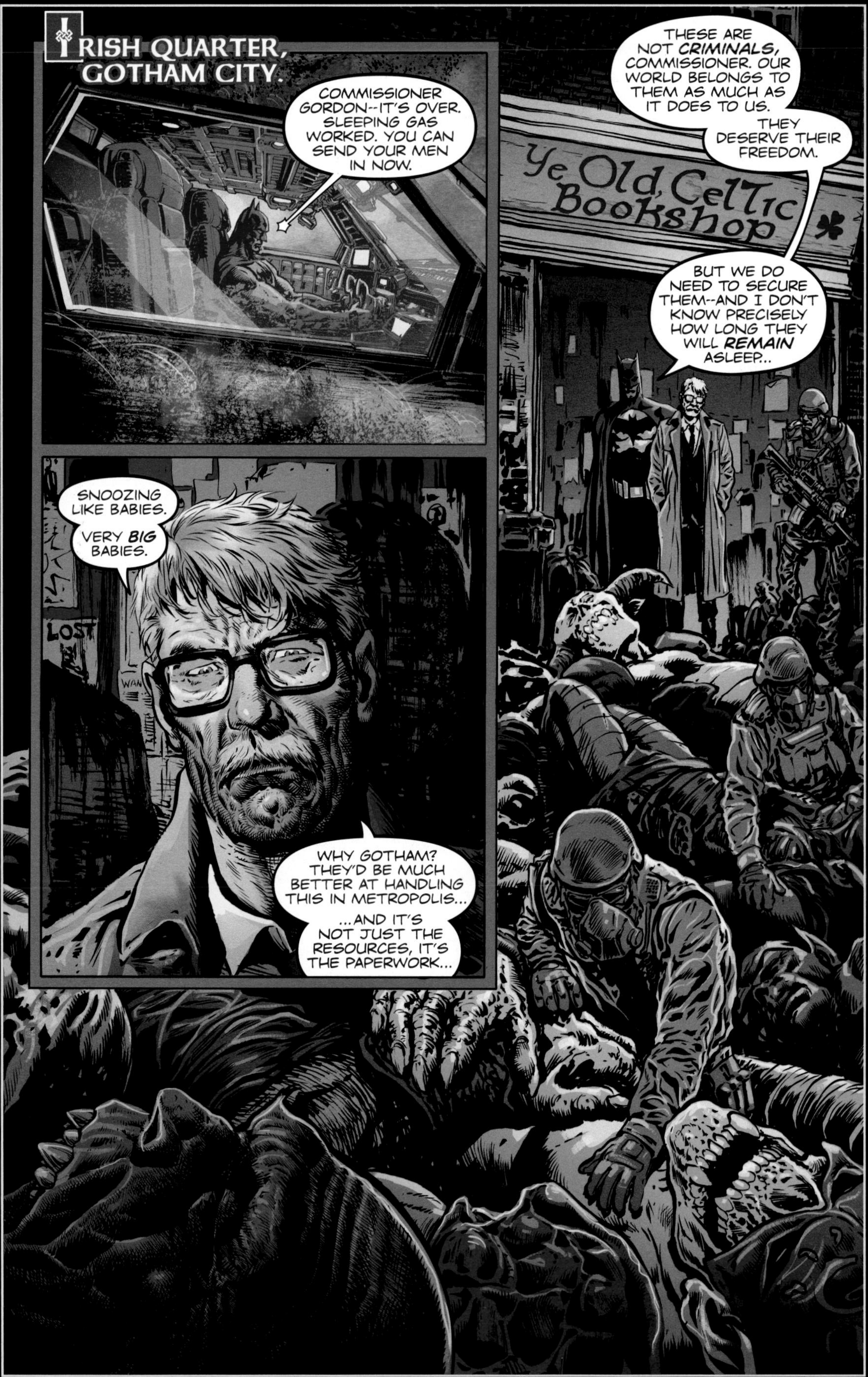
IRISH QUARTER, GOTHAM CITY.
COMMISSIONER GORDON--IT'S OVER. SLEEPING GAS WORKED. YOU CAN SEND YOUR MEN IN NOW.
SNOOZING LIKE BABIES.
VERY BIG BABIES.
WHY GOTHAM? THEY'D BE MUCH BETTER AT HANDLING THIS IN METROPOLIS...
...AND IT'S NOT JUST THE RESOURCES, IT'S THE PAPERWORK...
THESE ARE NOT CRIMINALS, COMMISSIONER. OUR WORLD BELONGS TO THEM AS MUCH AS IT DOES TO US.
THEY DESERVE THEIR FREEDOM.
Ye Old Celtic Bookshop
BUT WE DO NEED TO SECURE THEM--AND I DON'T KNOW PRECISELY HOW LONG THEY WILL REMAIN ASLEEP...
LOST

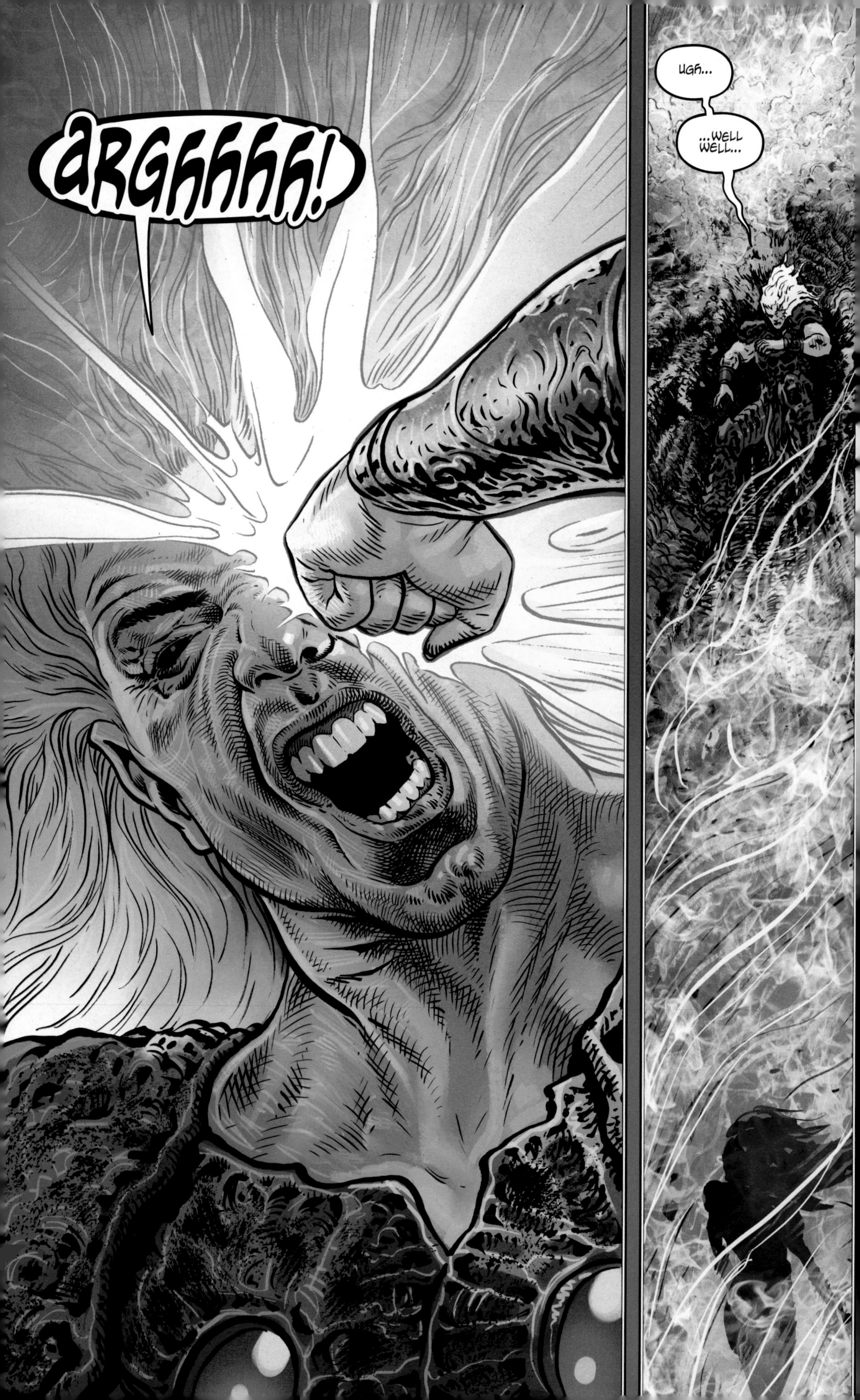
ARGHHHH!
UGH...
...WELL WELL...

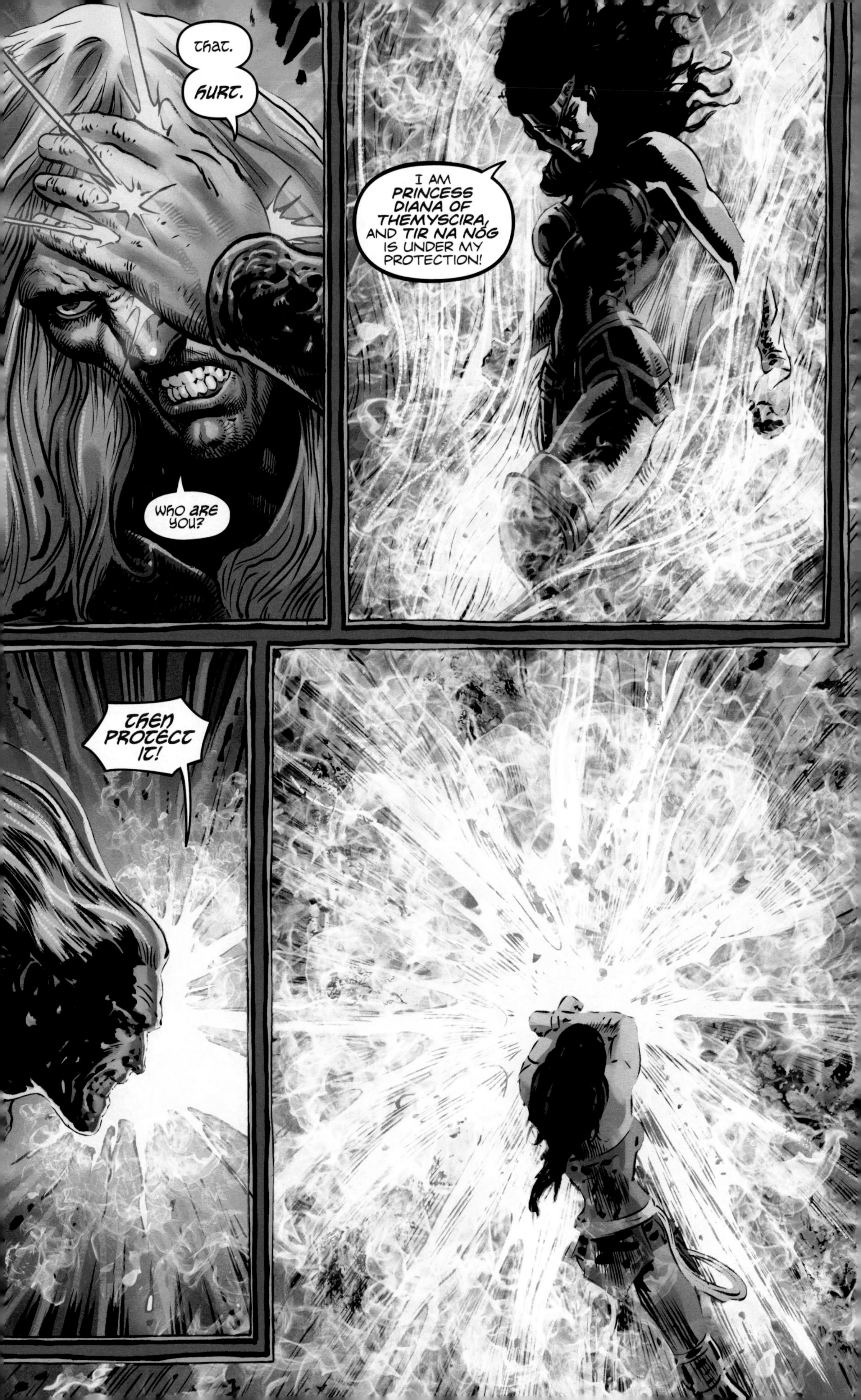
THAT.
HURT.
WHO ARE YOU?
I AM PRINCESS DIANA OF THEMYSCIRA, AND TIR NA NÓG IS UNDER MY PROTECTION!
THEN PROTECT IT!

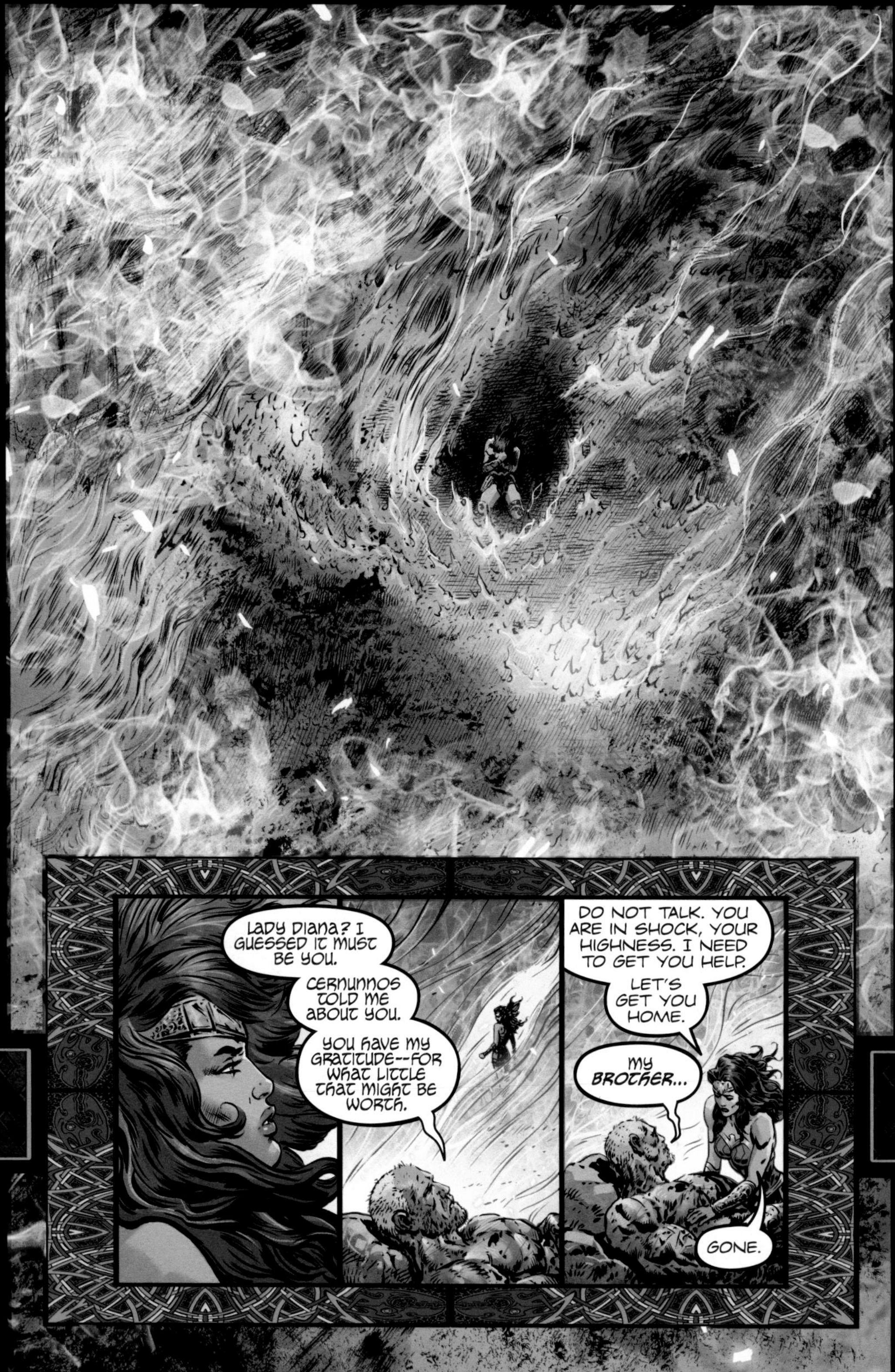
LADY DIANA? I GUESSED IT MUST BE YOU.
CERNUNNOS TOLD ME ABOUT YOU.
YOU HAVE MY GRATITUDE--FOR WHAT LITTLE THAT MIGHT BE WORTH.
DO NOT TALK. YOU ARE IN SHOCK, YOUR HIGHNESS. I NEED TO GET YOU HELP.
LET'S GET YOU HOME.
MY BROTHER...
GONE.

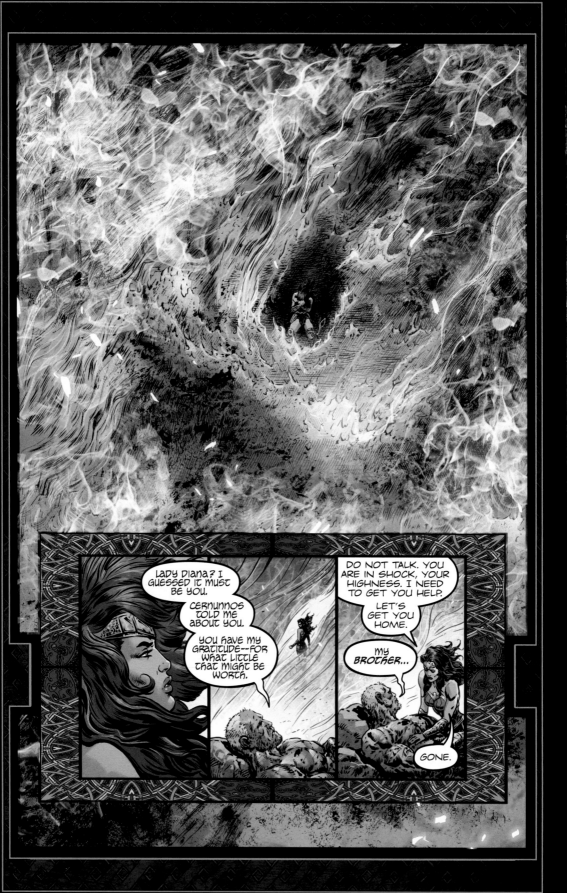

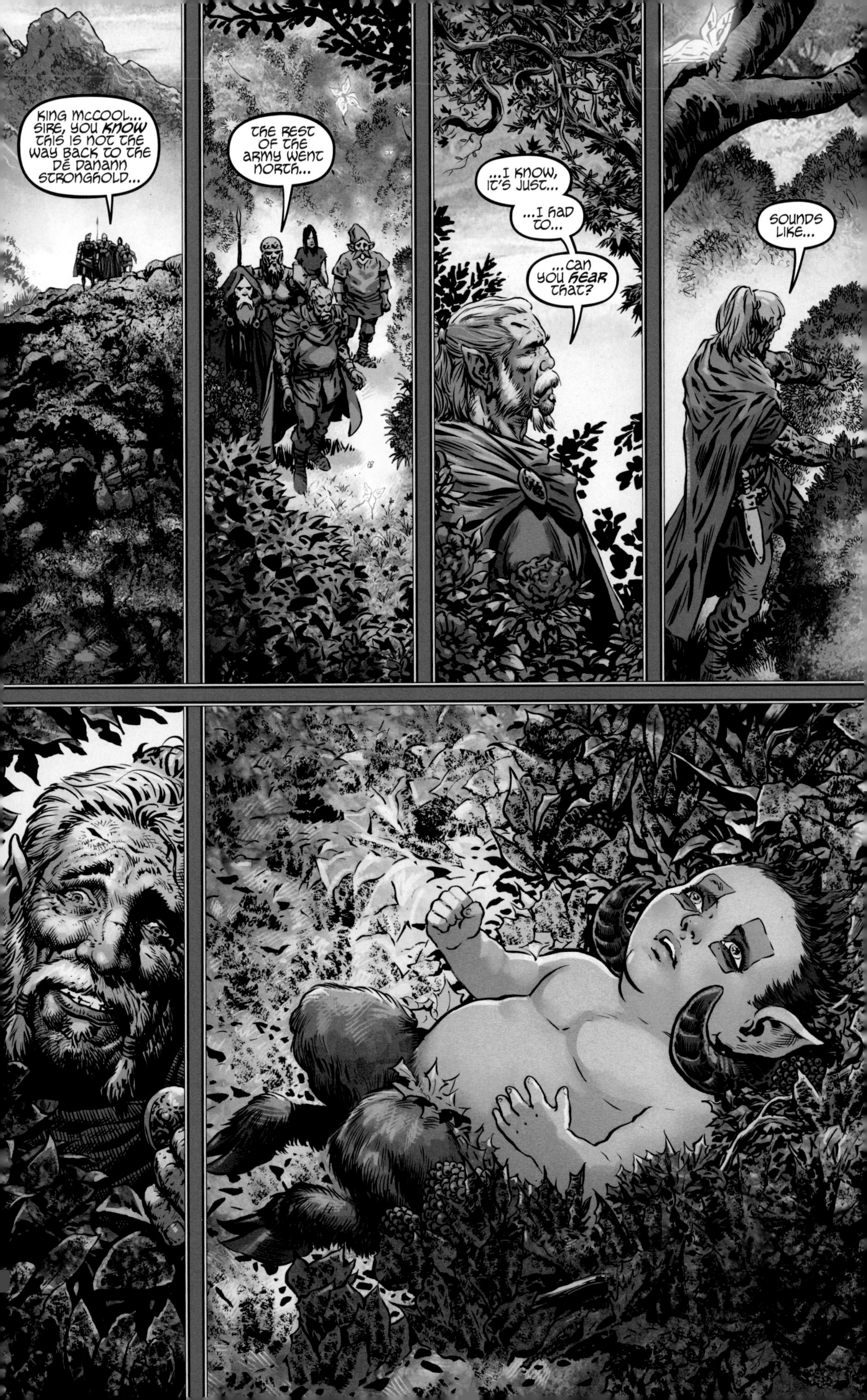
KING McCOOL... SIRE, YOU KNOW THIS IS NOT THE WAY BACK TO THE DÉ DANANN STRONGHOLD...
THE REST OF THE ARMY WENT NORTH...
...I KNOW, IT'S JUST...
...I HAD TO...
...CAN YOU HEAR THAT?
SOUNDS LIKE...

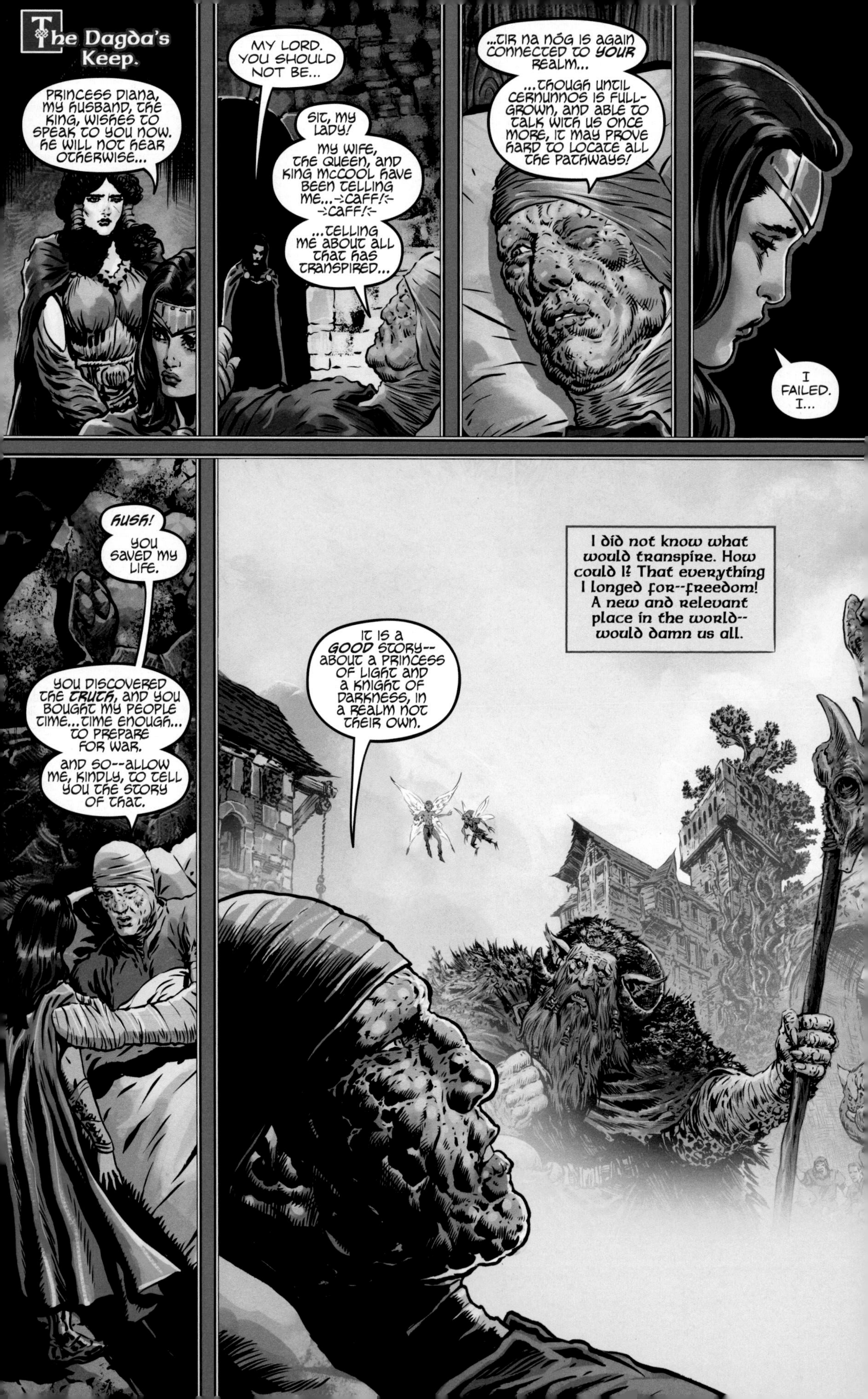

The Dagda's Keep.
PRINCESS DIANA, MY HUSBAND, THE KING, WISHES TO SPEAK TO YOU NOW. HE WILL NOT HEAR OTHERWISE...
MY LORD. YOU SHOULD NOT BE...
SIT, MY LADY!
MY WIFE, THE QUEEN, AND KING MCCOOL HAVE BEEN TELLING ME...CAFF! CAFF!
...TELLING ME ABOUT ALL THAT HAS TRANSPIRED...
...TIR NA NÓG IS AGAIN CONNECTED TO YOUR REALM...
...THOUGH UNTIL CERNUNNOS IS FULL-GROWN, AND ABLE TO TALK WITH US ONCE MORE, IT MAY PROVE HARD TO LOCATE ALL THE PATHWAYS!
I FAILED. I...
HUSH!
YOU SAVED MY LIFE.
YOU DISCOVERED THE TRUTH, AND YOU BOUGHT MY PEOPLE TIME...TIME ENOUGH... TO PREPARE FOR WAR.
AND SO--ALLOW ME, KINDLY, TO TELL YOU THE STORY OF THAT.
IT IS A GOOD STORY--ABOUT A PRINCESS OF LIGHT AND A KNIGHT OF DARKNESS, IN A REALM NOT THEIR OWN.
I did not know what would transpire. How could I? That everything I longed for--freedom! A new and relevant place in the world--would damn us all.

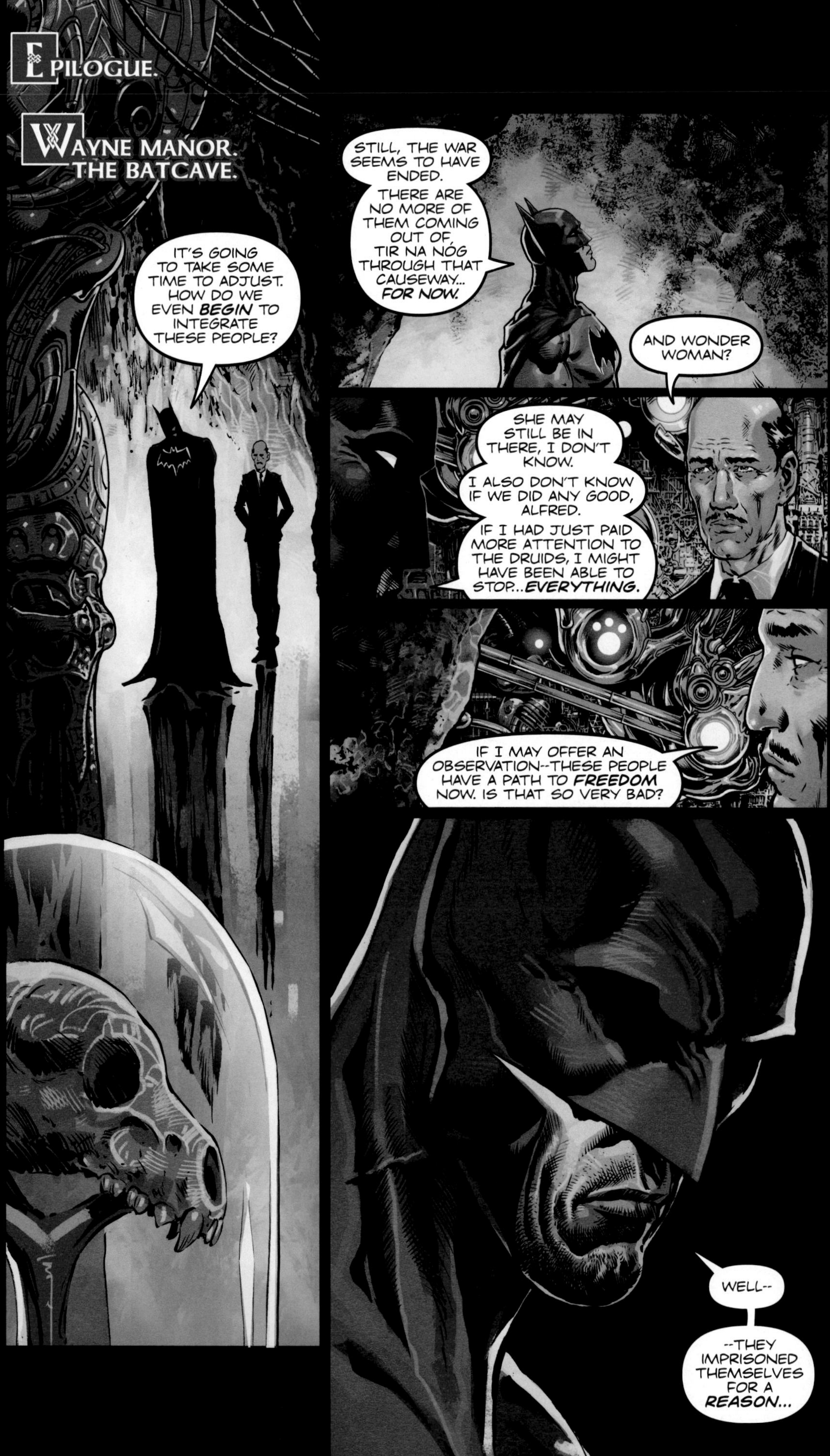
EPILOGUE.
WAYNE MANOR. THE BATCAVE.
IT'S GOING TO TAKE SOME TIME TO ADJUST. HOW DO WE EVEN BEGIN TO INTEGRATE THESE PEOPLE?
STILL, THE WAR SEEMS TO HAVE ENDED.
THERE ARE NO MORE OF THEM COMING OUT OF, TIR NA NÓG THROUGH THAT CAUSEWAY... FOR NOW.
AND WONDER WOMAN?
SHE MAY STILL BE IN THERE, I DON'T KNOW.
I ALSO DON'T KNOW IF WE DID ANY GOOD, ALFRED.
IF I HAD JUST PAID MORE ATTENTION TO THE DRUIDS, I MIGHT HAVE BEEN ABLE TO STOP...EVERYTHING.
IF I MAY OFFER AN OBSERVATION--THESE PEOPLE HAVE A PATH TO FREEDOM NOW. IS THAT SO VERY BAD?
WELL--
--THEY IMPRISONED THEMSELVES FOR A REASON...

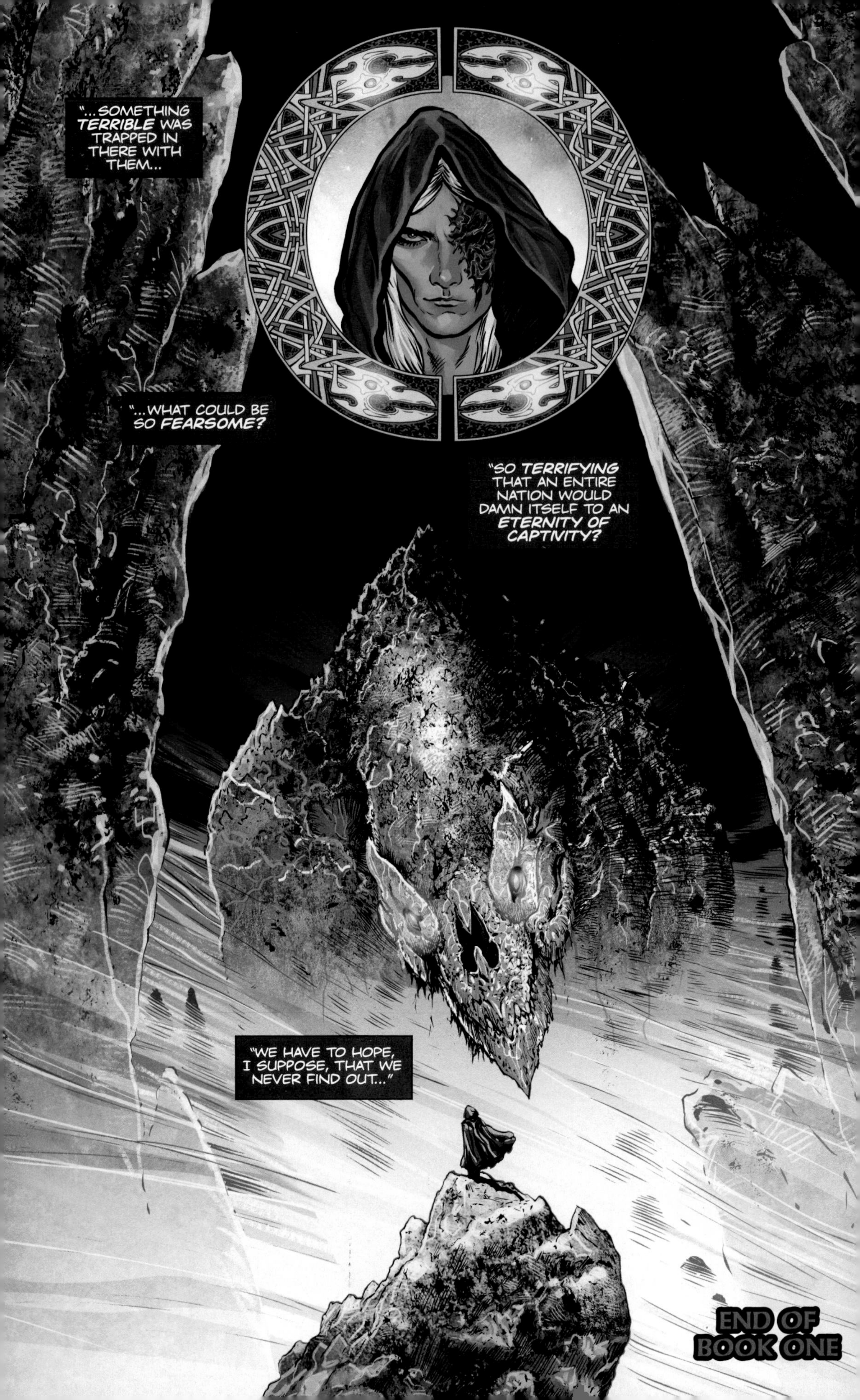
"...SOMETHING TERRIBLE WAS TRAPPED IN THERE WITH THEM...
"...WHAT COULD BE SO FEARSOME?
"SO TERRIFYING THAT AN ENTIRE NATION WOULD DAMN ITSELF TO AN ETERNITY OF CAPTIVITY?
"WE HAVE TO HOPE, I SUPPOSE, THAT WE NEVER FIND OUT..."
END OF BOOK ONE

REFERENCE GUIDE
By Liam Sharp

CERNUNNOS (Ker-nu-nuss): A widely worshiped god from the Celtic polytheist tradition of Europe, Cernunnos is a god of fertility—of life, animals and also of the underworld. Nicolai Tolstoy, in his book *The Quest For Merlin*, suggested that it was the image of this horned god of the underworld that invading Christians later adopted as a literal image of the Devil. Before this, the classic cloven hooves and horns hadn't existed in their mythology. This was used to convert early Celts, who were accused of devil-worship. Cernunnos has also been linked to the character of Conall Cernach from the *Táin*, or "Cattle Raid," of Irish mythological tradition.

KING McCOOL: King Mac Cuill was one of the last three kings of the Tuatha Dé Danann (see below), along with his brothers Mac Cecht and Mac Gréine. However, I opted to keep it simpler, with just one remaining king, and took the liberty of merging him with the much more famous Fionn Mac Cumhail, better known as Finn McCool, a mythical hunter and warrior whose exploits are recounted in the Fenian Cycle of Irish myth. McCool was a giant, associated with the Giant's Causeway, a natural wonder on the coast of Northern Ireland.

TUATHA DÉ DANANN: The Tribe of the Goddess Danu in popular folklore were once portrayed as giants, but as Christianity took over, they diminished, literally shrinking in size to become what would be known as faeries, then disappearing beneath the ground into Tir Na Nóg, "the Land of the Young." In my series, I decided to retain their original stature as giants—the former gods and warriors of ancient Ireland. I liked the idea that reports of their diminished size were really exaggerated by propagandists for a new faith. They would also eventually become the template for Tolkien's elves in his Middle-Earth stories.

THE SILVER ARM: My references and adaptation of this legend are largely based on the version presented by Jim FitzPatrick in his gloriously illustrated and influential book of the same name.

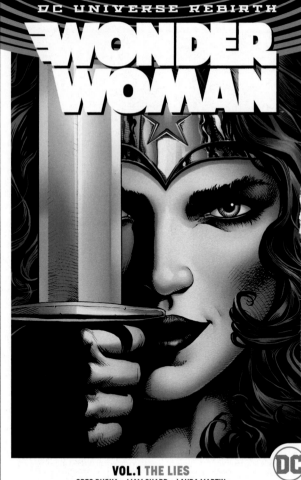